the mahatma *on* celluloid

Celebrating
30 Years of Publishing
in India

the mahatma *on* celluloid

A CINEMATIC BIOGRAPHY

PRAKASH MAGDUM

HarperCollins *Publishers* India

First published in India by HarperCollins *Publishers* 2022
4th Floor, Tower A, Building No 10, DLF Cyber City,
DLF Phase II, Gurugram, Haryana – 122002
www.harpercollins.co.in

2 4 6 8 10 9 7 5 3 1

P-ISBN: 978-93-5629-163-8
E-ISBN: 978-93-5629-170-6

Typeset in 11.5/15.5 Bembo Std at
Manipal Technologies Limited, Manipal

Printed and bound at
Thomson Press (India) Ltd.

To Motilal Kothari and A.K. Chettiar,
two passionate men responsible for preserving Gandhi on celluloid

Contents

Foreword

PRAKASH MAGDUM IS A noted film archivist and was the director of National Film Archives of India in Pune till recently. He is clearly very passionate about his vocation. Over a period of time, he has made a detailed inventory of the films made on and about Mahatma Gandhi.

The Mahatma was among the most photographed and filmed public figures of his time. He was the only great personality in history to free his nation from colonial servitude by leading a sustained campaign of non-violent resistance and protest with its focused appeal to human conscience.

The world media flocked to him. New reels and films, documentaries and features were made on and about him both in his lifetime and well after he passed away.

The most well-known of the films was *Gandhi* made by Richard Attenborough. Among several others, there was the one I made, titled *The Making of the Mahatma*, about his early life and experiences in South Africa where he had gone to take up the profession of law. Soon after reaching there, he was drawn into the anticolonial movement of the time. By the time he returned to India after a stay of twenty one years in South Africa, he had already earned the sobriquet 'Mahatma'.

Mr Magdum's book deals with cinema's tryst with Gandhi in documentaries and features made over the years. As an archivist, his work has great value for students, scholars and cineastes who can experience the *living* Mahatma through the medium of cinema.

Shyam Benegal
8 June 2022

Preface

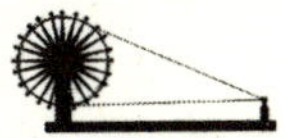

IN 1983, WHEN I was in the fourth standard in a small village school in Maharashtra, it was announced one day that a movie based on Mahatma Gandhiji's life was going be shown to school children. Not wanting to miss the chance to see the film *Gandhi,* I went along with friends, in the only tent-cinema theatre in my village. The film was directed by Richard Attenborough, and I was immediately transfixed by the amazing life of the saint-man depicted on screen. Though we were taught about him in school, and later in college, the experience of watching the life story of the Father of the Nation on film somehow stayed with me forever.

Then it became a ritual for me. On every 2 October, Gandhi's birthday, I would sit glued to the television to watch the film over and over again. Each viewing brought out a better understanding, not only of the various incidents in Gandhi's complex yet fascinating life, but also of India's freedom struggle.

More than seventy years have passed since Gandhi's death, but I find that the cinema industry is still fascinated with the man. Many films are being made by established as well as younger filmmakers who are keen to shed light on lesser-known incidents from Gandhi's life. As each year passes, we rediscover the value of Gandhi's thinking and perhaps try to apply it to the present times. In 2019, when the world started celebrating the 150th anniversary of Gandhi's birth, I thought of exploring how Gandhi has been portrayed through cinema. The initial idea was to compile a list of movies made on his life, and also those influenced by his values and principles apart from newsreels of the bygone era. Following my research, I found many film titles from various eras, and in many languages. To my surprise, the list ended up being extensive!

I also looked at the recent trend in Indian cinema where films were being made imagining Gandhi living in the present times. Disregarding the cynics who felt Gandhi and his values were outdated, some filmmakers thought otherwise. In recent times, various films have been released exploring how Gandhi might have responded to the challenges of today. This is quite a revelation! As a result, there is a large collection of films, both feature and non-feature, made on Gandhi that are now on my list. Some are available in the public domain, and others, at the time of the writing of this book, are under production.

In 2019, in a miraculous way, thirty reels in the 35 mm celluloid format, all films on Gandhi, were found. In my regular hunt for celluloid material, as part of my job as Director at National Film Archive of India (NFAI), I chanced upon a few metal film cans with the name 'Gandhi' written on them in a warehouse in Mumbai, not very far from Mani Bhavan, the place where Gandhi used to stay on his visits to the city. These cans, I discovered, contained mostly unedited footage, or what can be called stock-shots and rushes.

I started watching this newsreel footage—topical being the name for the form—on the flat-bed viewing machine at NFAI and was amazed at the extent to which Gandhi had been filmed in the pre-Independence era. The footage covers the major phases of his life. Some of the films made from this footage are available in the public domain, but many of them are not. The footage largely comprised shots that had not been edited into newsreels.

Watching this frail and exceptional man coming alive in the grainy images became my daily activity for weeks together. Some reels had sound, some didn't. Though some of these reels had inter-title cards (which helps in taking the narrative forward), it became quite a task to find any further information about the footage. That's what prompted me to explore the missing gaps and piece together a narrative on the unusual combination of Gandhi and cinema.

Unusual because, Gandhi was known to not like the medium of cinema! On many occasions he wrote and spoke about the 'evil' effect of the motion picture industry, and never changed his opinion. This may seem very strange. For an excellent public communicator like him, though he was being captured by cameras and his voice was being carried throughout the world, he failed to see the utility and power of the medium of cinema. Even though he had not watched films, he formed a negative opinion of them, believing that 'cinema films are often bad'.

There are very few leaders in the world who have been filmed as extensively as Mahatma Gandhi had been through his lifetime. And, after his passing, films continue to be made on him. Curiously, the growth and development of the Indian motion picture industry ran almost parallel to the Indian freedom movement led by Gandhi. While the first feature film in India was made in 1913, Gandhi had entered the scene of the struggle for India's independence in 1915.

Thereafter, the motion picture cameras followed Gandhi everywhere till his assassination in 1948. It was not only nascent Indian film companies but also the established foreign studios that sent their cameramen to capture almost every activity of Gandhi's. Newsreels, mostly one- or two-reelers, used to be shown before the start of regular feature films in theatres across the world. If we take into account the huge collection of motion picture footage of Gandhi, one can safely say that Gandhi lived in almost full public view.

During the early stages of Indian cinema, many film studios and directors, both openly and discreetly, had espoused the cause of the national freedom movement and brought it alive on screen through different stories. Many times, characters were made to resemble Gandhi, besides propagating the values and principles he advocated. The audience knew and understood what they were seeing and responded by participating in the struggle for India's freedom.

Gandhi's views on cinema were in stark contrast to those of most of his colleagues in the freedom movement, who were sympathetic and supported film as a mass medium. Film studios, in their own wisdom, ignored what Gandhi thought about cinema and continued to portray him, focusing on the issues dear to him: non-violence, village development, communal harmony, women's emancipation, removal of untouchability, cleanliness, village industries, etc. These themes formed the basis for the 'social' films produced in the country.

Then there were the topicals. A vast amount of footage on Gandhi is in fact available—right from 1912, when Gandhi is known to have appeared for the first time on screen, though only for a few seconds, and until his death in 1948. Cameramen, Indian and foreign, followed him like a shadow everywhere. So, what we have today in terms of moving images is of Gandhi in action in the true sense. Even though he disliked film as a medium, he allowed cameramen to shoot his activities on two conditions: that they refrained from using flash bulbs and did not disturb his routine.

His allowance made the humanity richer. When Einstein famously described Gandhi as 'coming generations would scarcely believe that such a one as this ever in flesh and blood walked upon this earth', it is the vast amount of film footage on Gandhi that will help all future generations to see and understand the man who is often equated with Christ and Buddha!

During his lifetime Gandhi immensely influenced the world and continues to do so even today. And the cameramen who came in close contact with him did not escape his spell either. As with so many people, their close physical proximity to Gandhi touched their lives and changed them forever. Their memoirs, some of which I consulted during the research, describe the intimacy and affection they received from their subject and how it impacted their lives. I also talked with some of the filmmakers who have fictionalized Gandhi's life on screen and tried to understand the motives as to why they were tempted to look again at Gandhi.

In a world of cinema, which thrives on glamour and beauty, here is an old frail man who still inspires filmmakers across generations and national borders. Some filmmakers have tried to critically examine his personality, while others have wanted to find answers in his philosophy that can be applied to the problems the world faces today. In the process of filming Gandhi, many filmmakers found themselves influenced by the man and his life.

The man who thought of initiating, for the first time, the idea of a full-length feature film on Gandhi was called Motilal Kothari. He came from a small village Tasgaon in Satara district in the then Bombay province. While working at the Indian High Commission in London in the late 1940s, Kothari thought Gandhi's story needed to be told in a grand way and worked tirelessly to realize his dream. Unfortunately, by the time his dream finally came true in the form of Richard Attenborough's *Gandhi* in 1982, Kothari was no longer alive.

There was another man, Pandit Narayan Khare, who too hailed from the district of Satara. Khare was the music teacher at Sabarmati Ashram, which he had joined on the invitation of Gandhi himself. One of the main disciples of Pandit Vishnu Digambar Paluskar, who established Gandharv Mahavidyalaya to train students in Indian Classical Music, Pandit Khare was instrumental in compiling *Bhajanavali*, a book of prayers in various Indian languages that were recited as part of the daily Ashram prayers. He was also among the chosen team of Gandhi's followers for the famous Dandi March.

When I came across these 'coincidences'—I too belong to the same geographical area of Maharashtra that Kothari and Khare did—I felt there was a cosmic connection between the three of us. Among generations after generations across the globe, this connection continues—it is a connection of universal love bound together by that divine soul named Gandhi.

There have been several books written on Gandhi in many languages across the world. No doubt, many more will follow in the future. He is a man whom many people have become fascinated with and have tried to analyse and interpret his life and philosophy in different ways. And, though many have done this, there is always something new to be discovered about Gandhi. In this book, I have tried to look at him through the lens of film. So perhaps, this could well be called Gandhi's 'Cinematic Biography'.

1

Raghupati Raghav Rajaram

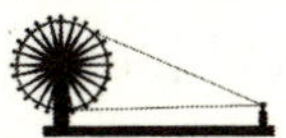

THE END CAME SUDDENLY and swiftly. A man of peace fell to bullets fired by one of his own countrymen. It stunned the newly born Indian nation and the entire world. Even though there had been attempts on Mohandas Karamchand Gandhi's life earlier and with an increased risk to his life in the aftermath of the bloodstained partition of the country, no one was prepared for the shock his assassination caused. The grief that engulfed every sane person in the world was unimaginable. A life lived on the purest of principles a human being could aspire to had been silenced by a brute weapon.

It was a normal winter evening at Birla House in Delhi on 30 January 1948. The clock showed ten minutes past five. Gandhi was unusually late for his daily evening prayer. People had gathered in large numbers for the prayer but, strangely, there wasn't any still or moving camera around at what turned out to be the last prayer meeting of the Mahatma. Margaret Bourke-White, the famous photographer from *Life* magazine, had left Birla House after taking a few pictures of Gandhi just before the prayer meeting was to start.

Gandhi's grandnephew, Kanu, who had clicked some of his most memorable photographs in his last years, was also far away in Noakhali in Bengal. For the man who lived most of his life in the constant gaze of cameras, his final moments were spent without the flashbulbs around, the light of which he did not like.

John Turner, a veteran British cameraman who had filmed many important events of the last days of India's freedom struggle, was a regular visitor at Birla House during that month. But on that fateful day he had decided not to go, having run out of raw film stock. Therefore, the absence of visual documentation of Gandhi's final moments has added to the ever-growing mystery of his persona. Gandhi had become a legend in his lifetime; the manner of his death put him on a pedestal alongside the Buddha and Christ. The day of week of Gandhi's martyrdom was the same as that of Christ's—Friday!

The apostle of peace had seen death from close quarters quite a few times before. Destiny intervened each time, miraculously, and Gandhi survived all these attempts on his life. On the night of 29 June 1946, while Gandhi was travelling to Poona on a train, there was a derailment caused by boulders deliberately placed on the track. Thanks to an alert engine driver, a major mishap was averted. The incident, though, did not affect Gandhi's sleep. The next day, during the prayer meeting in Poona, Gandhi observed:

> 'This is perhaps the seventh occasion when a merciful providence has rescued me from the very jaws of death. I have injured no man, nor have I borne enmity to any. Why should anyone have wished to take my life is more than I can understand. But the world is made like that. Man is born to live in the midst of dangers and alarms. The whole existence of man is a ceaseless duel between the forces of life and death. And even so, the latest accident strengthens my hope to live up to 125.'[1]

Sadly, that was not to happen.

Given the widespread popularity Gandhi had enjoyed across the world, it was but natural that the motion picture cameras tried to capture every possible moment of his last journey. When the news of his assassination spread, still and film cameramen with their crews rushed to Birla House. Right from the bloodstained white lengths of cloth at the site to the close-ups of Gandhi's serene face ... every single detail was filmed.

Some of the unedited film footage discovered in 2019 by National Film Archive of India (NFAI)[2] showed the actual spot where Gandhi fell. The footage showed the spot barricaded by rope and people taking away the bloodstained soil around in remembrance of the great soul. Film cameras captured visuals of a huge crowd that had gathered for their final darshan of the Mahatma. Some of these early shots might have been filmed by an enterprising young Indian cameraman, Ved Parkash, who had rushed to Birla House after hearing the news. The visuals also show the body of Gandhi being brought to the balcony of Birla House so that people could see Gandhi and pay their last respects. People of all faiths and races, with folded hands and mourning faces, are seen standing around Birla House silently. The body is then taken out and carried by some of Gandhi's faithful women followers.

It is a rare and unique sight to see women carrying the mortal remains of a human being. Even though the Indian tradition does not prohibit them from doing so, there have not been many instances, at least in public view, where such visuals were captured. But the man being carried on his final journey was not an ordinary one. He had fought to break all such traditions in his entire life; therefore, it was only fitting that those women, for whose equality he strived, carried his body to his final resting place. The motion picture cameras captured the scene of the body being transferred to a bigger vehicle, where it was received by prominent Indian leaders who were Gandhi's close colleagues in the freedom struggle.

Various Indian and foreign film studios put together their teams to cover events in India following Gandhi's assassination. The five-and-a-half-mile journey from Birla House to Raj Ghat, Gandhi's final resting place on the banks of Yamuna River in Delhi, took several hours. All along the way, a sea of humanity walked, chanting prayers and songs in honour of the Mahatma. His close associates Pandit Nehru, Sardar Patel, Sardar Baldev Singh and Acharya Kriplani, their faces grief-stricken, were sitting in the flower-bedecked carriage bearing Gandhi's body, along with two of Gandhi's sons.

Due to Gandhi's known reluctance to avoid the use of machines as much as possible, the carriage on his last journey was pulled by the men in uniform. The emotions of a million people, more or less held in restraint until that point, flew high after the procession reached Raj Ghat, and the visuals showed the police had great difficulty in ensuring normalcy. From all corners of the ghat, people tried to hand over pieces of sacred sandalwood they had brought for the pyre. It was their own way of participating in the final rites of the Mahatma. As the pyre was lit in accordance with the Hindu tradition, there was a massive outpouring of emotion from the crowd.

After the funeral, the ghat was a scene of personal prayer and tribute. People came one by one, silently, to bow at the samadhi. The motion picture cameras captured the great pathos of the mourning and grief of the common people by taking close up shots. Even today, these visuals give us an idea of the reverence in which Gandhi was held in the hearts of millions of people in India. Another visual taken a day later showed the collection of ashes by the priests and close relatives of Gandhi. The shots show the Yamuna flowing nearby, as if the river were a quiet witness to the solemn ceremony.

Despite the fact that the Indian freedom struggle had entered its crucial last stage, not many foreign newsreel companies had showed much interest in filming the key events after August 1947 in the subcontinent. They were content to rely on whatever was being sent by their Indian stringer cameramen working for American and British studios. But the new Viceroy, Lord Mountbatten, who had a keen eye for publicity, made special arrangements for a cameraman to fly in from Britain to cover the events of Independence.

Obviously, he wanted to turn the transfer-of-power event into a dazzling spectacle for the world to see, and thus, the Newsreel Association of Great Britain sent a cameraman to film the event on behalf of all newsreel companies from Britain. The veteran British cameraman John Turner was roped in for this special assignment. Turner had famously captured the sinking of the Royal Navy's battleship HMS Barham on film during the Second World War, apart from many other important events.

There is a fascinating story about the circumstances under which the visuals of Gandhi's last journey were filmed. Raw film stock, essential to carry out the filming, was a rare commodity in those early days of the domestic Indian film industry. Having missed the opportunity to be at the Birla House on the fateful evening Gandhi was shot, John Turner was determined to not take any more chances. But, Turner had exhausted all his film stock at the time, and procuring it was very difficult due to its rationing in India. The challenge was to get it by whatever means, and that too overnight.

It was Ved Parkash, Turner's friend, and a young Indian cameraman working for British Paramount News, who came to his rescue and managed to collect about 3,000 feet of raw 35 mm film overnight from various cameramen in the capital. Parkash knew many cameramen in the town since some of them worked with him as assistants. Turner remembered Parkash telling him, 'If anyone would not part with film, he would blackmail them by telling they would not get another job with him in the future. A true newsman!'[3]

To make judicious use of the precious stock, both Turner and Parkash decided to divide the work of filming the crucial moments of Gandhi's last journey. Accordingly, Parkash shot the scenes at Birla House by using about 1,000 feet of stock, while Turner captured the events at Raj Ghat with the remaining film. They didn't know whether the stock collected from different sources was good or not.

While recalling the challenges involved in covering this momentous occasion, Turner said, 'In addition to the camera, it meant carrying tins of different lengths and constantly having to reload the camera via the changing bag in the street and the crowds, and all the time wondering whether one was filming vital scenes with faulty stock. I can say without reservation it was the worst day in my whole career as a cameraman. But it transpired that all the film was usable and that was indeed a miracle.' [4]

The procession took about five hours to reach Raj Ghat, and that gave Turner sufficient time to make arrangements for the reloading of film without an assistant at hand. He walked with the cortege, taking several shots along the way. At the funeral site, he made use of a small platform, about ten feet high, already fixed by a local photographer. He had got a vantage position to film the last moments of the funeral, for which he had kept about 200 feet of film. Thus, what we have today is this seminal footage.

Turner has described the last funeral scene as he saw it: 'We were very close to the pyre and ideally placed to show it when it was alight. When the cortege arrived, drawn by members of the state services, Gandhi's body was placed on the pyre and the sandalwood logs set alight by his son. As the flames rose high, the crowd went wild through the police cordons. I managed to film the whole scene.'[5]

The poignant moments we see today of Gandhi's funeral is the handiwork of these two enterprising professionals. Parkash, a cameraman for British Paramount Newsreel, was awarded Britain's Academy Award for his coverage of the event, showing great visual sense.[6] Parkash later went on to work in the films division at United Nations at their New York headquarters. He developed a professional relationship with several leading cameramen of the times and reportedly visited the sets of *The Ten Commandments* when it was being filmed at Paramount Studios.

The Indian Censor Board's records of the time reveal details about the tremendous amount of film footage of Gandhi's last journey, the funeral, and the immersion of his ashes.[7] Indian and foreign film companies vied with each other to film these events from key vantage points. Hollywood-based *Motion Picture Daily*, a leading film magazine, reported in its issue of 4 February 1948 that the death of Gandhi was the highlight of all the current newsreels. It listed Movietone News, News of the Day, Paramount News, Universal News and Warner Pathe News, as the newsreel companies that widely covered Gandhi's assassination and the mourning that followed across the world.[8]

A lot of this footage was used in short films and documentaries from time to time, but some of it went into oblivion, only to resurface in recent times. The final journey of the mortal remains of Gandhi in Delhi was one of the biggest and the most filmed events in the world. The interest in Gandhi's life continued even after his death, and film companies sensed tremendous potential in showcasing Gandhi in film even after his assassination.

British Pathe, a major newsreel company of the time, made a topical film after a few days of Gandhi's assassination. It showed visuals of Birla House and Gandhi's room, which had a garlanded photograph of his placed on a white cushion on which he used to rest. The room was empty, save for two young girls reading newspaper reports of his assassination. The film then showed Raj Ghat, where people were sitting around Gandhi's Samadhi. Some were offering flowers and prayers and there were no security arrangement at the place. The visuals also showed a deserted India Gate and the Rajpath area in Delhi.

Regal Cinema, one of the popular theatres in Delhi's Connaught Place area, was at the time screening a Hollywood film, *The Foxes of Harrow,* starring Rex Harrison, and its poster, displayed prominently was shown. The notice board hung outside the theatre declared 'No Show Today'. Hotel Imperial was also filmed, showing the national flag flying at half-mast and a notice board informing 'Bar is closed'. In another topical film, Raj Ghat is shown barricaded with half-walls that had been erected around. Volunteers wearing Gandhi caps were seen taking the flowers offered by visitors and laying them on the Samadhi.

In their newsreel titled *Gandhi Assassinated,* British Movietone, another leading film company, described Gandhi as the leader with the largest following any man had ever had in his own lifetime. The film company Paramount also paid tribute to Gandhi in its newsreel, which covered the assassination and other events.

Immersion of the ashes of the departed, an important Hindu tradition, assumed more significance in Gandhi's case. Apart from being a deeply religious man, Gandhi was also the Father of the Nation. Therefore, his ashes were taken to different parts of the country for immersion in various rivers and holy places. Prayag (Allahabad in Uttar Pradesh) is considered a holy place because of the confluence of the three important rivers Ganga, Yamuna and Saraswati. In one of the ash-immersion ceremonies held at Prayag for Gandhi, Prime Minister Nehru, along with his cabinet colleagues, Governor Sarojini Naidu and the Mountbatten couple took part.

The entourage travelled in a boat to reach the immersion spot. The ashes had been brought to Allahabad by a special train and was received by Nehru and Sardar Patel. The urn containing the ashes was placed on a decorated amphibious vehicle to take it along the river. This journey of several miles saw people thronging on either side of the road to pay their respects to the departed. Aeroplanes flew low overhead and dropped flowers along the path of the vehicle while Gandhi's followers chanted holy prayers. Similar scenes were witnessed in Bombay, Jabalpur and Nasik, apart from other places. Many of these immersion ceremonies were filmed by various film companies.

The assassination of Gandhi was a watershed moment in the history of India. DG Tendulkar, who wrote a seminal 8-volume biography of Gandhi remembers, 'The manner of his death was the culmination and perfect climax to an astonishing journey. Even during his life, innumerable stories and legends had grown around him, and now, he seems almost a legendary figure, one in the great line of India's sages and heroes and wise men.'[9] The motion picture cameras also covered the ash-immersion ceremonies held across the country, capturing the grief-stricken scenes at each of these places.

It was not only the regular newsreel companies that came forward to make the topicals on Gandhi's assassination, but a few small production houses and distributors also thought it important to make films on the event. The Indian Censor Board records of the time reveal that many Indian film companies, both big and small, obtained the visuals of Gandhi's last journey and the ash-immersion ceremonies for screening across India. *Bapu Ki Antim Yatra* was a one-reeler film made by Motwane Motion Pictures and Eastern Movies in February 1948. Universal films made a one-reel topical called *Mahatma Gandhi's funeral*. Another newsreel on the same subject was made by Eagle Lion Distributors (India) Ltd.

British Movietone News produced a one-reel topical called *Mahatma Gandhi's funeral* and described the procession as one of the biggest funeral events in the world. A two-reeler topical, *Bapuji* was produced by Patel (India) Ltd. Dominion Pictures made a topical called *Indian National Flag* (with an inset picture of Mahatma Gandhi). Another two-reeler was made by Cine Film Service, titled *Immersion Topical of Mahatma Gandhi*. The topical made by Borkar Film Service Company was called *Raghupati Raghava Rajaram,* after Gandhi's favourite bhajan.

These topicals were not only made in English and Hindi but also in other Indian languages, obviously keeping in mind the huge viewership across India. Cine Film Service produced a one-reeler film *Immersion topical of Mahatma Gandhi* in Marwari, Marathi and Punjabi. A month after the assassination, Motwane Motion Pictures and Eastern Movies made a two-reeler topical *Mahatma: The Immortal.* Motwane Pictures also made a topical called *Amar Sangam,* consisting of two reels. Kala Pictures titled their topical *Shraddhanjali*, while Educational Films Guild made a one-reel film, *The Light that Shone.*

The production houses realized that the visuals of the ash-immersion ceremony and other events related to Gandhi's death were still in demand and continued to make topicals for months to come. One such event was the court-room trial of the Mahatma's assassins. In June 1948, Eastern Movies made a topical, *Mahatma's Assassination Trial,* which was released in English, Hindi and Tamil.

Another trend was to depict the entire life of Gandhi by putting together visuals of important events from his life. *Vishwadeep Bapu* (Light of the World Bapu) was one such topical made in Hindi. This three-reeler film was produced by The Screens, a Bombay-based distributing concern. It showcased a few principal events from the life of Gandhi, including his trip to England for studies, his work in Africa and in Sabarmati Ashram, the Dandi March, the Quit India Movement, the

Cripps Mission, his Noakhali tour, his Bihar and Delhi trips, and finally his last journey.

Tarachand Barjatya, who later started Rajshri Productions, produced the film while Dwarka Khosla directed it. Nilkanth Tiwari and Bharat Vyas wrote the songs, which were sung by renowned singer Mukesh. The commentary was written by Nilkanth Tiwari and delivered by Raj Mehta. The Tamil and Telugu versions of the film were released in October 1948.

Bapu Ki Amar Kahani, released in August 1948, was another such film from the banner of Famous Pictures. The film was exhibited at Metro Cinema in Bombay and was highly appreciated by the spectators.[10] *Pujya Gandhiji* was a topical made in Hindustani, Telugu and Tamil by Hindustan Information Films in January 1949. Then there was Films Division's short film, *Glimpses of Gandhiji*, made in both English and Hindi in August 1949.

The Indian film industry reacted to Gandhi's death by not only producing these topicals, but also decided to start a fund for a fitting memorial to the Mahatma. The executives of all the associations of the film industry, namely, Motion Picture Society of India, Indian Motion Picture Producers' Association, Indian Motion Picture Distributors' Association and the Cinematograph Exhibitors' Association of India met on 18 February 1948 and took this decision.

As an initial contribution, it was decided to earmark all the net proceeds from the screening of the short film *Bapu ki Antim Yatra* for this fund called Mahatma Gandhi Memorial Fund. Similar condolence meetings were held in Madras by the South Indian Film Chambers of Commerce and the Bengal Motion Pictures Association in Calcutta as well.[11]

The aura of Gandhi, his popularity, and the Indian masses' perception of him as 'saintly' had reached their zenith by the time India became independent. Despite his withdrawal from active politics, people revered Gandhi like a prophet. He was considered more of a 'saint' and not a typical politician. The response to visuals of his ashes being immersed showcased the hold Gandhi had on the minds of the Indian population, even after his death.

The celluloid material on Gandhi in 35 mm format recently unearthed by NFAI has two reels capturing the journey of his ashes on a train from Madras to Rameshwaram in Tamil Nadu.[12] As the special train moves from one railway station to another, people from all walks of life, irrespective of age and religion, can be seen lined up along the tracks with folded hands, just to catch a glimpse of the flower-decked urn placed prominently on board. The devotion in their eyes is of the kind reserved only for God; they were standing on the platforms as if they were offering prayers at a temple.

In his autobiography, Gandhi writes:

> A variety of incidents in my life have conspired to bring me in close contact with people of many creeds and many communities, and my experience with all of them warrants the statement that I have known no distinction between relatives and strangers, countrymen and foreigners, white and coloured, Hindus and Indians of other faiths, whether Muslims, Parsis, Christians or Jews. I may say that my heart has been incapable of making any such distinctions.[13]

That sentiment reflected in the mammoth crowds at various places paying homage to his ashes in the interiors of south India. Produced by Madras-based Documentary Films of India, this footage is a vivid depiction of the journey of Gandhi's ashes. It shows the train stopping at major stations along the way, where thousands of people had gathered to catch a glimpse of the holy ashes. The scene gets repeated at every station till the train reaches its destination, where an ocean of a crowd was present to witness the ceremony of immersion of the ashes in the sea.

It was a sheer coincidence that Gandhi had toured some of these very areas by train just a few months before his assassination. He had spent a considerable amount of time traversing the interiors of Tamil Nadu, including a visit to the famous Meenakshi temple in Madurai in

1947. These black-and-white visuals form part of another topical film, *Gandhi's South Indian Tour*. Everywhere, people had thronged to get a 'darshan' on his earlier tour of Tamil Nadu. Few months later, Gandhi was no more in flesh and blood but in the form of sacred ashes. These very same people were now standing with bowed heads to pay their last respects to his remains. The spectators had now become mourners.

Just a few days before Gandhi was assassinated, he was filmed in colour too, the footage of which has now become available for viewing. These were some of the earliest cinema pictures available in colour of any political leader in India. An enterprising Russian photographer, Constantin Joffé, had come to India in 1948 as a representative of the popular fashion magazine *Vogue*.[14] He managed to take his camera inside the Birla House and captured Gandhi's private moments.

The colour technology was new, and how Joffé got access to film Gandhi is not known. Gandhi's daily routine, including his walks around the house and his resting in the winter sun, have been shot beautifully by Joffé. Most of the shots were taken from a distance, so there are not many close-ups. But still, seeing Gandhi, who always wore white, in colour, is a wonderful experience. Apart from Gandhi's close aides Madeline Slade and Dr Sushila Nayyar, India's first President Dr Rajendra Prasad too is seen walking with Gandhi in Joffe's footage.

In another visual, Gandhi is shown resting while fully covered to protect from the cold winter. He looks very frail, lying on a cot in the lawns of Birla House and for a change, is seen wearing a straw hat. Even these long shots showed that Gandhi was quite weak and needed physical help to move. Joffé, who was in India for six months on a special assignment, also shot the poignant ceremony of immersion of ashes in colour held on Bombay Chowpatty.

'Raghupati Raghav Rajaram, Patit Pavan Sitaram' (O Lord Rama, descendant of Raghu, Uplifter of the fallen, You and your beloved consort Sita are to be worshipped) was Gandhi's favourite bhajan. Popularly known as 'Ramdhun', the commonly heard version of this song was composed by Pandit Vishnu Digambar Paluskar, the man credited with taking Hindustani classical music from the chambers and

royal courts to the common people. His prodigious son, Pandit D.V. Paluskar, popularized classical music even further.

Since his childhood, taking the name of Rama had been Gandhi's 'infallible remedy' for all problems. This bhajan has been permanently etched in the public memory with Gandhi's association. It is no wonder that many films featuring Gandhi used the tune of this bhajan as a motif. It was the surest way of evoking Gandhi's memory and highlighting the ethos of his mystic persona. The moving images of the holy fire that burnt the mortal body of Gandhi could not have had a more suitable background score than the soulful rendition of '*Raghupati Raghav Rajaram*'.

A Troublesome Guy, *Ghandi*!

More than 150 years have now passed after Mohandas Karamchand Gandhi was born in Porbandar, a small coastal town in India, but he is not merely a name. He is many things to many people. A bald and frail man with just one piece of cloth on his body, Gandhi is beyond adjectives. People love him, worship him, hate him, laugh at him, like him, ridicule him, imitate him; but he cannot be ignored. Not then, not now and not in the future.

When Gandhi appeared on the political stage in India in 1915, he was certainly not ignored. In fact, he was noticed—by the common people, by the contemporary political leaders, by the ruling British authorities, and also by the new emerging medium of cinema in the country. India was a large colony in the British empire and Gandhi had returned from South Africa after successfully experimenting with a new tool of political struggle. He had come back as the 'Hero of Natal', where he had successfully led a struggle to fight racial discrimination by the use of 'satyagraha' (truth force) and 'ahimsa' (non-violence).

As part of the movement, Gandhi had invited his political guru, Gopal Krishna Gokhale, a tall leader of India's freedom struggle, to South Africa in October 1912. It is believed that this was the first time Gandhi appeared on screen when a short footage was taken at the reception meeting. The footage shows Gandhi dressed in European clothes waiting to receive Gokhale at Johannesburg railway station. This footage, of only a few seconds, ranks as one of the rarest historical documents pertaining to the Indian freedom struggle; apart from capturing Gandhi for the screen for the first time, it also showcased Gokhale in moving images, most probably his only such appearance in film.

Cinema, one of the glorious inventions of the nineteenth century, was spreading fast as a mass medium across the world. The sheer magic of images moving on a big screen was a huge draw for people, and this new enthralling experience was hailed as no less than a miracle. The art of storytelling got a new tool and artists were trying to learn it to tell their stories. But it took some time, understandably, to explore the language and treatment of cinema.

Some of the earliest footages shot for cinema consist of private moments, as in a home movie. Slowly and steadily, topics of common interest found their way to the screen. Newsreels showing current events started getting made in a series format in the first decade of the twentieth century. Therefore, it is incredible that a complete 'stranger' like Gandhi, an Indian advocate in a foreign land, was filmed in the very initial years of cinema.

The story of how this footage of Gandhi was taken, preserved, and then secured, is fascinating. Even though we do not know who filmed this very important footage, it was Henry S.L. Polak, a close associate of Gandhi's during the African struggle, who managed to acquire it. He preserved it because he understood the value and importance of this precious piece of history. A.K. Chettiar, a young Indian filmmaker who had passionately searched for film footage on Gandhi across the world, met Polak in London in the 1940s and chanced upon this wonderful discovery.

Thankfully, the footage, a positive film of about 200 feet, had survived miraculously for twenty-seven years. When Chettiar saw it on screen, he could not immediately recognize Gandhi because the young Indian advocate was dressed in European clothes, with a Kathiawar turban![15] This particular footage was reported to have been screened in 1912 in a theatre meant exclusively for blacks in Johannesburg.

Even though film screenings had started in some parts of South Africa in the silent era, the first motion picture studio was established there only in 1915. Considering this, the production value of the footage showing Gandhi and Gokhale assumes greater significance. It was simply incredible that a local cameraman had filmed a leader from a foreign country in a nascent film industry. But it had indeed been made, preserved and then discovered after years. Gandhi was forty-three when he was filmed for the first time. Many people in India had heard of his heroics in a foreign land and they looked up to him to take on the mantle of leadership in India's freedom movement.

This was also the time when the cinema industry in India was taking its baby steps. India' first feature film was made in 1913, two years before the arrival of Gandhi in the country. D.G. Phalke, considered as the 'father of India's film industry', made *Raja Harishchandra*, a four-reel silent film. For his first feature film, Phalke decided to take the popular story of King Harishchandra to depict on screen. The story from the classical Indian epic, the Mahabharata, is about a righteous king who sacrifices his kingdom, wife and son to fulfil his promise to the sage Vishwamitra.

Gandhi often referred to the legend of Harishchandra as the epitome of selflessness and sacrifice. Truth as the most vital virtue, as depicted in the film, was to become the cornerstone of Gandhi's philosophy. Incidentally, Phalke was born just six months after Gandhi!

Aware of the nationalist sentiments of the freedom struggle, Phalke, chose another mythical legend of the birth of Lord Krishna for his film *Shri Krishna Janma* (The Birth of Shri Krishna) in 1918. Towards the end of the film, people of all castes from the audience used to pay obeisance to Krishna. Phalke inserted the title-card: 'May this humble offering be accepted by the Lord.' The idea of nation that Phalke espoused in this film closely resembled the ideas of inclusiveness propagated by Gandhi. The nascent film industry dived into many mythological tales from the rich history of India and started making films based on the heroes of the past. At the same time, taking a cue from the European and American film industries, Indian film producers also began producing topicals and newsreels on special events.

When Gandhi arrived in India in early 1915, the Indian movement for independence was led prominently by B.G. Tilak. A firebrand leader from Maharashtra, Tilak was known for his bold programmes and fiery speeches. He devised innovative methods to draw people from many walks of life into the struggle. Gandhi had immense respect for Tilak, although he differed with the ideology propagated by the latter. Both eventually met and discussed ways to take forward the movement, because freedom for India was their common aim.

By then Gandhi had toured the interiors of India on the advice of his political guru, G.K. Gokhale. This was the first of the many tours he was to undertake across India by the third-class railway coach. As Gandhi was preparing to launch a major mass movement, Tilak passed away in August 1920 in Bombay. Gandhi made it a point to be present at his funeral procession. Significantly, Gandhi also decided to shoulder Tilak's bier en route to the cremation ground at Girgaum Chowpatty.

Years later, when Gandhi's ashes were being immersed at the same Chowpatty, an enterprising cameraman from Films Division, in a flash of brilliance, captured the mammoth crowd in a top angle shot taken from the imposing statue of Tilak nearby. Gandhi's being a pall bearer at Tilak's last journey was more than just symbolic moment. The baton had already passed from Tilak to Gandhi to lead the freedom movement, and Gandhi announced commencement of the Non-Cooperation Movement, his first of many such initiatives, the very same day in Bombay.

Phalke's Hindustan Film Company made a small topical on Tilak's funeral ceremony. Again, it was A.K. Chettiar who managed to get hold of this footage, but unfortunately it is not available as of now. Another major studio of the silent era, Kohinoor Film Company, made a film (of 967 feet) on Tilak's funeral procession. Since Tilak was a popular leader, a few other companies, such as Oriental and Patankar Friends and Co., also produced one-reeler films on the event.

These films were among the earliest to be censored in India. The practice of film censorship started only in August 1920 in India, and these films were passed by the Bombay Board of Film Censors on the condition that only the funeral procession was to be shown and nothing else. Unfortunately, these films are lost as of now. These are a few of the early films—that too films made by Indian studios—in which Gandhi featured.

The same year saw two more Indian film companies making topicals on Gandhi. Aurora Cinema Corporation and Elphinstone Bioscope, both Calcutta-based film companies, made topicals on Lala Lajpat Rai and Gandhi's visit to Calcutta in connection with a special session of the Indian National Congress. Aurora Cinema Corporation was one of the earliest film companies in India established by Anadi Nath Bose in 1906. Elphinstone Bioscope was a precursor to Madan Theatres Ltd., founded by J.F. Madan, and produced two silent films on Gandhi's and Rai's Calcutta visit.

After the death of Tilak, Gandhi was anointed to lead the movement for India's freedom. He had already announced the Non-Cooperation Movement, with non-violence as a key aspect of it. The Non-Cooperation programme also involved boycott of foreign clothes, and people participated in large numbers by organizing bonfires of foreign clothes at various places in India. Two such major events, one in Bombay and the other in Ahmedabad, were filmed by Kohinoor Film Company in 1921. Both programmes were attended by Gandhi.

While addressing a historic meeting on 31 July 1921 at the Elphinstone Mills Compound in Parel in Bombay to inaugurate the Swadeshi campaign with a bonfire of foreign clothes, Gandhi said, 'We are purifying ourselves by discarding foreign cloth, which is the badge of our slavery.' [16] The first film was 980-feet long and the second 300 feet, both made in October 1921. These were also among the first public events of bonfire of foreign clothes in India.

In a full-length newsreel, *The Great Bonfire of Foreign Clothes* (1915), made by T. Jansen, an American freelance cameraman, Gandhi featured most prominently among the other nationalist leaders.[17] It ran for two weeks at Globe Theatre and West End Theatre in Bombay and received enthusiastic response. Ironically, as the existing rules of the regulatory authorities were not adequate to prevent the film's screening, the exhibition continued for almost one month without any authoritarian intervention.[18] In the absence of a Censor Board, the British administration could not prevent the film from being widely exhibited.

In July 1921, Gandhi was the chief guest at the unveiling ceremony of a statue of Tilak in Poona. A short topical was made by Kohinoor Film Company covering the event. A film was also made by the same company on an event marking the first death anniversary of Tilak at Chowpatty in Bombay, which was addressed by Gandhi. All these films were approved by the Bombay Board of Film Censors for unrestricted exhibition.

By then, the newsreel companies had realized the growing popularity of Gandhi. Their camera crew started following him and covering the major events he participated in. Several foreign film companies too, who specialized in capturing topical news, recognized the importance of this unusual Congress leader who was gaining pan-Indian appeal. The large crowds drawn to Gandhi's mass meetings made for ideal opportunities for filming small topicals.

Gandhi generated tremendous interest not only among the domestic audience but also among people around the globe, who were curious to know about him. 'Gandhi was independent, unfettered, unpredictable, hence exciting and difficult ... He dared to go anywhere without a chart.'[19] No wonder he made for a great subject for the motion picture cameras. Gandhi had successfully transformed the Congress Party from a minority group of the intelligentsia to a mass-based organization. People in large numbers thronged to his rallies, to see and to listen to him.

These public events naturally had tremendous news value. They also made for great visual appeal and impact on screen. No other leader till then had enthused the common man in India the way Gandhi had. The action and drama inherent in his public rallies, and also the way he dressed and interacted with the common man, ensured that the cameras went everywhere with Gandhi.

Paris-based Pathe Film Company was one of the earliest and leading film studios in the world. Through their wide network of cameramen, Pathe was always at the forefront in covering news across the world and was one of the first few foreign newsreel companies who started taking moving pictures of Gandhi. As early as in 1922, as part of Pathe Gazette, a longer and comprehensive account of the current events, the company produced a newsreel on Gandhi's imprisonment.

The inter-title card of the film said: 'Now condemned to six years imprisonment, the only cinema pictures ever taken of the notorious agitator.' In the film, Gandhi is seated on a raised platform wearing full clothes and a cap, which later became famous as Gandhi cap. He then gets up, gestures to people around to sit down, and makes a speech. There is no sound in the film, so we can only see his movements. The visuals also show him passing through the crowd.

There are a few close-up shots of Gandhi talking to people while some people standing nearby look into the camera amusedly. Gandhi was fifty-three years old at the time and looks much shorter in the film than his lanky appearance of later. This might be because Gandhi was fully clothed and had a shawl wrapped around him. There are strands of grey hair on his head visible underneath the Gandhi cap.

A year earlier, he had taken a vow to wear only khadi, but at this point he had not yet discarded the cloth covering his upper body. So, it is difficult to immediately recognize him because Gandhi later on wore only a dhoti, a piece of cloth wrapped around the waist. Foreigners called it loincloth and the word for Gandhi's regular garment has stuck since, even among Indians.

Quite often, his name was mis-spelt by the foreign media. In the initial few foreign newsreels, he is referred to as Ghandi. It is quite evident that the news editor at Pathe was unable to fathom the impact and spread of India's freedom movement, and therefore referred to Gandhi as a 'notorious agitator'! Around the same time, *Exhibitors Herald*, a major film trade magazine from Hollywood, mentioned Gandhi as a 'troublesome guy'!

It is really amusing to read such reports, indicating that the foreign media couldn't understand what to make of this unusual man. In fact, one news report talked about taking a bunch of motion picture actors from America to India to shoot some scenes for a film. The tour was to be for six months, with a plan to shoot in the interiors of India, 'where that troublesome guy is stirring things up', referring to Gandhi. [20]

Universal Pictures, another major global newsreel company, was comparatively sympathetic to the cause of India's freedom struggle. Their newsreel (No. 60) made in India in 1922 refers to the footage as 'exclusive views of mysterious India'! Their newsletter of December 1922 said:

> The first of these pictures clearing up the Mysteries of India appears in International News No. 60 and shows tremendous demonstrations by the followers of the patriot Gandhi, at present imprisoned, against the domination of white civilisation ... these exclusive pictures were taken at great personal risk by Captain Ariel Varges.[21]

Two months earlier, Phalke's Hindustan Cinema Film Co. made a two-reeler film on the thirty-sixth annual session of the Indian National Congress held at Ahmedabad. Gandhi had actively taken part in the proceedings and moved a resolution on non-violent non-cooperation. In September 1921, Gandhi had visited Calcutta and addressed various public meetings in connection with the boycott of foreign cloth. He was also in Delhi to attend Congress meetings.

These events were covered by the Calcutta-based Madan Theatres Ltd. and passed by the Censors in March 1922. Madan Theatres, founded by J.F. Madan in 1919, was the biggest film production house in the silent era of Indian cinema and the studio was very active in production and distribution of topicals as well as feature films. The company was also one of the biggest importers of film stock and at one point, owned more than 100 cinema theatres across the country.

In March 1922, Gandhi was sentenced to jail on charges of sedition for three articles that he wrote in *Young India*. He was lodged in

Yerawada jail in Poona, but was indisposed most of the time because of stomach ailments. In January 1924, he was operated at Sassoon hospital by Civil Surgeon Col. Maddock for appendicitis and was released from jail the next month. By then, his popularity had spread to the farthest corners of the country. This was an opportunity for some people to milk his name for advertisement. Sure enough, the film industry was one of the first to use Gandhi's name to attract audiences.

Sensing the importance of Gandhi's surgery, renowned Marathi playwright B.V. Warerkar, along with P.R. Lele, made a two-reeler film, *The Mahatma's Miracle,* which was released in February 1924. The writer, popularly known as Mama Warerkar, had earlier made a historical film, *Poona Raided*, depicting a daring and glorious chapter from the life of the Maratha king Shivaji. The makers supposedly secured a special permission for the filming of Gandhi's surgery from the Governor of Bombay, L. Wilson.

By the time Warerkar and his crew reached the Sassoon hospital, the surgery was over. Not one to lose the heart, they requested for 'action replay' of the procedure! Col. Maddock and the nursing staff were game to act, but not Gandhi. He refused to cooperate and reportedly turned his face the other way while holding a newspaper in front of him. Even so, the cameraman, Baba Anandkar, apparently managed to take few shots of him. The Bombay Board of Film Censors certified *The Mahatma's Miracle* for public release. While Warerkar claimed the two-reel film was the first documentary in India, his opponents alleged that Gandhi's dummy had been used for the shoot![22]

Whether the Gandhi in the film was real or a dummy, it was a clever ploy to use Gandhi's name in the title of the film and ensure footfall in the cinema theatres. Gandhi, unwittingly, had become a brand name in an industry he did not like. It was the poet-philosopher Rabindranath Tagore who had bestowed the title of 'Mahatma' (Great Soul) on Gandhi, and people soon started referring to him as 'Mahatma Gandhi'. Therefore, the film industry started using Mahatma in the title or publicity of the movie.

The entire surgical procedure also was nothing short of a drama. Due to increasing acute pain in his stomach, which was suspected as appendicitis, Col Maddock himself took Gandhi in his car from Yerawada jail to Sassoon hospital on 12 January 1924. As soon as the operation started in the night, the electricity failed and the procedure had to be carried out with kerosene lamps. The electricity came back just after the surgery got over!

This marketing trend caught on, and several producers used Gandhi's name to promote their films, whether he had any connection to the film or not. Most often, it was not. Gandhi was not amused by this trend. In 1925, a tea manufacturer in Ahmedabad had used Gandhi's name to advertise his brand. Annoyed by this, Gandhi wrote in *Navajivan*, 'The story of the misuse of my name is a long one. Men have been killed and falsehood propagated in my name; my name has been misused at the time of elections; cigarettes to which I am totally opposed, are sold in my name; as also medicines! When the evil is so widespread, what can one do against it?'[23]

After his release from prison, Gandhi was shifted to Bombay in March 1924 and he stayed at businessman Narottam Morarji's beachside bungalow in Juhu for convalescence. During this time, Majestic Films made a one-reeler film on the Mandvi Khadi Exhibition in March 1924 that featured Gandhi. Ardeshir Irani, who had established Majestic Films in 1923, went on to create Imperial Film Company, which produced India's first talkie film *Alam Ara* in 1931.

The cause of khadi was very dear to Gandhi and he had taken vow to wear only khadi in 1921. Therefore, Gandhi lamented the fact that an exhibition for khadi had to be held in the country, and in his message for the Mandvi Khadi Exhibition, which was read out by Kasturba Gandhi, he wrote:

> Is khadi, then, less useful than wheat and bajra? If we do not wish to eat oats imported from Scotland in place of our wheat and bajra, why do we then insult khadi by importing and wearing cloth from Manchester or Japan? Every patriot and everyone who loves his or

> her religion must consider this point. We shall surely remain under foreign rule as long as we cannot do without foreign cloth.[24]

Since Gandhi is known and viewed mostly as a serious political leader engaged in social and political causes, watching him walk on the beach is a pure delight! The visuals in the Majestic topical film show him coming out of the bungalow he is staying in and going to the beach. Here he seems to be enjoying himself in the company of his aides, including his son Devdas, and relishing a few placid moments, a luxury he rarely allowed himself.

A few months later, Art Theatre, a Calcutta-based production company, made a film titled *Mahatma Gandhi in Calcutta*, which was passed by the Bengal Board of Film Censors on 28 November 1924. Gandhi had visited the city in connection with a meeting with Swaraj Party leaders and had addressed two public meetings at Howrah Town Hall in early November.

All these moving images featuring Gandhi had visuals only, and no sound. The technology of mixing picture and sound in a film was yet to arrive, and therefore newsreels of the time contained only visuals of Gandhi. In them we see a Gandhi who is very different from the image of Gandhi in the public consciousness. Gandhi here is fully clothed and has some hair on his head. He appears a short man and had not yet started to wear his famous round spectacles. As a series of such newsreels and topicals started getting made in India and abroad, it was only a matter of time before filmmakers featured Gandhi in full-length feature films.

2

It's Not Vidur; It's Gandhiji!

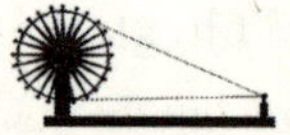

THE ENTRY OF GANDHI in a full-length feature film had all the elements of drama involved. Even though he was presented in the garb of a mythological character in the film *Bhakta Vidur*, people cutting across the society understood what they saw and cheered. This was the first time a Gandhi-like role, both in appearance and character, was presented in Indian cinema in 1921. The Censor Board soon realized the close connection between Vidur and Gandhi, and the film was first banned in Karachi, and then in Madras, for being 'a thinly veiled resume of political events in India with Vidur appearing as Mr Gandhi clad in Gandhi-cap and khaddar shirt'.[1] *Bhakta Vidur*, Kohinoor Film Company's silent era sensation, thus became the first feature film to be banned as part of the newly started censorship system in India. While banning the film, the Board said, 'We know what you are doing, it is not Vidur, it is Gandhiji. We won't allow it.'[2]

The story of *Bhakta Vidur* centred on the battle of the Pandavas and Kauravas, both sets of brothers being Vidur's nephews. Vidur was considered the epitome of knowledge and conscience, and the film very cleverly projected Mahatma Gandhi through his Character. Like Vidur, Gandhi advocated truth and ethics in life. When the film was released, the Indian National Congress led by Gandhi had launched an agitation to oppose the draconian provisions of the Rowlatt Act of 1919.

The Censor Board, therefore, observed that 'it [the film] is likely to excite disaffection against Government and incite people to non-cooperation'. Banning of this film, directed by Kanjibhai J. Rathod, under the Cinematograph Act in India, generated a huge controversy. The film was eventually re-released as *Dharma Vijay* in 1922 after ensuing some cuts, and people thronged to the theatres once again to watch it.

Dwarkadas N. Sampat, founder of Kohinoor Film Company, played the title role of Vidur with a close resemblance to Gandhi, wearing Gandhi-cap and khaddar shirt'.[3] Established in 1919, Kohinoor Film Company soon became one of India's leading film studios and focused on making films on subjects that were in tune with Sampat's Gandhian ideals. The songs, with specially written music score and performed live with every screening, in the film were in praise of the charkha (spinning wheel, as well as the Congress Party symbol then). '*Rudo mam rentiyo, rentiyama nikle taar, taare taare thai Bharatno udhaar*' (How beautiful is my spinning wheel, it spins out fine delicate thread, each thread helps elate Bharat). This song was first published by Virchand Dharamsey, a film historian of repute, who wrote the authoritative filmography of the Indian silent films.

The Gandhian connection in the film was vividly described by Sampat.

> Mahatma Gandhi's movement was in full swing at that time. I produced Bhakta Vidur. I was one of the artistes in the film and I played Vidur. I asked my artistes to treat me as Gandhi was treated by officials. I told them to forget that I was their boss. For the sake of realism, I asked them to beat me with sticks and stones when a scene required; my legs hurt, my back and shoulders ached. Where in one scene I was put in jail, I really cried. The fact, it was simulated

> Gandhi people saw on the screen was not disclosed at that time. There were people who saw the film six times or more. When the film reached Hyderabad (Sind), the British administration clamped a ban on it. *Bhakta Vidur* was screened at the Majestic Cinema in Bombay. The rush was so great that the police resorted to a lathi-charge to disperse the assembly.[4]

A leading newspaper, *Bombay Chronicle,* used the terms 'Swadeshi' and 'Glory of the East' to describe the film, where the acting skills displayed surpassed those of European cinema, according to the paper.[5]

It was interesting that a filmmaker imagined Gandhi in the mythological character of Vidur from the Mahabharata. The portrayal of Vidur to serve as an allegory for Gandhi and his freedom struggle was to return on screen after twenty-two years. In 1943, CIRCO Productions made a film *Mahatma Vidur* directed by Parshwanath Altekar and advertised it 'as the timely offering that brings to the screen in all glory and realism a page from India's greatest epic, the Mahabharata'. Though the film was initially announced as *Bhakta Vidur* in the promotional material,[6] the title was later changed to *Mahatma Vidur*, in all probability to highlight its connection to Gandhi.

The film, featuring Vishnupant Pagnis in the lead role, depicted incidents in the life of an unusual royal who renounces his position at the court and preaches the gospel of truth, non-violence and self-sacrifice. These very values were propagated by Gandhi as his tools in the struggle for India's independence. It turned out to be Pagnis's last film; the actor had become a living legend after his iconic title roles in *Sant Tukaram* and *Narsi Bhagat*.

In 1925, Kanjibhai Rathod, the maker of *Bhakta Vidur*, came up with a film, *Charkha,* under the banner of Rajkot-based Saurashtra Film Company. Rathod, considered by film historians as the first major professional director in Indian cinema, had left Kohinoor Film Company after directing many successful films. *Charkha* starred Ermeline and Madanrai Vakil in the main roles. The charkha featured prominently in this melodrama, whose alternative titles were *Spinning Wheel* and *Anath Abala,* indicating the values it showcased.

A year earlier, while directing *Sadguni Sushila* for Kohinoor Studio, Rathod had showed the female lead character spinning a charkha to portray her virtuous character. These cinematic efforts were clearly intended to establish a close connection with Gandhi and his values. Just six years had passed since Gandhi's arrival in India and he had successfully cast his spell not only on the general public but also on the nascent Indian film industry.

The charkha or spinning wheel, according to Gandhi, was the symbol of unity of Indian humanity. For him, spinning was a way to salvation for the poor and their linkage to God. 'While Khadi is good for the poor as an honourable occupation for earning bread, it has an additional and far greater value as an instrument of winning Swaraj through non-violent means.'[7] Independence for him was not just political independence but also meant Swaraj, seeing the nation as a republic where there would be freedom for the meanest of all countrymen. Therefore, Gandhi had purposefully included spinning as an essential activity for everyone in the struggle for independence. Moreover, he saw the charkha as an instrument to reach out to and connect with the vast rural masses.

Naturally, Gandhi spinning the charkha was a major visual opportunity for film companies. That is why several newsreels shot at various places show Gandhi spinning the yarn. For him, the activity of spinning was like a therapy and considered, 'The music of the wheel will be a balm to your soul'.[8] Sure enough, one sees Gandhi in these newsreels spinning away even while engaged in his other routine work; whether at the Ashram surrounded by his colleagues or at an important Congress meeting closeted with other leaders. His hands are constantly busy drawing out the yarn with meticulous precision, yard after yard, even while patiently listening to what others are saying. The charkha was his constant and essential companion even during his travels, and he used to carry a small foldable one everywhere. There is film footage showing Gandhi on the ship SS Rajaputana while on his way to attend the Second Round Table Conference in London, sitting on the open deck, busy spinning while curious co-passengers look on.

The charkha as a motif and symbol of the Gandhi-led movement for India's independence was to feature as a recurring theme in films across India. *Kalidas*, the first sound film in Tamil, was released in 1931 during the time when Gandhi-led Civil Disobedience Movement was launched. Even though the story was based on the life of one of the greatest Sanskrit poets, Kalidas, known for his epic poems *Meghaduta* (The Cloud Messenger) and *Raghuvamsha* (Dynasty of Raghu), the film had two songs praising Gandhi and the charkha.

Directed by the pioneering Tamil and Telugu director H.M. Reddy, the film had its lyrics written by Bhaskara Das. The lead actress T.P. Rajalakshmi sang these two patriotic songs: '*Ratina maam Gandhi kai banna maam*' (The charkha is an arrow in Gandhi's hand) and the other one with a nationalist overtone, '*Indiargal namma varakul eno veen sandai*' (We Indians, why are we fighting amongst ourselves?) The songs were meant to foster national unity. Incidentally, the film was shot in Bombay on the sets of *Alam Ara*, the first talkie film made in India.

Another Tamil film, *Seva Sadanam* (House of Service), was released in 1938 as part of a nationalist project by veteran director K. Subramanyam. Gandhian ideals were the focus in the film while emphasizing the cause of equal rights for women. The film is considered lost as of now, but the available publicity material shows the protagonist leading a group of women engaged in spinning yarn on the charkha, alluding to the Gandhian way of social reforms. Next year, Subramanyam came up with *Thyagabhoomi* (Land of Sacrifice) in Tamil, which again showed newsreel footage of Gandhi spinning the charkha. The main character of Sambu Sastri, played by Papanasam Sivan, was closely modelled on Gandhi, and the credits roll with the song '*Bharata Punya Bhoomi*' (The Holy Land of Bharat) sung by the well-known Carnatic musician and playback singer D.K. Pattammal.

The virtues of spinning yarn at the charkha continued to resonate in films across India. *Aaj Ka Hindustan* (India Today), a 1940 Hindi film produced by Shree Ranjit Movietone Co., had a song highlighting the importance of the charkha. A tale of two brothers, one nationalist and the other anglophile; the film exhorted women to spin yarn, which would turn the fortunes of the country. The song boldly proclaims Gandhi as the leader of the country: '*Charkha Chalao, Behno, Kato ye Kachhe Dhaage Dhaage ye kah rahe hain Bharat ke bhaag jage, Charkhe ke geet gaao, Duniya ko ye sunao Charkha chalanewala Gandhi hai aage-aage.*' (Sisters, spin the wheel and weave. The yarn proclaims the awakening of Bharat's destiny. Sing a song at the spinning wheel and tell the world that the man who is spinning is leading us.)

In the same year came a Hindi film, *Hindustan Hamara* (Our India), directed by Ram Daryani under the banner of Film Corporation of India. A feudal melodrama, the film prominently deployed the Gandhian symbol of the spinning wheel throughout. The song '*Charkha chal ke kaam banaye*' (Let us work through spinning the wheel) is a tribute to the spinning wheel. One of the best demonstrations of charkha was shot in a mass-spinning sequence in the epic documentary *Mahatma Gandhi* by A.K. Chettiar. It was filmed in Tirupur, now the hosiery town of Tamil Nadu. Two thousand women were seen spinning the charkha to the song '*Aadu ratte*' (Let the spinning wheel turn), written by Namakkal Kavignar Ramalingam Pillai and sung by D.K. Pattammal.

The symbolism of the charkha in films and its close connection with Gandhi were not lost on the British government. The Censor Board, its full control in the hands of government authorities, deleted several sequences in many films where the charkha was shown or mentioned and linked with Gandhi. A ten-reeler film made by Kohinoor United Artists had to change its title from *Naujawan Hoshiyar* to *Daring Youth* or *Shree Jawan* for these reasons. Scenes displaying the national flag as well as spinning wheel, takli, and the charkha (constituting 272 feet of film) were also cut by the Bombay Board of Film Censors.

In another film, *My Mother* or *Meri Ma,* made by National Film Co. Ltd., as many as sixteen scenes (106 feet of film) where the charkha and the flag of the Congress were exhibited, were cut. The axe of the Censor Board also fell on the words 'Gandhi the Great' wherever they occurred in the seven-reeler *The Slide Show* by Columbia Pictures of

America, and were replaced with the words 'Rama the Great'. Another Columbia production faced the same fate. Their two-reel production *Entertainer* was certified and passed for exhibition only after an entire portion, showing a player imitating Gandhi, clad in a loincloth and with a stick in hand, was cut.[9]

In 1931, Ardeshir Irani's Imperial Film Company produced *Khuda Ki Shaan* (Glory of God). Directed by R.S. Chaudhury, this silent film featured the character Garibdas Sadhu, played by Cowasji Makanda, who looked exactly like Gandhi. The caste system in India and its effect on society was the major focus of the film. Still, the film ran into trouble with the Censor Board on account of this character having been deliberately made to resemble Gandhi. And its original name, *The Wrath,* had to be changed to *Khuda Ki Shaan.*

But the most moving sequence involving the charkha appeared in a short film made on Gandhi's visit to Madras in 1946. The film, made by Projection of India Pictures, was titled *Mahatmaji's South Indian Tour and Harijan Yatra.* It started with visuals of the engine of the Gandhi Special train, which was decorated with flags and his portrait. At various places, Gandhi appeared outside the coach for darshan and made small speeches, including one at Trichinopoly Junction. A special mass spinning demonstration by villagers on the Manapparai station platform was the highlight of the footage with delightful Gandhi watching it from the train!

The Civil Disobedience Movement had gained momentum in the far-flung corners of the country in the 1930s. The motion picture companies, both Indian and foreign, had sent their camera teams to film these protests. It was estimated that about fifty film news crews were operating in early 1930, covering various events across the world. A report in one of the leading film trade magazines from Hollywood indicated the reach and importance of the Gandhi-led freedom movement among the newsreel companies. It said, 'Topping all these in importance at the moment, however, is the Fox Movietone News outfit in India, where Gandhi is leading a revolt against British rule that is fraught with possibilities of universal import. The attention of the world is focused on India as is a Fox Sound camera.'[10]

Takli: Machine Gun of Civil Disobedience

A closer look at the charkha, the spinning wheel, reveals its uncanny resemblance to the film projector! Both have a round spool around which one has to knead out the cotton or reel using the fingers or hands, and both make a revving sound while being operated. It needs basic training to operate these two machines—one produces yarn and the other projects moving images on a screen. Gandhi's charkha, a simple instrument, had steeped into the consciousness of the Indian masses. People from all strata of life had adopted spinning as part of their daily life. Visuals of people at the spinning wheel thus became a regular feature in newsreels as well as feature films. So, regardless of the clippers in the hands of the censors, the charkha continued to fascinate film companies.

One of these companies was British Movietone, which came out with a very interesting two-minute film on the charkha called *The Indian Takli*. The inter-title of the film read: 'The Machine Gun of Civil Disobedience: Spinner explains how the Takli will keep British cloth out of India.' This short film is a live demonstration of how the takli, a spinning wheel, works. It describes why it is a key part of Gandhi's Civil Disobedience Movement and would help India gain freedom by allowing its people to boycott foreign cloth.

The film opens with a visual of a khadi-cloth-clad volunteer wearing a Gandhi cap. The spinner, a dark-complexioned young man, explains in English that the takli is a substitute for the spinning wheel and is meant for those who cannot devote time at the charkha. The takli cost just one cent and could be conveniently carried about, he says. Spinning on the takli was very easy and could be learnt by anyone, even children.

While demonstrating the simple process, the young man elaborates with a straight face the logic behind the Swadeshi movement and emphasizes that if anyone spends four hours a day at the spinning wheel, the entire requirement of yarn for one's shirt, cap and dhoti would be taken care of, and in this way eliminate the need for purchasing foreign cloth. The entire economics behind the movement is explained without much fanfare in a short time. It is this clarity of thought that touched the minds of common people and sustained the movement for years.

We do not know whether this short film, made in English, was essentially meant for audiences in India, but given the wide reach of such topical films as part of a newsreel package, this wonderful demonstration film must have reached and amused audiences across the world. It was the best exhibition of Gandhi's novel idea and an apt advertisement for India's freedom movement.

'She's All for India!'

If British Movietone got an Indian volunteer to demonstrate how the takli was operated, Paramount News, their competitor, was not to be left behind. In fact, it went one step further and got Madeleine Slade, a disciple and a close aide of Gandhi's, to spin for the screen and explain the workings of this magic wheel. The curiosity of Western audiences who were far away geographically and culturally from India about this piece of equipment Gandhi had introduced as the panacea for the many ills of Indian society and as a weapon to fight British rule, could be satisfied to an extent only through such newsreels.

Already, the Western world was intrigued that Slade, a daughter of a senior British Admiral, had left everything, including her family, and joined the cause of India's freedom as one of the closest disciples of Gandhi. Getting Slade to talk on screen about the importance of the charkha was, therefore, a major coup of sorts for the studio, and Paramount rightfully termed the interview as 'exclusive'.

She is all for India!, the title of the Paramount topical film itself was a giveaway. Madeleine Slade, in her interview, which was shot in Bombay in 1932, explains how the charkha works. There is another film showing the same visuals but with a different title, '*Miss Slade Imprisoned*', and it added, 'Gandhi's English Disciple gives exclusive interview, prior to receiving 3-months gaol sentence.' The film opens with a long shot of Slade wearing a white khadi saree, sitting at the spinning wheel. She says:

> You had asked me to speak to you on the West, on the subject of the spinning wheel. Most of you may not know and you should have no idea about its possibilities. Well, here is the wheel. A very simple and beautiful thing you will see. And I propose to spin a little bit to show you. This is Mahatma Gandhi's great constructive idea for his suffering people. But it is an idea which exploiting buyers do not like. For it means India will learn to lead a simple, self-dependent life and stakes independence we have come to fight.

While Slade talks about the virtues of both the charkha and Gandhi, she is engaged in working the wheel and spinning a bit of yarn. She continues:

> As I speak here, I look across the blue sea to the distant mountains of Maharashtra. Up there in the Yerawada prison, he (Gandhi) is a simple silent figure. It is not for India alone that he suffers, but for all humanity; for a truer, simpler, happier life. By its aid, our impoverished peasant women can double their income. By this thread, our villages can produce limitless quantities of yarn which peasant weavers can turn into cloth. In this way, our village people can find their way back to the work and wealth which they enjoyed in the past. Mahatma Gandhi has done and is doing this with all the other means. For him it is forty years, he has led a life of … And now, at the age of sixty-three, he is lying in jail for the seventh time in his life … [The missing words are due to poor audio]

There are a few close-up shots of Slade with a wry smile, showing a shaved head under the drape of her saree, worn just the way Indian women did. Gandhi was already in jail at the time and she was to follow her mentor there. But it was a major triumph of Gandhi's ideas and thoughts that a Westerner, though his disciple, was seen on the screen propagating use of the spinning wheel in a fight against her own country of birth.

The title of the earlier short film, *Machine Gun of Civil Disobedience*, was clearly explosive and would not have fetched the approval of Gandhi, for his means were purely non-violent in his mission of attaining freedom for India. But the charkha surely played a very prominent role in easily mobilizing people in a country of the size of a subcontinent. Gandhi was very clear in his methods of non-violent civil disobedience, which was baffling to most of the Western world. His explanation for adopting this strategy was very simple, 'The British want us to put the struggle on the plane of machine guns where they have the weapons and we do not. Our only assurance of beating them is putting the struggle on a plane where we have the weapons and they have not.'[11]

If this two-minute film provides a glimpse of the power of a small handy instrument as a weapon in the hands of the common man, a master strategist was at work in conceptualizing it. The genius of Gandhi was to go further in choosing to walk for breaking a law concerning an item that was part of daily life for the same common man. It was salt, which he picked up at a small sea-side village in Gujarat, which catapulted him, through the images of the motion picture, firmly on the world stage.

3

Hail, Deliverer!

THE AMITABH BACHCHAN STARRER *Mard,* set in pre-independence India, was one of the highest grossing films of 1985. Bachchan's character Raju, in this Hindi film, is the son of an Indian king in British India called 'Mard' (Man)—meaning a true man, who does not feel any pain (*Mard ko dard nahin hota*). In one particular scene, Raju's love interest, Ruby, played by Amrita Singh, chains him and lashes him with a whip. She goes on to rub salt, literally, all over his wounded body. But instead of writhing in pain, Raju laughs aloud and declares, 'For this salt only, a Mahatma had started a movement. The blood of thousands of freedom fighters had become a part of this salt then. Today, by rubbing this salt on my body, my blood is getting assimilated with those of the martyrs!'

The genius of Manmohan Desai, the director of many such successful commercial pot-boilers, including the iconic *Amar Akbar Anthony* (1977), was at work here in evoking the memories of Gandhi's epic Dandi Salt March even after fifty-five years of the event. The sequence from *Mard* described above was indeed a true reflection of how the historical Dandi March is etched in the public imagination, and also how the Indian film industry tried to capitalize on Gandhi and events from his life cinematically and commercially.

The Dandi March was not only a significant event in India's quest for freedom, but it also firmly established Gandhi as a tall political strategist on the world map. His sheer imagination in drawing up a public campaign involving a few days' walk and the breaking of the salt law provided an excellent opportunity for film companies to capture something dramatic on camera. In the process, newsreel companies, both Indian and foreign, carried Gandhi's name and image across the world.

From the beginning of 1930, all eyes were on Gandhi as to what he was up to in the fight for India's independence. The speculation was rife that he was going to announce some major programme as part of the Civil Disobedience Movement. But nobody had any clue what it was going to be. Gandhi himself was struggling in the dark and searching for his inner voice to show him the light. In January that year, when poet Rabindranath Tagore met Gandhi in Sabarmati Ashram, the latter had confessed to Tagore his dilemma. Since the atmosphere was filled with anticipation, representatives of the media, including cameramen from motion picture studios, were hovering around the Ashram near Ahmedabad to catch the news.

In such a charged atmosphere, Gandhi announced on 5 March 1930 his intention to walk 241 miles towards the coast of Gujarat and break the salt law at Dandi. The idea was simple; challenge the British law ordaining that sale and production of salt by anyone but the British government was a criminal offence, punishable by law. The general reaction to Gandhi's dramatic announcement was sheer disbelief. Most of the Congress leaders too, leave alone the common man, could not initially appreciate the full import of the campaign of marching to the sea to break the law. His closest colleague Pt. Nehru said, 'We were bewildered. We could not quite fit in a national struggle with common salt.'[1]

Curiously, the British government also did not know how to react to this masterstroke by Gandhi. The event attracted huge eyeballs across the world. It indeed had all the characteristics of cinema; drama, suspense, sound and action. The British authorities, though initially bewildered, later dismissed the idea of boiling seawater in a kettle as 'the kindergarten stage of political revolution'. They thought not to make Gandhi a hero by arresting him at the start of the campaign itself, and they sincerely believed that the so-called march was going to end in a fiasco. The government, therefore, in its own wisdom, decided not to intervene and instead wait for events to unfold.

This provided an excellent opportunity for Gandhi and his band of followers to gain an enormous amount of goodwill and publicity. Every passing day, for twenty-five days, was filled with action and excitement. The inherent drama involved in conceptualizing the march and its execution made for more than enough material tailor-made for the motion picture camera. The visuals captured during the march led by Gandhi reached across Europe and travelled beyond the Atlantic to theatres in the USA. A simple act of walking to symbolically break the law captured the imagination of crores of people, and these moving images of the act enhanced its impact multifold.

Gandhi's close colleague Pandit Nehru, who was sceptical initially about the entire idea, later captured this impact in his vivid words:

> Many pictures rise in my mind of this man, whose eyes were often full of laughter and yet were pools of infinite sadness. But the picture that is dominant and most significant is as I saw him marching, staff in hand, to Dandi on the Salt March in 1930. Here was the pilgrim on his quest of Truth, quiet, peaceful, determined and fearless, who would continue that quest and pilgrimage, regardless of consequence.[2]

As Gandhi made his epic journey, accompanied by seventy-eight chosen men representing mini-India, several film companies came forward to shoot this historical event. There was excitement in the air, mounting every day as Gandhi marched towards his destination leading his pack of faithful followers and common villagers. While announcing the decision to march to break the salt law, Gandhi made it more dramatic by taking a vow not to return to the Sabarmati Ashram until India got independence! In such a charged atmosphere, the villagers on the way chose to walk with him till the next village, returning with memories of a lifetime.

Along the way, Gandhi, now sixty-one years of age, generated tremendous curiosity, and the cameras filmed these moments, to be screened across India for lakhs of viewers who couldn't take part in the march. Every day it was speculated that Gandhi would be arrested and put in jail. Gandhi himself thought so and had prepared an action plan in the event of his arrest. Noted psychoanalyst and author Sudhir Kakar describes the scene vividly:

> A cloud of dust, thrown up by trucks racing up and down the length of the column, settled on the marchers like a shroud. Hired by movie companies, the trucks carried camera equipment and newsreel crews trying to film the march from different angles. Gandhiji's odd challenge to the might of the British Empire had aroused a good deal of interest in many parts of the world. Fox Movietone, J. Arthur Rank and Paramount News were immediately recognizable from the logos pasted on the sides of their trucks. But there were also other, less familiar names; Deutshe Wochenschau from Germany or Cinepathe from France, for instance, names we never saw on our cinema screens. The technicians, even the British ones, waved to us as the trucks finally sped past the column to wait ahead at the village Gandhiji had announced as the first halt for the day.[3]

Even though Kakar's book *Mira and the Mahatma* is a fine blend of fiction and non-fiction, his description of the march is near perfect. In the available footage of the Dandi March, the moving image cameras sent by motion picture companies from across the world are seen mounted on the mobile trucks. The cameramen can be seen busy rotating their camera cranks by hand. The visuals also show these trucks moving in the midst of the march, with the cameramen atop them filming it.

This was not Gandhi's first such march though. While in South Africa, he had led about 2,000 people, including women and children, on 6 November 1913. He was arrested many times during that march from Charlestown to Natal. That march, for the cause of coal workers, brought laurels to Gandhi and he was hailed as the Hero of Natal.

Many prominent Indian film companies also filmed the Dandi March. These topicals were certified by the Censor Board of the time and released immediately. *Mahatma Gandhi's March for Freedom* was a two-reel (2,100 feet) film made by Sharada Film Company. *Mahatma Gandhi's Historic March* was also a two-reel (1,993 feet) film, produced by Shri Krishna Film Co. It was certified and passed by the Censor Board on 12 March 1930 for general release. Sardar Chandulal Shah's Shri Ranjit Film Co. made a one-reeler film titled *Mahatma Gandhi's March*.

Though these topicals had no sound, watching Gandhi sprinting towards his destination on screen is nothing short of exhilarating. With a bamboo stick in hand and vermilion smeared across his forehead, he walks so fast that his followers have to break into a trot to catch up with him. He is in total command, leading his followers with a gentle smile on his face. The visuals in these topicals show the villagers along the path of the march, waiting for Gandhi with folded hands on both sides of the road and garlanding him with flowers. True to his inclusive approach, it was his band of women followers who came out in significant numbers. Even though the walkers marched in line, it was not a regimental march. In the visuals, the march is a beautiful flow of a mass of people, striding along pleasantly.

Walking on dusty roads under the hot sun in the scorching summer is an exhausting exercise, to say the least, but Gandhi does not appear tired at all. For him, the simple solution of placing a towel on his bald head, as seen in the footage, is enough to give energy to sprint ahead.

In one visual, he is seen entering a house at the end of the day's walk and a volunteer welcoming him. He walks inside, enquires about others and then proceeds to take a well-deserved rest. Along the path of the march, sometimes there was no road at all, and the team had to trudge through fields.

In some visuals, a retinue of trucks carrying motion picture camera equipment can be clearly seen. At various stopovers, Gandhi held public meetings and spoke about the importance of the action he had initiated. His first stop was at a small village Aslali, where he said: 'If, out of Gujarat's population of 90 lakhs, we leave out women and children, and the remaining 30 lakhs get ready to violate the salt tax, the Government does not have enough accommodation in jails to house so many people.'[4]

A leading French film studio, Gaumont Film Company, shot some of these meetings, which went into a film titled *Gandhi Starts Campaign of Civil Disobedience.* The inter-title card reads, 'Exclusive Gaumont Graphic pictures rushed from India by specially chartered aeroplane!' Another caption describe the scenes: 'Village folk of Aslali hear from Gandhi his final plans.' In one of the topicals made by Bombay-based Shree Krishna Film Co., the inter-title cards are in Gujarati. The cameramen had travelled to the next village, where the march was to make a stop, to shoot the volunteers carrying the necessary supplies for the satyagrahis in advance.

The inter-title card explains the scene thus: 'The day before the march, Bapuji sent a team to make advance arrangements.' Another inter-title card says, 'In prayer meetings held in villages along the march, Bapuji explained [to] the people how to break the salt law.' An interesting third card reads: 'The government banned the filmmakers from showing the film to the public.' There is also footage of a retinue of musicians taking up the front of the march and playing their instruments. Some of the men are dancing impromptu.

On the last day of the march, senior Congress leader and Gandhi's trusted lieutenant Sarojini Naidu received him at Dandi. Like her colleagues, she too was not sure initially about the efficacy of breaking a salt law. But after seeing the tremendous response for the march, Naidu was a changed person and decided to join her leader. There is a very endearing visual from that day. Even after having walked ten miles every day under the hot sun, Gandhi has only a smile on his lips. He is energetic and chivalrous, and can be seen offering a hand to Sarojini Naidu, ten years younger than he, to climb up to the podium! Gandhi's address to the large crowd from the podium under a large leafy tree has been filmed too. In words befitting the occasion, he said:

> Dandi was chosen not by a man but by God. How otherwise could we have chosen for the battlefield of satyagraha such an out-of-the-way place—a place where no food grains are to be had, where there is a scarcity of water, where thousands can assemble only with difficulty, walking ten miles from the railway station, and where if you are travelling on foot, you have to negotiate creeks full of slush and mud? The truth is that in this struggle we have to put up with suffering.[5]

'India's Nightingale' Sarojini Naidu was at her poetic best while standing beside the man of the moment and cheered, 'Hail Deliverer!'. The visuals show Gandhi having a bath on the morning of 6 April at the seashore in Dandi. While taking a pinch of salt in his hand, Gandhi delivered those prophetic words, 'With this, I am shaking the foundations of the British Empire.'[6] Strangely enough, even though cameras had followed him all the way to the coast on this historical march, the climax of the march, of Gandhi picking up the salt from the seashore in his hands, was probably not filmed. If it had been, then the footage is not to be found now.

A month later, the British government, which had made all the wrong moves till then, decided that enough was enough. Thus, Gandhi was arrested at midnight at Karadi near Dandi on 5 May 1930 and taken to Yerawada jail in Poona. Universal Studios immediately reported this development with a newsreel titled *Leader of Millions Jailed by Authorities*, and showed visuals of Gandhi speaking from a raised platform. Gandhi is also shown moving among the crowds, his followers coming up to him one by one and touching his feet. Women come up to him and smear vermilion on his forehead. Gandhi was arrested, but he had already ignited the imagination of the people.

It was also the beginning of the Civil Disobedience Movement, the protests being on a scale never seen before in India. Gandhi had galvanized the entire nation with patriotic fervour. Bombay was the major centre of agitations, and the topicals of the time show stirring visuals of peaceful protests being lathi-charged by police.

Apart from the Indian and foreign film studios, there was one gentleman who also shot two rolls of film on the Dandi March at a great personal risk. A.K. Chettiar, creator of the epoch-making documentary 'Mahatma Gandhi: 20th Century Prophet' approached him and managed to get about 2,000 feet of the rushes. It consisted of visuals of the Dandi March, from beginning to the end. This individual had shot the footage at his own expense. He had also shot scenes of the huge processions in Bombay, risking lathi charge by police. According to Chettiar, 'The film on the Dandi March was wonderful and the shooting was of very high standard.'[7] Unfortunately, Chettiar's documentary is not yet available in full in the public domain, so neither is the Dandi footage acquired from the unknown gentleman.

Some films on the Dandi March, though, faced the wrath of the Censor Board. Two films made by Shree Krishna Film Co., titled *Civil Disobedience at Dandi 6th April 1930* and *Civil Disobedience at Dandi 7th April 1930,* of one reel each of 1,000 feet, were prohibited from being screened by the Bombay Board of Film Censors (BBFC) on 22 April 1930. The Censors said the films were calculated to foster resistance to the government and promote breach of law and order.[8]

Two newsreels made by Universal Pictures Corporation having No. 38 (1930) and No. 44 were ordered by BBFC to omit the scenes showing Mahatma Gandhi at Dandi at the time he was engaged in breaking the salt law. It was also ordered to cut the inter-title 'First round pictures from scene of the great Hindu uprising show all Bombay backing Gandhi's fight for freedom from British Rules', as well as the scenes thus captioned by it. Hearst Metrotone News No. 1 newsreel of MGM also faced the same fate. The Censor Board asked the makers to omit the sub-title, 'Bombay becomes Venice for day, Gandhi's cohorts call it all when streets of Indian City are flooded by the heaviest monsoon in 50 years.'

The impact the historic Dandi March created has been corroborated in the British official records. In a report by the Director of the Intelligence Bureau to the Home Member in August 1930, just a few months after the event, he wrote:

> The Congress was able to command whatever support it wanted in that town; its volunteers and picketers were fed free by the people; its 'stranglehold' on business of every sort was complete; many businessmen were prepared to continue in the movement, even though ruin stared them in the face; in short, the Congress was 'completely in command', with the initiative entirely in its hands.[9]

To some extent, this impact could be attributed to the short films and topicals made by the Indian and foreign film studios, which were screened in theatres across India and elsewhere. Gandhi told the villagers at Dandi:

> You have made the road from Navsari to Dandi famous throughout the world by arranging for free drinking water at frequent intervals all along it ... Dandi should be a sacred ground for us, where we should utter no untruth, commit no sin. Everyone coming here should come with this devout feeling in his heart.[10]

It was not just the topical and newsreel makers who were interested in the Dandi March. Indian filmmakers had realized the dramatic value of this movement and tried to portray it in some of their nationalist projects, which were made in several different languages.

Ten years after the Dandi March, the film *Uthama Puthiran* was made in Tamil. An adaptation of the English film *The Man in the Iron Mask*, the film was directed by T.R. Sundaram. The promotional poster announced it as a nationalist film in Tamil. Gandhi and Bharat Mata (Mother India) were mentioned in the first reel of the film and there was a vivid reference to the Dandi March. The singing star P. Chinnappa played a double role in the movie. In Telugu, the film *Padandi Munduku* was made in 1962; basing its core theme around Gandhi's Dandi Salt March. Directed by V. Madhusudhana Rao, the film showcased people's participation in the struggle against British economic monopoly.

Valorizing Gandhi's leadership in the nationalist struggle, the film also highlighted Gandhian self-dependence as a fundamental prerequisite for freedom. Inspired by Dilip Kumar's Hindi film *Shaheed* (1948), based on India's freedom movement, the veteran producer–director Rao decided to make one in Telugu. The story, written by P. Chengaih, featured a family of freedom fighters that had a strong connection with Gandhi's salt satyagraha. The film also contained old newsreel footage of speeches by Gandhi and of the hoisting of the tricolour flag at Red Fort by Nehru. The critically acclaimed movie was screened at the prestigious Moscow International Film Festival as well as the Tashkent Film Festival.

Even in the new millennium, the magic of the Dandi March has not yet worn off. Seventy-seven years later, a film production team followed the trail of the original Salt March, stopping at the same villages and towns, in search of Gandhi's legacy. Made by the Wide Eye Film in 2008 in Hindi, English and Gujarati, the film was directed by Lalit Vachani. *In Search of Gandhi* is a road movie about issues of livelihood in the present times and the future of democracy in India. It is a documentary about 'the salt stories' of our times.

News of Gandhi's innovative form of struggle had reached the far corners of the world and people got to know about India's unique freedom movement led by him. How it influenced the minds of common man in UK has a fascinating story told by Lowel Thomas, one of the most successful radio stars and newsreel commentators. While talking to his audience on the National Broadcasting Company (NBC), one of the two major nationwide networks in the United States, in 1938, he said,

> Years ago, in London, I was talking on India just at the time Gandhi was campaigning against the salt tax. In the midst of my speech, one night, a woman in the audience stood up and began shrieking, 'Down with salt tax! Down with Lowel Thomas!' over and over again. She kept at it for several minutes and turned up next day and did the same thing and continued her protest for three days. On the fourth day, she was arrested, and Thomas went to Police station and got her released. He said, 'If I could, I would have paid her to make the disturbance every night! You have no idea how it electrified the audience and made them aware of what I was telling them about India.'[11]

After India became independent, there was another Dandi spectacle planned. An American theologian, E. Stanley Jones, who knew Gandhi well, proposed a reverse march, back to Sabarmati Ashram. It was to fulfil the vow Gandhi had so dramatically taken before leaving for the Dandi March. When Jones wrote to Gandhi in 1948 about his idea of holding a pageant to come back to Sabarmati, eighteen years after he first set out, Gandhi replied, 'The withdrawal of the British troops from India would be the greatest pageant conceivable.' He also said, 'I don't know when I will be able to leave my present haunts.' He was then in Bihar, busy restoring peace in the areas where Hindu-Muslim riots had taken place.

Jones persisted in pushing the idea through Gandhi's secretary Rajkumari Amrit Kaur, who later became India's minister of health. After Gandhi's death, she wrote, 'When I presented the suggestion to him, he smiled and said, "I must do or die here in Delhi. Nothing else matters now."'[12] Sadly, this reverse march was not destined to happen. Otherwise, the event would have received the kind of motion picture coverage that might have surpassed the publicity fetched by the original event.

A day before Gandhi was to break the salt law at Dandi, he had declared, 'I want world sympathy in this battle of right against might.' The moving visuals of this historic march were splashed across the world, ensuring not only sympathy for India's freedom movement, but also firmly establishing this battle as a 'right' one, in tune with Gandhi's ideals of right means for right ends. The motion picture images of the Dandi March also firmly placed Gandhi as one of the most popular leaders on the world map.

4

Gandhi's Talkie Debut

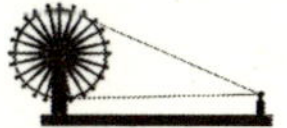

IT WAS A HOT and sunny day on 30 April 1931 in Borsad, a small mofussil village in central Gujarat. In the afternoon, a bullock cart came up the courtyard of a house where Gandhi was staying. The cart was loaded with huge film equipment consisting of picture and sound cameras from the American motion picture company Fox Movietone. Walter J. McInnis, a cameraman dressed in a khaki short-sleeved shirt and shorts, who came with the cart, took off his hat, greeted a gentleman wearing a suit in the courtyard and exchanged pleasantries with him.

The short man in a suit was the veteran American journalist James A. Mills from a leading news agency, Associated Press (AP). McInnis enquired about the presence of Mahatma Gandhi in the house and asked about the chances of taking talking pictures of Gandhi. Mills was surprised at the mention of talking pictures. He then cautioned McInnis that Gandhi was one of the most difficult subjects in the world for a talkie picture because he had a very feeble voice, apart from having a very deep aversion to being photographed. The Fox crew was not to be disheartened by these warnings because they had travelled far, enduring the tropical heat and other vagaries of nature, to accomplish their mission in India. After confirming Gandhi's presence, McInnis gestured to his colleague William K. Hawk, the sound operator sitting in the bullock cart, to move inside along with equipment.

The efforts and perseverance of these three gentlemen, Mills, McInnis and Hawk resulted in what we have today a historical document; the first talkie interview of Gandhi. Almost one year after the famous Dandi March, Mills sat down cross-legged on the floor to interview Gandhi while the motion picture camera rolled. Unlike all the earlier footages on Gandhi, this had recorded sound too. It indeed was a major coup. Mills managed to get Gandhi to talk and got both action and sound recorded for the first time. It was historical event for the cinema industry because Gandhi was one of the first political leaders of India whose voice was recorded while he was so being filmed.

Mahatma Gandhi Talks is the title of the first ever motion picture talkie interview of Gandhi. Taken by James Mills, the interview was broadcast by Fox Movietone News and British Movietone, and also by several other film companies across the world. Fox Movietone was quick to highlight the uniqueness of the film in their opening inter-title card that said, 'Fox Movietone News brings to you the first talking picture ever made by India's famous leader, given exclusively to us at his home in Borsad.'

Several versions of this special interview were made by Fox, British Movietone and also by Hearst Metrotone News Company. The newsreel actually starts with the visuals of Gandhi and his wife Kasturba returning from their daily early morning walk, with his secretary Mahadev Desai and his disciple Madeline Slade following. Gandhi, wearing nothing but a loincloth, walks taking long strides. He throws a glance at the camera but moves ahead without acknowledging it. The walking party, busy in animated talk, enters the house.

Incidentally, the Gandhi talkie interview was recorded only a month after sound technology had been introduced in Indian cinema. *Alam Ara*, the first Indian talkie film, made by Ardeshir Irani for Imperial Film Company, was released on 14 March 1931. Being the initial days of the technology, recording of sound was a really challenging task. We already know that the Fox Movietone team had to carry heavy sound equipment by bullock cart to Borsad to record this interview of Gandhi. Mills was dressed in a full suit and tie for the special interview, and it was quite a task for him to sit cross-legged opposite Gandhi and ask questions in the hot and humid weather!

Amusingly, throughout the entire interview, Gandhi didn't care to turn towards the camera and answered questions with his head bowed down most of the time. He did not even look at Mills, the interviewer, and was busy, uncharacteristically, picking his toes. Was he nervous at facing the motion picture camera at very close quarters? But even if he was, it didn't show on his face. His voice was steady, and he spoke in a low and measured tone during the entire conversation.

What a contrast these two men presented—Gandhi sitting with his legs in a scissor-cross position resting his back against a big white cushion, wearing his customary dhoti and bare-chested; and Mills, a short, well-built man, fully clothed with a tie. Gandhi was wearing his famous round spectacles. A bit of grey hair was visible on his bare chest, and his head was completely bald. Mills asked questions from his notebook, and while Gandhi answered, he took copious notes.

The setting was very simple. Rather, there was no setting at all for such an important interview. It was filmed in a room of the village house Gandhi was staying in, with possibly no use of flashbulbs or artificial lights. The only source of light was the natural light coming in from the windows behind Gandhi. There were no decorative items, and no furniture was visible. Both gentlemen sat on a carpet on the ground and talked.

Mills started the interview by asking Gandhi, who was going through a paper in his hand, 'Mr Gandhi, you may tell us, please, when you expect to leave for London for the Second Round Table Conference.' Gandhi answered without looking at either Mills or the camera, 'Well, I have no notion. And I don't expect to go there if the Hindu-Muslim question is not effectively solved.' In answer to a question about what course of action he would follow if England did not grant his demand,

Gandhi said, 'Of course, Civil Disobedience. And all other phases of Satyagraha are always at our disposal. But whether we shall resort to this weapon immediately or what other steps we shall take, I cannot state at present.'

Gandhi spoke in a slow and low voice and offered a benign smile at this moment. In the event of England accepting his demand, would there be complete prohibition in the new Indian state, was the next question. Gandhi was emphatic in his answer, 'Oh, yes!' Mills probed further, 'Absolute prohibition?' Gandhi affirmed, 'Absolute.' Mills then asked about the possibility of abolition of child marriage in India after Independence. Gandhi answered, 'I should very much like to [see child marriages abolished], even before.'

The next question was about extermination of the caste system and the future of 60 million untouchables in India after Independence. Gandhi was again firm in averring that it would be exterminated 'most decidedly'. While answering a question about communal and social harmony between Hindus and Muslims in independent India, Gandhi replied, 'I look forward to seeing complete social harmony and unity and I should be severely disappointed if it was otherwise.' Mills proceeded to ask, 'Do you expect England, this time, will give India self-government?' Gandhi thought for a while and said, 'That also not I can say.' Mills then asked, 'But you are hopeful.' Gandhi's answer was characteristic of him: 'I am an optimist.'

The Western world was always intrigued about Gandhi's scanty way of dressing which they called as loin-cloth. On this issue, Gandhi himself had made a tongue-in-cheek remark, 'Mr Churchill has been kind enough gratuitously to advertise my loin-cloth to the whole world.' It prompted Mills to ask whether he would wear the same dress while attending the Second Round Table Conference in London. Gandhi had no qualms in answering, 'I shall certainly not be found in European dress. And if the weather permitted, I should present myself exactly as I am today!' Mills was probably not taken in by Gandhi's honest answer and persisted with another question, 'And, if the King of England invited you to a dinner at Buckingham Palace, you would go in a customary Indian dress?' Gandhi was candid this time when he said, 'In any other dress, I should be most discourteous to him because I should be artificial.'

As the interview progressed, Mills was clearly in discomfort sitting on the ground and was shuffling his legs continually. He then asked, 'If England does not grant your demand, are you prepared to return to jail again?' Gandhi, with his head bowed, managed a smile and answered, 'I am always prepared to return to jail.' It was now Mills's turn to offer a half-laugh at Gandhi's answer. But he was not yet finished, and asked, 'Would you be prepared to die in the cause of India's Independence?' Gandhi thought for a while and dismissed the question with a smile, 'It is a bad question!'

Towards the end of the interview, Mills thanked his subject while saying, 'It was a brief expression of bridging a friendship through Fox British Movietone News for British public please, Mr Gandhi.' In response, Gandhi said:

> Well, I am glad to be able to say that the circle of British friends is ever increasing, and it could not be otherwise as the Satyagraha movement, however much it may be misrepresented, is nothing but a movement for promoting goodwill amongst those against whom we seem to be fighting. Therefore, I have no misgivings as to the ultimate result.

Gandhi then suddenly realized that the allotted time for the interview was over and glanced at his famous round watch lying on his lap. With an apologetic smile he said, 'There is no time left now!' Mills was gracious in expressing his gratitude. 'Thank you very much, Mr Gandhi, for your kindness and patience. I should also like to thank you on behalf of Fox Movietone News for the message given today to the American Public, and through Fox British Movietone News for the British Public.'

The camera was still focused on Gandhi and there was a wide toothless grin on his face while Mills offered his gratitude. 'Thank you,' said Gandhi, and gestured his aide to come and help him resume the work even while the camera was still rolling. It is most likely the interview was not edited, and the last visuals of Gandhi talking to his aide revealed the humane side of the man in an unguarded moment!

Gandhi's first-ever talkie interview for the screen was heralded as a great achievement for the film industry. *Motion Picture Herald*, a leading international film magazine from the USA, was quick to highlight its importance in an article headlined 'Another clear-cut triumph for the brute power of movies'.[1] The report put Gandhi in the list of other world leaders who were filmed on camera while talking including Mussolini, King Carol II of Romania and Alfonso XIII, King of Spain. Their sub-headline was 'Filming a great soul', and the report said:

> It would be safer not to trust too much the movie cameramen when they say they found Gandhi, the Mahatma, more capricious and temperamental than Hollywood stars. The really interesting thing is not his manner. It is his submission to even a short session before the camera. That is another clear-cut triumph for the brute power of the movies. The news accounts say he broke a twenty-five-year resolution never to be formally photographed and put away his dislike for things mechanical to go through with the business. To many it will seem a curious identification of the Eastern ascetic with these typical Western ways of life which previously he has rejected.

The report goes on to add that,

> Western high-pressure publicity, Western entertainment for the masses, Western exploitation of a personality—these are scarcely things one would have thought of in connection with the Hindu philosopher and advocate of spinning by hand. Whether he was motivated by some desire to conciliate the large though vague popular following attracted to him in the West; or by some political motive not yet disclosed to us; or just possibly, by some secret vanity, we shall not guess ... Whatever his motive, the movies have had their way with another 'world leader', who is also an authentic 'great soul'.

The leading newspaper of the world The *New York Times* was also quick to highlight the importance of the event and reported the news of the interview the next day. Its report was headlined, 'Gandhi tortured by Talkie Debut'[2] and gave a full account of the interview. The report said he discussed prohibition, his mode of dressing, and America in the film interview. It added that Gandhi was uncertain of his visit to the USA and he hoped not to be regarded as a 'freak' if he managed to come to the USA after India won the fight.

Motion Picture Herald, in its issue immediately following James Mills' first-ever talkie interview of Gandhi, carried an article titled, 'Recording Mr Gandhi'. It said,

> The recording of the elusive and reluctant Mahatma Gandhi by Fox Movietone News, presented this week at the Embassy on Broadway, is one of the romantically adventurous achievements of the sound screen. The labours of "Crew 42", struggling with ponderous equipments through jungle villages in a tropic temperature of 130 (Fahrenheit) degrees and their struggle with the moods of the strange Gandhi, surpass in heroic quality many a more loudly proclaimed feat of the cinema.[3]

The same journal devoted two full pages in colour to showcase the importance of this Gandhi interview with a collage of various current newspaper headlines. A similar two-page colour coverage was given by *The Film Daily* in their 19 May 1931 issue. A cursory glance at these headlines would reveal the significance imparted by the media. 'Gandhi in a Talkie Role Breaks 25-year Rule; Sets All India Rabbling'; 'Gandhi Gives First Movie Interview'; 'Gandhi persuaded to pose and talk for news cameras'; 'India is surprised by Actor Gandhi'; Gandhi's Talkie Debut Amazes Followers'; 'Gandhi Poses for Talkie Pictures'.[4]

Another New York-based film magazine, *Film Daily*, in its issue of 31 May 1931, carried a prominent report on the interview. The report highlighted the lack of interest Gandhi showed in granting such an interview, and it remarked that this was really an unusual phenomenon in the era of newsreels. 'When the newsreel fellers want to photograph some celeb in an interview, most everybody jumps at the chance … from Mussolini up or down … but not so Mister Mahatma Gandhi, the uncrowned ruler of millions of Hindus … who would die for him if he said the word.'

The magazine further highlighted the challenges faced by the Fox Newsreel team and called Gandhi a 'temperamental actor'! Again 'He refused to prepare a speech or talk extemporaneously … he said they could photograph him at his work.' Therefore, the only chance for the team to get him to talk was to have a third man (in this case James Mills) question him while they worked the apparatus. Apparently, on one occasion, Gandhi agreed to take his work outside where the light was good but changed his mind next morning! He also refused to move closer to the window, and so the team had no light but back light, and had to keep their lenses wide open. With the microphone placed 12 inches from Gandhi's face, ensuring quality recording of sound was a herculean task.'

Exasperated with the whole experience, McInnis and Hawk in their report said, 'He is temperamental and conceited … a hopeless case for sound picture. But if, in the future, he loses his conceit and egotism and becomes normal, he will possibly make a good subject.' The commentator then cheekily remarked, 'from all of which you can gather that Mr Gandhi didn't want to appear in a Newsreel and tell what a Big Shot he is … but if he ever loses this conceit and egotism, he will become normal … like the rest of the Hollywood actors.'[5]

Extracts from this historic talkie interview of Gandhi were also screened by other motion picture companies across the world. Hearst Metrotone News, a US film studio, had an arrangement with Fox Film Corporation to use their material. Using the Fox Movietone Sound System, they made a topical film carrying the pictures and sound recording from Gandhi's interview by James Mills. It was titled *Mahatma Gandhi Makes First Talk for Metrotone*, and added another inter-title, 'India's renowned leader gives film interview at his home in Borsad.' The narrator described its significance by saying, 'You are about to hear for the first time, the voice of the most remarkable man in the world today ... Listen to this extraordinary man.' There is advice and caution added, 'You must listen carefully as his natural shyness makes him speak almost in whispers.'

British Movietone came out with their own topical film using the same footage, titled *Gandhi is Persuaded to Talk.* It said, 'Movietone is present at an interview given by Indian leader to a representative of the American Press.' The next title card says,

> In retreat, in the village of Bosgad [read Borsad], the nationalist leader sits and plays for the Hindu-Moslem settlement which will substantiate his claim to represent all India. Our associates, Fox Movietone News, surprised Gandhi giving an interview to an American Press Correspondent and were able to record the following questions and answers.

The footage showing Gandhi walking with his wife Kasturba and others is then shown. The narrator then adds, 'Gandhi believes in early morning exercise. Here we see him returning from his 6 o' clock walk accompanied by his wife and Ms Slade.' The group is then shown entering the house, and then the interview starts.

The British subsidiary of Fox Movietone had all along tried to toe the government line, and therefore it was understandable that they played down the importance of this historic interview. Their editorial line and the tone and tenor of the inter-titles in their topical film clearly indicated this bias.

While Gandhi's talkie interview was being celebrated as a major achievement for the cinema industry worldwide, one also has to remember that India's foremost revolutionary freedom fighter Bhagat Singh was hanged just few days before the interview and arguably found no mention in any of the newsreels of the time. A fiery Bhagat Singh embraced death for the cause of India's freedom along with two of his colleagues, Sukhdev and Rajguru, on 23 March 1931. Though Gandhi differed with them in their ideology, he had pleaded their case with Viceroy Irwin for commuting their death sentence. But the British government was hell-bent on it, and in fact brought forward the hanging from the scheduled time by eleven hours, for fear that pressure might build to save them. Bhagat Singh, a handsome, young twenty-three-year-old was, arguably, an equally popular in India, but even his heroic sacrifice was not considered worthy of a newsreel. What was denied to him in his lifetime has now been more than compensated for, and many biopics have been made post-Independence to celebrate his patriotism.

Gandhi's political bête-noire Winston Churchill also had one of his talks filmed just a few days before Gandhi's talkie interview. Churchill was slated to address a public meeting on the subject of India in London, and the small talk that was filmed was like a curtain raiser for this event. Churchill clearly had a flair for publicity, about which UK's former Prime Minister Lloyd George later remarked: 'He would make a drum out of the skin of his own mother in order to sound his own praises.'[6] At that time, Churchill was one of the emerging leaders of his party. His talk was filmed on camera by Fox Movietone News on 12 March 1931 in London. He spoke about the current situation in India while sitting at his desk. Known for his oratorial skills, Churchill's talk was pointed and forceful. In fact, the available unedited footage showed that the interview was rehearsed many times before both Churchill and the crew were fully satisfied. For good measure, Churchill told his viewers that there could be interference and disturbance by the communists in the proposed meeting and not to worry about the same!

If things had happened as envisaged by a German director, Gandhi's moving visuals, along with dialogue, could have been taken much earlier. Noted German cinematographer and director Walter Ruttmann had planned to film Gandhi and Rabindranath Tagore in conversation for his talking film *The Melody of the World* as early as in 1928, almost three years before the Fox Movietone interview. *Exhibitor Daily Review*, a film trade magazine, reported that Ruttmann was leaving for America to engage notable people in his talking film, which it described as a 'world sound-film symphony'.[7] It also said the sound system he planned to use was the Tri-Ergon Music A.G. which was same as Movietone.

Fox Movietone News had also managed to film a small speech by Indian philosopher J. Krishnamurti on 14 April 1928. The film was called *Youthful Prophet from India*. Looking almost like a dashing Al Pacino from the popular Hollywood classic film *Godfather*, Krishnamurti, then thirty-three years old, was filmed speaking on the way to spiritual happiness. This could have been filmed during his trip to the USA. There was also a small speech filmed on Indian leader and poet Sarojini Naidu by Fox Movietone News in their studio during her visit to the USA on 1 November 1928. Wearing an exquisite Indian saree, she stood and spoke in the most graceful language about the important historical role of women in Indian civilization.

James Mills, Gandhi's interviewer, was a veteran American foreign correspondent from Associated Press (AP). He was active during the two decades between 1920 and 1940, having covered fifty-four countries across five continents. Mills was one of the very few media men who filmed Gandhi extensively from November 1930 to mid-1932, and also took several of his iconic photographs. He had also managed to do a full-fledged interview of Gandhi in January 1931 in Poona. After being tipped off about Gandhi's imminent release from prison, Mills waited for ninety-six long hours at the gates of Yerawada jail. Then, at last, Mills spotted Gandhi and recalled, 'a tiny fragment of humanity, shivering in the chilled peach blue in the Indian dark.'

It was known that Gandhi didn't like being photographed and therefore, he didn't cooperate in posing for the camera. This was keeping with his distrust of modern machines, but he also did not object to being photographed. Talking about his experience, Mills said, 'Of the thousands of public men I have filmed or interviewed, none have been more difficult to handle than Mahatma Gandhi, that curious combination of politician, mystic, philosopher, saint, and seer, who is fighting for the freedom of 36,00,00,000 Indians.'[8]

This historic talkie interview of Gandhi by Mills is not available in its entirety. Only a few minutes of footage exists in the public domain. Still, what is available is a great piece of history. It was not that Gandhi was inaccessible to media. He had been interviewed by both Indian and foreign media regularly on a variety of topics. In the month of April 1930 itself, when this talkie interview happened, he had granted interviews to three different print media houses, viz., *Statesman*, *Tej* and *Associated Press of India*. An active journalist himself, Gandhi had been editing two journals, *Young India* and *Navajivan*, apart from running *Indian Opinion* during his South Africa days.

But this interview was unlike others. Despite his dislike of being photographed, here he was, filmed from close quarters, and his speech recorded too. It is a great mystery how Gandhi allowed himself to be filmed because he did not hold the medium of cinema in high esteem. It could be only due to the close proximity James Mills had developed with Gandhi that such an interview could take place.

Gandhi was not too keen to be interviewed for camera, and he made his displeasure known, 'I do not like this kind of thing, but I shall reconcile to it, if not more than few minutes have to be given.' But he also knew its importance and said, 'Although I know this sort of enterprise will advertise you, which is your primary object, I know also that it will serve to advertise the cause which I represent—India's independence.'[9] In keeping with his solemn vow taken in 1905, Gandhi declined to pose for the interview. It was supposed to be conducted in the courtyard of the house for better visibility, but had to be held in his room finally.

Due to a certain familiarity with Gandhi's way of dressing, of wearing only a loincloth, we do not realize the fact that sitting for this all-important interview with his upper body uncovered was a big deal. Considering the special occasion and the fact that he was being recorded on film from close quarters for an audience spread worldwide, he had no qualms about not dressing up for the occasion. It is to his credit that he was his natural self, without any hint of awkwardness. It is unthinkable for any political leader to do this in today's times of constant media onslaught, where looking good in crisp designer clothes is a must.

Arguably, this was the only instance when Gandhi could be seen answering questions in a sit-down interview. Gandhi has been filmed many times talking to the press and in motion pictures over the years.

But they showed him simply speaking, not being interviewed. There is no such footage available of an interview of Gandhi in moving images. And it is likely he did not grant any to any other journalist since this interview.

The US-based Fox News started its services in 1919, and when sound technology arrived, it came to be known as Fox Movietone. The network was a pioneer in bringing sound to newsreels when it screened news of the first transatlantic flight piloted by Charles A. Lindberg on 20 May 1927. The Italian dictator Mussolini became the first political leader on which a talking picture was recorded on 6 May 1927. Fox Movietone started producing newsreels along with sound, and one of the earliest in the series featured George Bernard Shaw and was released on 25 June 1928. Fox Movietone News was one of the earliest and also longest running of all the American newsreels. In the UK, it was known as British Movietone News. It is estimated that at least 40 million people in the United States and more than 200 million people worldwide watched newsreels each week in the late 1930s.[10]

A veteran Fox Movietone cameraman, Charles Peden, described the difficulty in chasing the elusive Gandhi, and then arranging and managing the interview the studio had been trying so hard to get. He remarked,

> Mahatma Ghandi is a tough old bird. He thinks he is a pretty hot subject, but he is testy and cranky to deal with. He heartily detested the ordeal of being filmed at Broad [Borsad] India and did everything to discourage the interview. When the boys finally pinned him down, he refused to move out where the light would be favourable and would not speak above a whisper. He was nailed only after chase in over half of India, through terrific heat and untold discomforts.[11]

Bombay-based Imperial Movietone Studio did not encounter so much difficulty in getting a message from Gandhi. After his hectic parleys with Viceroy Irwin, there was an announcement of a truce known as the Gandhi-Irwin Pact. Imperial Studio prepared a topical film based on these events for the screen. It was titled *Mahatma Gandhi after Truce*. It was reported that Mahatma Gandhi cooperated with the company: 'Mahatma Gandhi was pleased to afford special facilities to the Imperial Movietone Company and the Company has brought out a sort of unusual interest. Mahatma's message is made available to the public and they were pleased to hear his message from his own lips about the utility of Khadar.'[10]

Far away in Lahore, Punjab Film Corporation also made a small topical on the Gandhi-Irwin truce. Established in 1926, the studio started making educational films, thus marking the beginning of the Punjabi film industry.

James Mills was to continue his special relationship with Gandhi even after this historic interview. When this legendary foreign correspondent of Associated Press (AP) died in 1942, Gandhi was profuse in paying tribute to Mills: 'I have pleasant recollections of James Mills' numerous interviews with me. I remember his keeping awake the whole night when, in January 1932, I was arrested in Bombay.'[12] In fact, Gandhi told Mills that he might die in the prison and might not be able to see Mills again. Gandhi wrote, 'I can never forget the brave American breaking down as I was descending the staircase in custody of guardians of law just after my morning prayer.' He continued, 'Therefore, I thank you and the Associated Press for the thorough and impartial way in which you have always reported my activities and the progress of India's nationalist movement.' Months later, when Gandhi was released from prison after midnight, he spotted Mills at a remote railway station in the dark and exclaimed,[13] 'Mr Mills, if I should die and start to enter heaven, I should expect to see you waiting to interview me at the gates!'

5

The Mystery Man in London

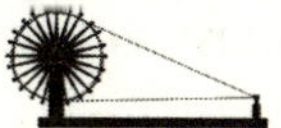

> Mahatma Gandhi will be the voice of 31,80,00,000 natives in the epochal London Conference to decide the country's status in the British Empire. Regarded as a Saint by his people, Gandhi is received with wild acclaim wherever he goes. These pictures show his reception at a typical mass meeting in Western India.

THIS WAS HOW A leading newsreel company of the world, Pathe News, described Gandhi in their topical in August 1931. The accompanying visuals were taken at a Congress meeting before Gandhi had embarked on his historic visit to London. The context and significance of the meeting were important and Pathe News was spot on in their assessment. Of all the people attending the conference, Gandhi was to be the centre of attraction, and that was exactly what happened in the British capital later that year.

The stage was set for Gandhi to go beyond the geographical borders of India and showcase to the world the man he was. Towards the end of 1931, a Second Round Table Conference was organized in London by the British government to discuss issues related to India. As the sole representative of the Indian National Congress, Gandhi also claimed to be representing people from all walks of life in India. But on the eve of his epoch-making journey to London, he was not in high spirits. He said,

> When I think of the prospects in London, when I know all is not well in India ... there is nothing wanting to fill me with utter despair. The horizon is as black as it possibly could be. There is every chance of my returning empty-handed. But believing as I do that God has made the way to London clear for me through the 'second settlement', I approach the visit with hope.[1]

Even before Gandhi was to travel to attend the Conference, there was a buzz among film companies about the impending visit. The visuals captured in some of the newsreels showed excitement in the air when Gandhi was amongst the people. He would walk through a melee of people jostling with each other to catch a glimpse of him, and he would respond to their affection by joining his hands. Whether in a big city like Bombay or a small village in the interiors of India, the only difference in the visuals was the difference in the attire of people. For the film cameras, such a moving mass of people was always an exciting visual, ideal for the screen.

And there was James Mills again on Gandhi's journey, movie camera in hand! He travelled on board the SS Rajaputana along with Gandhi and his party from Bombay to Marseilles. Mills' first-ever talkie interview of Gandhi just a few months before this journey had facilitated spread of the cause of India's freedom struggle in USA, Britain and other countries. On this voyage, he took some of the most memorable visual images of Gandhi that would be played again and again, up to the present day.

On 29 August 1931, Gandhi embarked on this important journey onboard the SS Rajaputana from the Bombay docks. There was a festive atmosphere among the huge crowd assembled to see off Gandhi. In the visuals taken on the occasion, several major Congress leaders can be spotted, including Pandit Nehru and Sardar Patel. James Mills can also be seen on the ship deck, trying to capture footage from close range with a camera in his hand. Bombay Port Trust Hotel was thronged by a large number of people in another visual taken from the ship. It is obvious that many film companies had positioned their teams at various vantage points to capture these moments.

For fourteen days, during the journey from Bombay to Marseilles in France, Gandhi looked a free man; free from the burden of leading the struggle for independence of one-fifth of the human race. One of the most popular leaders of the world, who was always in the midst of people and who had no time for himself, found a certain quietude and calmness in those days. That serenity clearly showed in the moving visuals taken on the ship by Mills. He shot extensive film footage capturing some of the most intimate moments of Gandhi never seen before. Mills was able to shoot many thousand feet of film with his Bell & Howell camera, and these visuals were screened across the world.

Subsequently, this footage formed an integral part of any film or documentary made later on Gandhi. Due to the special rapport between the cameraman and his subject, what we see today are some of the most wonderful moving images of the Mahatma. Mills recorded his thoughts on this journey from a cameraman's perspective and said, 'Never did he willingly lend himself to pictures. Yet never did he forbid me to photograph him. He always maintained a curiously detached, impersonal, negative attitude towards my efforts to capture his features for screen and for history.'

Though initially, Gandhi was non-cooperative while being filmed, he later became much more comfortable. Mills recalled, 'It was no easy task for a photographer to break down this formidable barrier of prejudice on Mr Gandhi's part toward being filmed. But I accomplished it by simply "taking the bull (or shall I say the lamb) by the horns", and filming the Mahatma without his permission. When, at first, I levelled my turret-head FILMO and EYEMO at him, he seemed somewhat pained and displeased, but he soon became accustomed to my frequent visits. When I came within a few feet of him for a close-up, however, he would exclaim, "You are torturing me."[2]

It was a torture for Gandhi then, but in the process Mills managed to take some excellent close-up shots of Gandhi, which have now become iconic images. Despite his reluctance, Gandhi at no time became impatient with Mills. The professional relationship between the two blossomed into a personal one during the journey, and by the time the voyage was over, Gandhi was calling Mills by his first name. In the end, Gandhi also developed an interest in the cameras being used. Mills said, 'He showed so much interest in my FILMO and EYEMO that (in spite of his deep prejudice against everything mechanical) he asked to see these two magnificent specimens of the art of cinema camera construction. He was amazed at the precision, compactness and smooth running of the 'baby' camera of the Bell & Howell products, no less than that of its big brother, the 'EYEMO'.[3]

The importance and value of this extensive visual coverage were immediately taken note of everywhere. America-based *Movie Makers Magazine* published a report stating that Gandhi was one of the most difficult men in public life to be photographed, and it also carried a photograph of Mills capturing Gandhi on camera onboard the ship.[4] Though Gandhi was not known to look directly into the camera, Mills had special magic on hand which he explained,

> On the steamer, between Bombay and Marseilles, however, he actually looked squarely into the Cooke lenses of my cameras. One of the most original shots I made of him showed him holding a laughing baby, while the Mahatma himself wreathed in smiles. Another showed him on the Captain's bridge of the 'Rajaputana', piloting the big liner through the Indian Ocean. A third fine shot showed the little 93-pound Hindu agitator grinning from ear to ear as I collared him at his spinning wheel.[5]

Even as Gandhi was not very optimistic about the outcome of the Conference he was going to attend, he was full of joy and energy during the sea voyage. Slade, his close disciple, who travelled with him on the ship, recorded the pleasant memories later. 'As a sailor, Gandhi was out and away the best among his party.'[6] Even his private secretary Mahadev Desai, also part of the tour, in a letter to Pandit Nehru wrote, 'Bapu is thoroughly enjoying himself—if I may use the word "enjoy" about anything he does.'

A cheerful and serene-looking Gandhi is the highlight of the images captured by Mills on that journey. In what was reminiscent of his public life, Gandhi spent almost the entire time on the deck in full view of fellow passengers. The visuals showed him spinning yarn while curious passengers, including the captain of the ship, looked on. Like in today's times, where the camera pervades the private lives of celebrities, Mills followed Gandhi into the washroom too, where he was filmed shaving.

Gandhi, for a change, had no qualms about it, and he actually laughed looking into the camera, a very rare sight indeed. The passengers on board were of different nationalities and were keen to interact with him, including the children. Gandhi obliged each and every one of them with a smile. He also sat coyly for photographs with passengers and gave autographs, which too was captured by the movie cameras. Gandhi was also seen putting a life jacket on, following instructions from the captain.

Captain H. Jack Morton seemed proud that Gandhi was travelling on his ship. He was more than willing to entertain Gandhi and was seen giving him a detailed overview of the functioning of the ship. He took Gandhi and his colleagues to the captain's cabin. The visuals of the visit show Gandhi taking a keen interest in whatever was being shown to him. In his trademark humour, Gandhi said, 'I hope I do not capsize the boat!' while handling the wheel. On board, he was most candid with the children, of all people. In one of the most famous photographs of Gandhi taken by Mills, he is enjoying an ear-to-ear laugh with an amused small kid in his arms. While Gandhi was busy spinning, some European children are seen approaching him with curiosity, and he entertained them with a smile.

On the other hand, his co-passengers Madan Mohan Malviya, Sarojini Naidu, his secretary Mahadev Desai, his son Devdas Gandhi and Margaret Slade appeared most conscious while facing the camera, and none of them could hide their nervous smiles. In a few visuals, Mills is seen talking with Gandhi and Sarojini Naidu. Among the many highlights of the footage shot on board, the standout heart-warming visual is of Gandhi standing alone on the deck in a contemplative mood, looking far beyond into the horizon. It is a scene that lingers in the mind of viewers and one of the very rare private moments of Gandhi, a public man.

Pathe News continued to broadcast Gandhi's tour and included these visuals in their newsreels. Their editor's note captured the mood succinctly. 'No man in centuries has stirred India's teeming millions as much as this little brown Hindu. With the world watching him while the London Conference determines his country's future, these pictures show Gandhi enjoying the simple life aboard ship.'

When Gandhi disembarked from SS Rajaputana on 11 September 1931 at Marseilles, a large number of European and American cameramen and photographers were waiting at the dock. A crowd of about 200 to 300 French people had also gathered in an impromptu reception for Gandhi. The long voyage and much-needed rest had freshened up Gandhi and he looked cheerful. The visuals of that day show he had a difficult time making his way ahead through the jostling crowd, which wanted to take a closer look at him. One of the journalists present at the occasion was the American correspondent of *Chicago Tribune*, William Shirer, who had been in regular touch with Gandhi since the Gandhi-Irwin talks in India.

It was clear that the British government had learnt their lesson well after their strategic error in handling the Dandi March. Therefore, arrangements were in place not to allow Gandhi to run away with any media mileage during the Second Round Table Conference. When Gandhi was to catch a boat train, (a train for incoming passengers from a ship to transport them to city), from Marseilles to London, no journalist or cameraman was allowed to board that train. Simply put, no tickets were sold, and no passes given to any media men. When William Shirer, who was determined to cover Gandhi for this all-important conference, failed to get a ticket on the train, he was left with no other option than to plead with Gandhi. Like a magician, Gandhi produced two tickets instantly and handed them over to him, much to the delight of Shirer! Once again, Gandhi had outsmarted the British government, as the reports filed by Shirer from Gandhi's onboard journey got splashed on full pages as the Indian leader reached London.

While attending the Round Table Conference, Gandhi was the centre of attraction for the world media. Pathe Gazette in their newsreel reported, 'Gandhi is here! The Indian nationalist leader whose personality is intriguing the whole world, arrives!' The visuals taken of his arrival at Marseilles on 11 September 1931 in France were shown in theatres. Almost every action after his momentous arrival was filmed and reported with great interest. Here was an old man, with a toothless smile, clad only in a loincloth in the bitterly cold weather of London, preferring to stay with commoners and amidst laughter. He thus caught the imagination of the Britishers.

When Gandhi arrived, it was a typical London day on 12 September 1931 with an overcast sky. It had rained in the afternoon when Gandhi moved out of the railway yard by walking towards his car. A big crowd was present, braving the cold and rains, waiting to have a glimpse of what this mystery man looked like! For a change, Gandhi was wrapped in thick shawls but the 'loincloth' remained, true to his words spoken to Mills in the talkie interview. Gandhi, without any visible discomfort on account of the cold weather, walked towards his car. He was wearing sandals and not covered shoes.

As his car moved, there was a huge crowd on both sides of the road braving the pelting rains to catch a glimpse of him. When Gandhi finally reached his destination at Kingsley Hall, he stepped into the balcony and greeted the large crowd gathered there. The entire scene looked like a reception reserved for a film star, and Gandhi proved to be much like one, greeting the crowds in Indian style by joining his hands to acknowledge their loud cheers.

Several film companies extensively filmed the proceedings of the Round Table Conference, Gandhi's important meetings and his visits to various places in England. Prominent among these events was his meeting with British Prime Minister Ramsey McDonald at 10 Downing Street. The films show him coming out of the PM's residence and getting into a car.

Muriel Lester, a social reformer and close associate of Gandhi's, was his local hostess at Kingsley Hall in East London. Her account vividly tells us of the frenzy and interest Gandhi's visit had generated among the newsreel companies. She was chased by representatives of many motion picture companies for securing media coverage rights for the various events related to the visit. A few of them went so far as to offer her a share of the profits their footage would generate. Lester wrote, 'The luggage brought by the Movietone people intrigues us greatly. On three different occasions films were made of Kingsley Hall (where Gandhi stayed during his London visit) and helping make them was a thrilling experience.'[7]

Pathe News chronicled the Kingsley area where Gandhi stayed in their special topical film. It was captioned *Gandhi's London Home in the East End*, and introduced Lester as his hostess during his stay for the Conference. She explained in detail the set-up at Kingsley Hall, while the camera showed Gandhi's room and other areas in the building. Such film reportage was an early indicator of today's television news, which invades the bedrooms of celebrities to show how they live and what they eat!

British Movietone also made a special topical film showing the Kingsley Hall rooms where Gandhi was to stay. It was titled *Gandhi's Apartment Is Made Ready,* and viewers are shown the view that Gandhi would see from his room. Viewers were shown the competitive hospitality being offered to Gandhi at Hampstead, that he had declined. One can imagine the interest in Gandhi's visit to London, as all this coverage constituted preliminary reports, even before Gandhi had arrived in the city.

Lester had by now become a celebrity in the UK on account of the continuous publicity associated with Gandhi's stay at her cottage. So, a textile factory worker in Lancashire wrote a letter to her on 1 July 1931 inviting Gandhi to visit their factory. The worker, A.B., wrote,

> I, as a working man who depends upon the Lancashire cotton industry for a living in common with a few other million workers who have no other means of earning their daily bread, would only be too pleased if Mr Gandhi would visit Lancashire, for I believe that some good of a permanent and lasting character would accrue to the mutual benefit of the Lancashire cotton worker and our fellow working men in India. I have a profound admiration for Mr Gandhi and a great many of my fellow co-workers in Lancashire share that spirit of admiration for Mr Gandhi.[8]

He requested Lester to show the letter to Gandhi and expressed his wish to meet and talk with him. When Gandhi eventually visited Lancashire, he captured the imagination of the cotton mill workers too. Echoing the sentiments expressed in the letter, a huge crowd had gathered at the cotton town to welcome him. Many of them had become jobless as a result of the boycott of foreign clothes by Indian people as part of the Non-Cooperation Movement led by Gandhi. But that didn't prevent the mill workers from showing their affection and admiration for Gandhi.

It was perhaps Gandhi's innate political acumen that led him to spend time with these mill workers during their difficult times, and the film footage of his visit showed him getting mobbed wherever he went. As always, it was a group of women that surrounded him at Darwen, and cheered the most. The cold weather did not hamper the spirits of the visitor, a sixty-two-year-old man, or the hosts. Gandhi was immensely pleased with the love and warmth he received despite the misgivings expressed about his visit, and spoke about the possibility of future cooperation between Lancashire and India.

Pathe Gazette's topical film on this visit described him as 'the Indian nationalist leader whose personality is intriguing to the whole world'! The spell cast by Gandhi and his politics was difficult for the Western world to understand. Therefore, it was no wonder that the editor could not find any other words to describe him than 'the mystery man of India' and 'bizarre little man'. After showing some shots from Lancashire, the topical described the scene: 'Gandhi feels goodwill for those whom he appears to be fighting.'

British Movietone, though, had a different viewpoint to offer on the visit. Their topical film, in tune with their cautious and pro-government policy, was titled *Hush-Hush Publicity on Gandhi's Journey*. It said, 'Little man from India in shawl and loincloth lands quietly in Marseilles and proceeds to London.' Before he started his train journey to London, Gandhi was surrounded by a horde of press people, including motion picture cameramen present on the platform. Gandhi looked to be in a very jovial mood. William Shirer, who had managed tickets to travel on the boat train courtesy Gandhi, stood near him at the window and asked him to give a quote. Gandhi responded cheekily 'I know your trick' and went on to cover Shirer's mouth with his hands to stop him from asking further questions!

The media contingent was not ready to leave him easily and pressed for a quote for the French people, to which Gandhi replied with a broad smile, 'I thank all the French.' It was such a rare visual to see the humorous side of Gandhi on screen. It was visibly clear that he enjoyed all the attention showered on him on the occasion. Though a man of the masses, Gandhi was not often seen expressing his inner emotions to the outer world. But here he was, in full public view, engaging in banter like a friend, smiling ear-to-ear all the way.

Charlie Meets Gandhi

During his London stay, Gandhi met several eminent people and visited universities and public institutions as part of his outreach efforts. One such meeting on 22 September 1931 grabbed eyeballs across the world. The cinema legend Charlie Chaplin was in London to promote his new film *City Lights* (1931) and had sought a meeting with Gandhi, 'the newest sensation in London'.[9] Even though Gandhi didn't know who

Chaplin was, he agreed to meet the comedian because he was told that the latter made millions laugh! The great comedian had already made *The Kid* (1921) and *The Circus* (1928) and had achieved an iconic status in world cinema.

The meeting was supposed to be a closely guarded secret but somehow the news spread, and a huge crowd thronged outside the building at Canning Town where they were to meet. Motion picture companies positioned their cameramen to capture this historic meeting. Both Gandhi and Chaplin arrived by car separately and had to make way through the surging crowd that was cheering them. The cameramen had a hard time filming the scenes because of the huge crowd. They could not manage a vantage point to get close-ups of the two men, and all they could film were few long shots of the two celebrities alighting from their respective cars and proceeding to Dr Katial's house in Beckton Road, Canning Town, the venue of the meeting.

The visuals of their meeting were splashed everywhere. A Pathe topical film was captioned *Charlie meets Gandhi* and its inter-title read, 'East-enders, in thousands, turn out to greet the two famous little men, with cries of "good old Charlie" and "good old Gandhi".' Both the gentlemen can be seen in the film waving from a balcony window at the crowd downstairs. The same film also had French inter-title cards with the title *Gandhi Et Charlot* with drawings of Gandhi and Chaplin on either side. It also said, 'Who could have imagined that two personalities of such a different order would have met.'

During his four-month long whirlwind tour of Europe, Chaplin had hobnobbed with Kings, Lords and Prime Ministers and one Hollywood report asked, 'Has Chaplin stayed abroad too long?' It mentioned only two people as different from the list of who's who; Gandhi and a British judge. The report said, 'Only Gandhi and a British judge took him down during all his holidaying. Gandhi, living on a strange world of dates, goat's milk and meditation, averred that he had never seen a Chaplin picture, while the judge criticized Charlie pointedly for his behaviour in a courtroom.'[10]

Chaplin, the great artist, and twenty years younger than Gandhi, was full of praise after meeting the old man. Like most of people who came under Gandhi's spell, Chaplin was clearly elated while describing Gandhi. 'Gandhi is a tremendous personality, tremendous! He is a great international figure! More, he is a great dramatic figure.'[11] Chaplin was to make his masterpiece *Modern Times* five years after the meeting. The film underlined the idea that machinery should benefit humanity and not destroy the worker. If it sounded more like Gandhi's views, then it is open to anybody's imagination whether this London meeting had any role to play in influencing Chaplin's creative mind!

Oranges for the Mahatma!

There was another interesting meeting Gandhi attended that attracted the attention of the movie cameras. On the morning of 9 September 1931, James Phillips, the Pearly King of Hoxton, called on Gandhi along with his children. The Pearly royal family represented an iconic image of London and were recognized by their unique, colourful sense of dressing. Their distinctive garments have pearl buttons sewn into meaningful patterns and symbols. The visuals filmed at the entrance of Kingsley Hall showed the fun and banter Gandhi had with the royal children. Gandhi came out of the Hall smiling and placed his hand on the shoulder of the King. While the King and his children, a son and a daughter, were in their colourful traditional attire, Gandhi was in all-white gear, in his 'loincloth' and a shawl to cover his body.

The contrast in their dressing styles was tailor-made for the movie cameras. A big crowd had gathered at the venue, including cameramen with their still and moving-image cameras. When the royal boy presented Gandhi an orange, Gandhi in his mischievous voice said, 'Take the orange? ... thank you ... thank you.' It was now the turn of his sister to offer him an orange. Gandhi, now laughing profusely, continued with his playful banter, 'Why take only one, I take two!'

The kids were amused at all the attention, and there were cheers from the assembled crowd even as their royal father looked on approvingly. They offered Gandhi another set of oranges, which he gleefully accepted. Paramount Sound News filmed this delightful event and aptly titled it *In the Limelight*. It also said, 'Mr Gandhi, on his way to attend Round Table Conference, meets some real Cockneys.'

Paramount Sound News made several newsreels on Gandhi's London visit. *India's Man of the Hour, This Little Man Gandhi, India's Hope,* and *That Elusive and Mystic Personality* were some of the titles of these newsreels that were shown across Europe and America. At the conclusion of his eventful visit, Gandhi gave an interview where he was seen in his characteristic wrapped dhoti surrounded by smiling Englishmen. His departing words were captured on camera, 'I shall carry the pleasantest memory of my stay among poorest people in East London.'

A newsreel, *Gandhi India Bound,* showed visuals of him at Boulogne, and carried an inter-title that said, 'To report Round Table progress to his disciples, Mahatma lands in France on first stage of voyage home.' While Gandhi was in Paris, the newsreel covering his movements there said, 'Station crowds surge to get view of Hindu leader'. It showed people jostling with each other to see Gandhi. Another newsreel by Paramount was titled *Gandhi Going Home* and showed footage of the last leg of his visit in Lancashire. The inter-title card said, 'Mahatma commemorates English visit by planting tree at East End lodging, as the Round Table Conference ends.' Surrounded by mill workers, Gandhi planted a sapling with a shovel in hand, amidst cheers and clapping.

British Movietone also made a topical on his return journey and titled it *Gandhi Starts His Homeward Trek*. Gandhi was filmed walking with Sarojini Naidu at Folkestone, and he spoke to the motion picture representatives, 'I carry with me the pleasantest recollections of many happy friendships.' He boarded the ship and then posed again for photographs.

Paramount News followed Gandhi in Geneva during his stopover there on his return journey to India. The topical film made on the occasion was titled *Gandhi at Peace City-Geneva*. The visuals showed him explaining India's stand to a large audience in Victoria Hall on

10 December 1931. In the clip, he was seen reading from his written speech while the huge crowd clapped in unison at the end of the meeting. Hearst Metrotone News also filmed this speech. Their topical was titled *Gandhi's Farewell Talk in Europe,* and the inter-title card said, 'India's leader stands by his policy of non-violence–answers queries through interpreter at Geneva.' Gandhi is shown seated alone on a raised platform while the interpreter stood beside him. As Gandhi read from a prepared note with a firm and clear voice, the audience listened in rapt attention. He said,

> I regard myself as a soldier, though a soldier of peace. I know the value of discipline and truth ... I must ask you to believe me when I say that I have never made a statement of this description that the masses of India, if it became necessary, would resort to violence. I regard myself as incapable in my lucid moments of making a statement of this character ... It is complete independence we want.[12]

Gandhi also made a brief halt in Rome. This visit, however, seems to have been orchestrated by Mussolini's army, as most of the time Gandhi was surrounded by the state military officials. They, in fact, organized a parade of small boys in uniform in honour of Gandhi while showcasing their military equipment to this apostle of non-violence! His response was a trademark toothless smile and a gesture of namaste with his hands. He is seen in the company of Slade and Mahadev Desai during the visit. Since his request for an audience with the Pope was turned down, a Universal Newsreel report said, 'Gandhi's scant garb bars Papal audience; honoured by Cadets.'

Even though his journey back home on board the SS Pilsna was not filmed by anyone, there is an interesting visual of Gandhi preparing his 'drink' on the ship! After boarding the ship, Gandhi is seen waving goodbye to people on the shore. He then sits quietly on the deck and prepares himself a drink with lime and soda. He then uses a spoon to mix it before drinking it all in one go, while the gentlemen surrounding him look on amusedly.

One of the newsreels showing his trip to London and back decided to innovate a bit from the routine coverage. So, it depicted the entire route of his journey on a map. The audience gets an idea of Gandhi's historic visit and the places he visited along the way both to and from London, indicated by dotted lines on the world map.

His entire London visit and the film footage of it are very good indicators of Gandhi's character, personality, and his relationship with the motion picture camera. Despite so much attention and despite the relentless focus on him, he is most natural in his actions. He does not look into the film camera unless specifically asked to; he goes about his routine work without taking note of the presence of the camera; he doesn't give any special consideration to the fact that he is being filmed.

Gandhi is totally oblivious that several cameras, both moving and still, are constantly around him and clicking away almost every moment of his life. Only on some rare occasions does he allow himself to look into the camera, sometimes smiling and posing. All along there is a smile on his face—that charming toothless smile that endeared him to the camera and the entire world. This has been Gandhi's trademark demeanour throughout while being filmed.

Indian film studios were also in the forefront in making films on Gandhi's visit to London. It is most likely that Indian companies sourced the footage from their foreign counterparts and distributed their films in the local languages. Bombay-based Saraswati Film Laboratory made several short films and screened extensive footage on this important event. Their one-reeler film titled *Epoch Making Voyage of Mahatma Gandhi to London* was passed by the Bombay Board of Film Censors (BBFC) on 31 August 1931.

Saraswati Film Laboratory made yet another film, *Arrival of Mahatma Gandhi in London*. They also made a one-reel film after the conference got over with the title *Mahatma Gandhi returns from the pilgrimage of Peace*. *Mahatma Gandhi in London* was the title of a one-reeler film made by British Screen News and distributed by Shree Krishna Film Co. The latter also made a one-reel film, *Mahatma Gandhi's Return from London*.

Topical of Mahatma Gandhi and Others was a one-reeler made by Indian Topical Co. *Bombay Welcomes Mahatma Gandhi,* with vernacular sub-titles, was made by M.B. Bilimoria. Imperial Film Co. produced a one-reel film, *The Return of Mahatma Gandhi from Round Table Conference.* They also made a short feature called *Mahatma Gandhi after the Truce. Mahatma Gandhi's Arrival in Bombay* was the name of a one-reel film made by Pathe Film Company. Krishnatone Film Company made a two-reeler film called *Mahatma Gandhi's Speech in Public Meeting.* All these topical films were passed by the Bombay Board of Film Censors without any cuts for public exhibition.

When Gandhi returned to India, a huge crowd waited at the Bombay docks to welcome him back home. The British Movietone topical made on the event described it as 'How India Greeted Gandhi's Return' and said that excited crowds filled the streets leading to the quayside as the Mahatma disembarked at Bombay. The crowd was visibly elated to see Gandhi back and there was clapping and yelling, with chants of '*Mahatma Gandhi ki Jai*'. The visuals also showed Gandhi addressing a huge crowd in Gujarati on the esplanade at Bombay. The moving visuals captured on his arrival showed a smiling Kasturba waiting patiently at the docks in Bombay, while Pandit Nehru's wife Kamla was seen going up the ship and then accompanying Gandhi as he came down the ship.

Fox Movietone News continued its extensive coverage of Gandhi even after his arrival back home. They made a short topical film which described Mahatma Gandhi as the sixty-three-year-old leader of 300 million people, who was ready to give his life for the cause of political independence for India. It also remarked that Gandhi was back home after unsuccessful London parleys to initiate a non-violent war against British rule. Shots of Gandhi disembarking from the SS Pilsna, to claps and cheers, were captured. One British officer is even spotted taking off his hat in honour of Gandhi. Gandhi is also seen standing in the balcony of the house where he went after his disembarkation, while a huge crowd cheers him.

His entire journey from the Bombay docks to Mani Bhawan was filmed, showing the tumultuous reception he received from the citizens.

The visuals also showed him addressing a mammoth crowd in Gujarati. Another topical was made by Fox Movietone News on the arrest of Gandhi, just after his return from London. The inter-title card said: 'India feels the hand of new Viceroy—Gandhi is sent to Central Prison for an indefinite term.' And the movie showed visuals of thousands of his followers going to barbed-wire prison camps with shouts of '*Mahatma Gandhi ki Jai*' and '*Inquilab Zindabad*'.

Paramount News was also in Bombay with their cameramen, shooting the demonstrations in January 1932. Their topical was titled *Indian Unrest Grows* and it shows visuals of Gandhi closeted with his colleagues for discussions. The inter-title card says, 'No cooperation with British! Mr Gandhi, awaiting arrest, has final conference with disciples.' While Gandhi is in the midst of discussions with political leaders, the visuals show Kasturba Gandhi sitting anxiously along with a few other women followers of Gandhi. The narrator describes the man of the moment as frail, emancipated, and Sphinx-like!

All these newsreels and topical films, many of them focusing on Gandhi's Dandi March and his visit to London, were subsequently banned by the Bombay Provincial Government. Clearly, the large-scale spread and appeal of these visuals had rattled the government. The Indian media condemned this ban vehemently, with the *Bombay Chronicle* writing that the films could be prohibited but not Gandhism.[13] The *Free Press Journal* attributed the ban to the Gandhian ideas depicted in these films.[14]

As many as twenty-six newsreels, from both Indian and foreign film studios, were on the banned list, and it took five years for the ban to be lifted by the Provincial Government of Bombay, in August 1937. A Gujarati newspaper reported, 'The Govt of Bombay has published a public notice to lift the ban on films and film companies considered to be illegal by the Cinematograph Act, 1918.'[15]

The services of Associated Press (AP), a leading newswire agency, had reached more than 2,600 newspapers and radio stations worldwide by 1945, which was double the figure in the 1920s. Their newsreels, in their heydays, were being watched by one out of ten persons across the world. Add to this the combined wide reach of Fox Movietone News and British Movietone News, and that of Hearst Movietone, who had agreements for news sharing, and one can imagine the reach and spread of Gandhi's interview as well as visuals taken on board the SS Rajaputana by James Mills and the coverage of his subsequent London visit. Within fifteen years of his arrival in India to lead its struggle for freedom, Gandhi had thus truly become a global phenomenon, aided in no small measure by the visual splash he made through the motion picture camera.

6

Mahatma in the Popular Consciousness

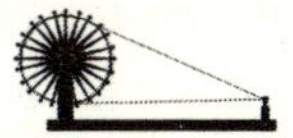

VIJAY BHATT WAS A leading filmmaker in the Hindi and Marathi cinema industry in the 1940s and 1950s, and also a staunch follower of Gandhi. Bhatt, who established Prakash Pictures in 1934, a major production house in Bombay, had gone to meet Gandhi along with his friends one day and seek his 'darshan' at Valsad in Gujarat in 1939. They approached Gandhi during his morning walk and sought his blessings. In a brief talk Gandhi asked Bhatt, a fellow Gujarati, 'What are you doing?' 'I make films,' said Bhatt. 'Have you thought about making a film on Narsinh Mehta?' was the second and only other question asked by Gandhi. Bhatt responded, 'I will try to make it, Bapuji.'[1]

Gandhi's wish, naturally, was considered as a command by Bhatt, and thus he made the 1940 bilingual devotional biopic *Narsi Mehta/ Narsi Bhagat* in Gujarati and Hindi, respectively. Vishnupant Pagnis, who had become immensely popular after portraying Tukaram in Prabhat's *Sant Tukaram,* played the lead role of Narsinh Mehta. The veteran actress Durga Khote also acted in the film. Narrating the life story of the popular saint-poet, written for the screen by Mohanlal Dave and Vishnupant Aundhkar, the film contained Narsinh Mehta's most popular bhajan, '*Vaishnava Jana To Tene Kahiye Je Pida Parayi Jane Re*' (One Who is a Vaishnav, Devotee of Vishnu, Knows the Pain of Others). It was Gandhi's favourite bhajan. Gandhi mixed religion and politics in his unique way, and he was largely inspired by the teachings of this Gujarati saint-poet Narsinh Mehta. The bilingual film was well received, but even though Gandhi had recommended that Bhatt make a film on Mehta, he did not see it.

During the decades of the 1930s and 1940s, the filmmakers in India were exploring different stories to tell. Even though the majority of the stories depicted on screen were based on mythological tales, some progressive filmmakers had started to explore different themes. Many of them were politically conscious and staunch followers of Gandhi. They took up such projects that would showcase the values and principles advocated by Gandhi. These values were nothing really new but rooted deeply in Indian culture. The social reform movements led by many reformers in different parts of the country had also created a conducive atmosphere in society for the reception of such films.

Again, the common man viewed Gandhi not just as a political leader. The movement he was leading was not only for the political independence of India. Gandhi's goal was 'Swaraj', which meant freedom for the poorest of Indians. His dream was to create a new village-centred society, and based on a new awakening among the masses. The Indian film industry, after about twenty years of existence, was now ready to explore new subjects, going beyond the usual fare they were dishing out till then. Gandhian ideals, time and again emphasized in Gandhi's writing and speeches, were therefore found suitable for screen adaptation. The new breed of directors, who were liberal in their approach and nationalist by nature, took these ideas and converted them into stories for the screen.

Before Bhatt had made his screen version of the saint-poet's life, there had been another film on Narsinh Mehta made in 1932. Bombay-based Sagar Movietone had produced the film, which was directed by Nanubhai Vakil, who too was a Gandhi admirer. The film included the song '*Vaishnav Jan To*' in its soundtrack and met with a stupendous reception at each show, when the entire audience would stand up with folded hands and hail Gandhi.[2]

One of the most significant filmmakers of the time who dared to depict Gandhian themes before Independence was K. Subramanyam. A progressive director in the Tamil film industry and a keen Gandhi follower, Subramanyam made three films that distinctly advocated nationalist and reformist themes in tune with Gandhian ideals. *Balayogini* (1936), *Seva Sadanam* (1938) and *Thyagabhoomi* (1939), a trilogy directed by him, brought in a new wave of 'social' films in the Tamil cinema industry. *Balayogini,* written by Subramanyam, along with Papanasam Sivan and B.T. Raghavacharyar, was one of the first reformist social films, marking an important milestone in Tamil cinema.

A saga of the struggle of a Brahmin widow and her young daughter in a society steeped in irrational caste prejudices, *Balayogini* was released in an environment where the social rights movement had started taking root in Tamil Nadu. Such was the commitment of the filmmakers towards the cause they were trying to depict that they did a completely unthinkable act and cast an actual Brahmin widow in the lead role. Gandhi had always espoused the cause of women's empowerment, encouraging them to actively participate in the social spheres. This had a visible effect, and a large number of women came forward to take part in the freedom movement responding to his call. Even though Gandhi was busy in the freedom movement, he had found time to condemn the tradition of 'sati', prevalent particularly in north India, in his many articles.

Next to come in Subramanyam's trilogy was *Seva Sadanam*, which highlighted Gandhian ideals in critiquing the conservative social malpractices that caused great harm to women's dignity. After *Balayogini*, K. Subramanyam made this film based on the renowned Hindi writer Premchand's novel *Bazaar-e-Husn* focusing on women's empowerment. Even though the film is considered to be lost, the available publicity material provides a glimpse of the protagonist leading a group of women engaged in spinning yarn on the charkha, alluding to the Gandhian way of social reforms.

Gandhi considered the charkha as an essential tool in the daily life of the common man in India. Even while working at his ashram or while speaking in public meetings, Gandhi was busy spinning yarn, wasting no time. Gandhi had said, 'The message of the spinning wheel is much wider than its circumference. Its message is one of simplicity, service of mankind, living so as not to hurt others, creating an indissoluble bond between the rich and the poor, capital and labour, the prince and the peasant. That larger message is naturally for all.'[3]

Thyagabhoomi (Land of Sacrifice), the third film in Subramanyam's series, released in 1939, was a classic reformist social. The film, produced and directed by Subramanyam under the banner of Madras United Artists Corporation, liberally employed Gandhian themes and actively advocated the Temple Entry Movement in Tamil Nadu. The character of Sambu Shastri, closely modelled on Mahatma Gandhi, was played by the well-known composer Papanasam Sivan, and the film incorporated some documentary footage of Gandhi spinning the charkha.

A Congress government was in power in Tamil Nadu when the film was being made, and it helped Subramanyam deal with the subject of freedom struggle in a bold way. 'The film opened with a song glorifying India and Gandhi ... In fact, some of the sequences in the film, like the picketing by Congress volunteers and the marches, were semi-documentary in character.'[4]

By the time the film was completed and released, there was a change of power in Tamil Nadu. Since the film glorified the freedom movement and boldly propagated Gandhian values, the British government banned the film even while it was running successfully in the theatres. *Thyagabhoomi* is considered to be Subramanyam's best-known film and Tamil cinema's biggest hit in the 1930s. The story, first published in the journal *Ananda Vikatan*, was brilliantly adapted by the celebrated filmmaker for the screen.

The film opens with a scene where Harijans are waiting in front of a closed temple during a cyclone. Sastry, the lead character, is punished for sheltering them, and he goes to Madras, where, together with the Harijan Nallan, he embarks on Gandhian social uplift programmes, including the picketing of liquor shops. The obvious context here was to the famous Vaikom Satyagraha in Kerala in 1924–25, where Gandhi had actively intervened on behalf of the untouchable castes to get the temple roads opened to all.

The trend of social reformist themes based on Gandhian ideals and nationalist projects had already been reflected in *Kalidas* in 1931 in Tamil cinema. It was also seen in other Tamil films such as *Dharmapathni* (Devoted Wife, 1929) which highlighted the issue of alcoholism, and *Anadhaipenn* (Orphan Girl, 1931); there was a clear shift away from themes dominated by mythology and towards the 'tradition of socially-conscious cinema'.[5]

Around the same time, in faraway Bengal, the New Theatres, established by B.N. Sarkar, produced one of the first devotional films in India, *Chandidas*. Released in 1931, the film was directed by Debaki Bose, a Gandhian. Bose had actively taken part in the Non-Cooperation Movement launched by Gandhi. *Chandidas,* based on the story of a legendary fifteenth-century Bengali Vaishnavite poet, brilliantly captured the democratic aspirations of the poet wherein, along with his lower-caste beloved, Rami, he rejects the traditional form of religion for their right to worship and practice.

The film was remade in Hindi in 1934 by Nitin Bose, with the popular singer-actor K.L. Saigal playing the main character of Chandidas. Debaki Bose made another outstanding bilingual film, *Bidyapati/ Vidyapati,* in Bengali and Hindi, respectively, in 1937. Written by Bose and Kazi Nazrul Islam, the film portrayed the Mithila King Shiva Singha's love for his wife. The figure of the court poet Bidyapati, who has a great influence on the King, takes the iconic form of a motivational saint, much like the transformation of Gandhi into a Mahatma.

There was another film taking off on Gandhian ideas, made by the Poona-based Prabhat Studio in 1935. Both its Hindi and Marathi versions directed by V. Shantaram were originally titled *Mahatma,* a devotional offering narrating the story of the medieval Maharashtrian poet-saint Eknath. Seen as a bridge between his illustrious predecessors

Dnyaneshwar and Namdev and the later saints Tukaram and Ramdas, his teachings dealt with social injustices like untouchability and propagated equality and humanity.

The title role was played by the iconic Marathi musical theatre singer-actor Bal Gandharv. A year before *Achhut Kanya* (Untouchable Maiden) was released, *Dharmatma* showcased the efficacy of the screen as an effective medium of propaganda. The censors took objection to the title *Mahatma,* after which it was changed to *Dharmatma.* Several films had used the name of Mahatma in their publicity campaign to attract the audience in theatres and censors were very harsh on anything concerning Gandhi. Notwithstanding the change in title, it was acclaimed as a brilliant film targeting the issue of untouchability.

Even though Bal Gandharv's much anticipated acting debut on screen didn't enthuse the audience, the major highlight of the film was a very close correlation between saint Eknath and Gandhi. It was a portrayal of the message of truth, non-violence and equality, which caught the imagination of the viewers, according to the message of Ahimsa (non-violence), Satya (truth) and Samanata (equality). These were principles associated with Gandhiji's movement of non-violence, truth and national consensus. The fusion of Eknath's active idealism—in seeking equality between the castes without upsetting the authority of tradition—and Gandhian practice was nearly complete.[6]

V. Shantaram went on to explore Gandhian ideals and principles in films through his bilingual classics *Duniya Na Mane* and *Kunku* (The Unexpected) in 1937, and *Admi (Life is for the Living)* or *Manoos* in 1939. Produced under the Prabhat Film Company banner, the former film raised questions about the practice of young girls being forced into marrying much older men. Based on a landmark Marathi novel by N.H. Apte, this Prabhat offering is considered a classic, and it earned both critical acclaim and commercial success.

The main protagonist, Shanta Apte, wears a khadi saree as a mark of protest against the marriage imposed on her, and that gives the young woman a very dignified aura. Empowerment of women in India was on the agenda of social reform framed by Gandhi. The film successfully projected the valiant fight of the young bride, Neera, brilliantly played by Apte, against forced marriage to an old man. Shantaram went one step further in his next film *Admi,* which told the story of a policeman who marries a sex worker to improve her social status, only to face the wrath of a conservative society. The humanist narrative highlighted the Gandhian disapproval of social customs that discriminated against women.

Untouchability is considered to be one of the major social evils of Hindu society in India. Gandhi gave the lower-caste people who were considered untouchable the name 'Harijan' (children of God) and even named his weekly magazine *Harijan.* Having seen the indentured Indian labourers in South Africa from close quarters, Gandhi was very clear in his attitude towards this evil. 'Swaraj or independence is a meaningless term if we desire to keep a fifth of India under perpetual subjection ... Inhuman ourselves, we may not plead before the Throne for deliverance from the inhumanity of others.'[7] He termed untouchability as an 'excrescence' and went to the extent of saying: 'If it was proved to me that it is an essential part of Hinduism, I for one would declare myself an open rebel against Hinduism itself.'

It was against this background that Bombay Talkies' *Achhut Kanya* in 1936 brought forth the issue of untouchability in Indian cinema. The non-violent way of fighting against the social injustice, as depicted in the film, brought into sharp focus Gandhi's crusade for social equality. The character of a fakir in the film was reminiscent of Gandhi, and the film tried to convey that Harijans are equal participants with others in India's freedom movement.

In Telugu, the issue of untouchability was cinematically tackled by Gudavalli Ramabrahmam in his film *Mala Pilla* (The Outcast Girl) in 1938. A film adaptation of G. Venkatachalam's short story *Mala Pilla,* it narrated a tale of love between a Brahmin boy and a Harijan girl. Ramabrahmam's social drama focused on the Harijan movement aimed at permitting Harijans to enter Hindu temples, which itself was inspired by Gandhi. The film, a tribute to the Maharaja of Travancore who had passed a law allowing people of all caste to enter temples, presented vivid visuals celebrating the spirit of the Non-Cooperation Movement and Gandhi's indisputable leadership of it.

The musical film turned out to be a major hit that year, with popular songs that had direct reference to Gandhi, such as '*Kollaayi Gattite Nemee Maa Gandhi Maaladai Thirigithe Nemee*' (What's wrong even if our Gandhi wore only loincloth, what's wrong if a SC [Mala caste] girl wanders around), written by Basavaraju Apparao, with music composed by Bhimavarapu Narasimha Rao.

Next year, Ramabrahmam came up with a film that touched upon another aspect of the reformist agenda attacking the zamindari system. *Raitu Bidda* was released in 1939 against the background of the emerging Kisan Sabha agitations in rural Andhra Pradesh during the 1930s. The Kisan Sabha was formed during the All India Congress session in Lucknow in 1936 to mobilize peasants against the zamindari system to secure their rights. Ramabrahmam was greatly influenced by Gandhi's anti-untouchability campaign, and this film was dedicated to the Maharaja of Travancore who had opened the temples in his state to all castes.

Two major films were made in Tamil in 1938, on the theme of untouchability. The first film, *Harijana Singam* (Madras CID) was directed by the leading stunt artiste in Tamil films, Battling Mani, who played the lead role too. Produced under the banner of Zenith Film Company, it was a pathbreaking film on the issue of Harijans. The second film, *Desa Munnetram* (Development of the Nation), was directed by Mahindra, and it touched upon issues of social reforms relating to untouchability as well as temple entry for all castes. Film historian Randor Guy called the film a 'masterstroke of communal equality' while concluding that the film would be 'remembered for its thematic content, patriotic songs and the performances by Baby Rukmini and Natesa Iyer'.[8]

Chandulal Shah, who helmed Ranjit Studios, one of the biggest film studios in Bombay, produced a major social film, *Achhut* (The Untouchable), in 1939. This film addressed the burning issue of untouchability, whose eradication was a cause dear to Gandhi. *Film*

India, the leading film magazine of the time, underlined the relevance of the issue and said,

> The nation will remain indebted to this brave producer Sardar Chandulal Shah for bringing to the screen the burning problem of our eighty million untouchables, whose silent sighs have yet remained a shameful blot on Hinduism. Sardar Chandulal has produced *Achhut* which even our revered leader Mahatma Gandhi can't afford to miss.[9]

By all accounts, *Sant Tukaram* in Marathi was one of the most popular devotional film offerings from Prabhat Films. The life of the seventeenth-century bhakti poet-saint Tukaram was brilliantly directed by V. Damle and S. Fattelal in 1936, and it came to be known as one of the best portrayals of Gandhian values on screen. The film, deeply rooted in a traditional discourse, touched upon many contemporary social and ethical issues prevalent in the society. At the same time, the narrative also focused on larger nationalist and religious ideas because Gandhi's politics was deeply rooted in religion.

Gandhi has often been viewed as a saint by many because of his constant emphasis on religion in almost everything he practised in his daily life. His way of life, adopted consciously after his coming back to India from South Africa, presented a stark contrast with that of the regular politicians of the day, and it really endeared him to the common people. He often quoted from religious texts, and his ideas of truth and non-violence thus found echo in the stories of these 'social' films. The structure of these films and the images they portrayed bore close parallels to Gandhian ideas and motifs. Audiences across the country knew and understood this completely, irrespective of whether the stories were told directly or discreetly.

Because of his emphasis on religion in politics and his personal way of life, Gandhi was often identified and compared with the medieval Saint Tukaram, at least in the state of Maharashtra. The contemporary social and political discourse placed Gandhi and his principles of love and non-violence in the league of Tukaram while B.G. Tilak, a firebrand nationalist leader, was often associated with Saint Ramdas because of his militant nationalism. There are interesting works by several Marathi poets and writers on the parallels between Tukaram and Gandhi. One such fictional story describes an imaginary meeting between the two. Tukaram gives his blessings to Gandhi for his cause of social reforms and the freedom movement. Therefore, it was no wonder that Prabhat's *Sant Tukaram*, released in the heyday of the freedom struggle, was considered a true cinematic representation of Gandhi's ideals.

The motifs running through these films often took direct inspiration from Gandhi's life itself. *Deshdasi*, directed by Chandulal Shah under Ranjit Movietone, was produced in 1935. Its story involved both a love triangle and a nationalist project. It starred Gohar, E. Bilimoria and Raja Sandow in the main roles. The characters Veena Kumari and her lover Dr Rasik come to an ashram run by Dileep Kumar (Sandow). The ashram was itself the result of its founders having been inspired by Mahatma Gandhi. Veena Kumari decides to serve the downtrodden, and eventually Dr Rasik also joins in the medical efforts to serve the workers. The publicity poster for the film shows the lead pair wearing khadi and Dr Rasik wearing a Gandhi cap.

Gandhi had taken a vow of celibacy while in South Africa.[10] Master Vinayak, a leading film director in Marathi, decided to portray this theme on screen and made *Brahmachari* (The Celibate) in 1938. He used satire so effectively that the film became one of the most successful of its times. A strong critic of old-world traditions, Vinayak masterfully presented the story employing hilarious scenes. The publicity campaign for the film featured photographs of Gandhi prominently, week after week, making the film's association with the Mahatma very clear in the minds of the audience so as to draw them to the theatres. One of the advertisements said it loud and clear, 'Mahatma Gandhi wants Brahmacharis and why?'![11]

Next year, Master Vinayak explored another theme—prohibition—which Gandhi strongly believed in. Master Vinayak's Marathi-Hindi bilingual film *Brandichi Batli/Brandy Ki Botal* (Bottle of Brandy) was a brilliant narrative on the evils of alcoholism, delivered in a hilarious manner. It advocated the need for prohibition. Made during the heydays of the nationalist movement, the film opens with a patriotic song, which is followed by a mass procession for prohibition using patriotic slogans and flags. A social satire written by the renowned author, playwright and director P.K. Atre, the film had vivid references to Gandhi, who was referred to as '*Azadi ki Devta*' (Angel of Freedom) in the film. The documentary footage of Sardar Patel delivering a speech on abstinence, which was used in the film, was snipped by the Censor Board.

The same subject was tackled in Tamil in T. Marconi's *Vimochanam* (Deliverance) in 1939. The film revolved around the theme of ill-effects of alcoholism, which Gandhi believed was one of the important problems needing social reform in India. Incidentally, when this film was released, the Congress session was being held at Salem, where prohibition was imposed, in Tamil Nadu. The film was inspired by Rajaji, one of main colleagues of Gandhi, who was instrumental in imposing prohibition as well as the upliftment of poor when he headed the Congress government in Madras presidency.

Around the same time, two Telugu films made by two prominent filmmakers brought the issue of widow remarriage on screen in an effective manner. *Malli Pelli*, directed by Y.V. Rao, was released in 1939. This reformist film was a trendsetter that took up the issue of widow remarriage strongly. According to music historian V.A.K. Ranga Rao, this was the first Telugu film that had playback singing. Interestingly, Y.V. Rao had directed the first Kannada talkie film *Sati Sulochana* in 1934. Then, veteran filmmaker B.N. Reddy made *Sumangali* in 1940, inspired by the Telugu social reformer Kandakuri Veeresalingam Panthulu's ideas. Again, this film narrated a realistic tale of widow remarriage, becoming one more example of Gandhi's influence on the spread of reformist ideas and their manifestation in popular culture.

The motif of the charkha and its vivid portrayal on screen was another way of paying tribute to Gandhi and his chosen weapon while depicting the freedom struggle. Released in 1940, a Hindi film, *Aaj*

Ka Hindustan (India Today), made by Jayant Desai, was a tale of two brothers, one nationalist and the other anglophile. The film, produced by Ranjit Movietone Co., had a song that praised the virtues of the charkha and exhorted women to spin yarn, which would turn the fortunes of the country. The song boldly proclaimed Gandhi as the leader of the nation:

'*Charkha Chalao, Behno, Kato ye Kachhe Dhaage Dhaage ye kah rahe hain Bharat ke bhaag jage, Charkhe ke geet gaao, Duniya ko ye sunao Charkha chalanewala Gandhi hai aage-aage.*' (Sisters, spin the wheel and weave. The yarn proclaims the awakening of Bharat's destiny. Sing a song on the spinning wheel and tell the world that the man who is spinning is leading us.)

The imagery of Gandhi and Bharat Mata (Mother India) features prominently in the film *Uthama Puthiran*, made in 1940 in Tamil by R. Sundaram. An adaptation of the English film *The Man in the Iron Mask*, the poster of the film announced it as a nationalist film in Tamil. There was a vivid reference to the Dandi March undertaken by Gandhi against the unjust salt tax. The singing star P. Chinnappa played a double role in the movie.

Poona-based Prabhat Film Studio came up with yet another 'saint' film, *Sant Dnyaneshwar,* in 1940. Made in two languages, Marathi and Hindi, the film was directed by V. Damle and S. Fattelal, makers of the iconic *Sant Tukaram*. It was a biopic on a young man who was instrumental in starting the Bhakti movement in twelfth-century Maharashtra. The film turned out to be an all-time classic. It was a simple yet sincere film made in the true Prabhat tradition.

Noted American filmmaker Frank Capra liked it so much that he said he was surprised to find such a technically well-made film produced in Poona, a town smaller than Bombay, where the industry was well established.[12] It was hard to miss the parallels between the humanism propagated by Dnyaneshwar and Gandhi's ideas of social reform, so delicately portrayed in the film. Dnyaneshwar staged miracles to educate the masses; and Gandhi's life was also nothing less than miracle. At another level, the film showcases the development of Dnyaneshwar's character, who goes on to make a huge impact on the masses, just like Gandhi.

Released during the peak of the nationalist struggle and exactly a year before Gandhi's call for the Quit India Movement, Sohrab Modi's historical epic *Sikander* is best remembered for its populist political metaphors. Based on the legend of Alexander the Great's (Sikander in Hindi/Urdu) invasion of India, the film invoked strong nationalist impulses when the Indian king Puru requests the neighbouring kingdoms to unite against the common foreign enemy. Prithviraj Kapoor played the role of Alexander the Great while Sohrab Modi played Puru, the Indian king. One particular song by Sheela, '*Jeete Desh Hamara*' (Let the victory be ours), written by Pandit Sudarshan, is noteworthy as a prayer song in which people cutting across social strata pray for success in the battle against the common enemy. The movie aroused nationalist sentiments, and even though it was approved by the Censor Board, it was later banned in some of the theatres serving British Indian Army Cantonments.

Loosely based on Gandhian social values, Homi Wadia's reformist film *Ekta* was made in 1942 and marked the beginning of Sindhi cinema. Dedicated to the 'glorious cause of Hindu-Muslim unity', the film focused on inter-communal relationships.

Even though Gandhi had not featured in these films and it was his values and principles that were depicted, the British government adopted a draconian approach and clamped down on some of them. The Censor Board duly cut a few scenes wherever references were made to Gandhi in *Preetam* (The Loved One), made in 1942, and in *Raja* (The King), produced in 1943.

Gyan Mukherjee's super-hit crime drama *Kismet* in 1943 was produced by Bombay Talkies and underscored the patriotic sentiment through its plot. The song in the film, '*Door Hato Ai Duniya Walon, Hindustan Hamara Hai*' (Go away foreigners, India is ours) became an instant hit in what was an atmosphere of rising nationalistic fervour during the post-Quit India phase. Even though the song was clearly anti-British, it was ostensibly against the Japanese invasion and had a cleverly inserted line against the Germans and Japanese. The song described the map of India, which consisted of Afghanistan in the east and Burma in the west! Ashok Kumar played an anti-hero in the film, which turned out to be a trendsetter in many aspects for the Hindi film industry.

Next year, Mukherjee came up with another film, *Chal Chal Re Naujawan,* taking the popular lines from the hit song of the movie *Bandhan* (1940). The film underscored political ideas, with nationalist songs like '*Jai Bharat Desh*' (Victory to India) and the communal-harmony number '*Bolo Har Har Mahadev Allah-o-Akbar*' (Praise to Mahadev and Allah), depicting the theme of Hindu-Muslim unity propagated by Gandhi. Noted filmmaker Bimal Roy's debut Bengali film *Udayer Pathey* (Towards the Light), released in 1944, told the story of an impoverished novelist's tryst with destiny. The title was taken from a Tagore poem. The film referred to the Swadeshi programme, and the Gandhian protagonist's involvement in trade unionism pointed towards the changing landscape of politics in Bengal. The tune of the present national anthem '*Jana Gana Mana*', composed by Gurudev Rabindranath Tagore, was played for the first time in the title track of this film.

'Meera's bhajans! How can they be not beautiful? I am very familiar with many bhajans of Meerabai,' Gandhi had exclaimed in an interview. Ellis R. Duncan, an American filmmaker who worked predominantly in Tamil cinema, directed *Meera* in 1945. 'India's nightingale' Sarojini Naidu, a Gandhian to the core, spectacularly introduced the famed singer M.S. Subbulaksmi in the lead role of Meera in the Hindi version of the film. The songs became immensely popular, especially its gramophone records.

Two years later, Nanabhai Bhatt made *Meerabai* in 1947 in Gujarati. The musical film reproduced the well-known story of Meera's devotion in the wake of Indian Independence. 'In my Sabarmati Ashram these bhajans are sung repeatedly and with love and devotion to Her. Such rare joy is experienced from her bhajans,' Gandhi had told well-known musician Dilip Kumar Roy in February 1924.

A.V. Meiyappan's staunchly patriotic Tamil film *Nam Iruvar,* released in 1947, begins with the legendary Tamil poet Subramanya Bharati's death anniversary and ends with Gandhi's seventy-seventh birthday celebrations. Dealing with the challenges of the black market and corruption faced by newly-independent India, the protagonist in the film understands his misdeeds in the climax of the film and becomes a Gandhian nationalist. To emphasize nationalist sentiments, the characters in the film greet each other with '*Jai Hind*' and wear Congress (Gandhi) caps.

The success of the film owed much to the generous use of slogans in praise of Mahatma Gandhi and photographs of freedom fighters. The film's dialogues captivated audiences. After India attained freedom in August, a new song was added at the end of the film, sung by the well-known Carnatic singer D.K. Pattammal. '*Thayin Manikkodi*' (Flag of Mother India), written by Bharati, created a sensation, and people thronged to watch the film again.

Kovai Ayyamuthu, a nationalist leader and a great campaigner for khadi, came out with the film *Kanjan* (Miser) in Tamil. He wrote the story and script, and also directed the film, along with T.R. Gopu. When the shooting of the film was completed, Gopu, in a fine gesture, presented khadi cloth to all the workers. Gandhi's visit to Palani and the Independence Day celebrations at Coimbatore were shown in two reels along with the main film, which was released in November 1947.[13]

Film Land Ltd. produced *Message of Mahatma Gandhi,* which was directed by Muzammil and advertised as a national epic. The story was written by Begum Muzammil and carried the sacred message of truth, love, unity and brotherhood. The film had Leela Chitnis, Muzammil, Shashikala, Jillobai, Rekha and Prakash in the main roles.[14]

Two films were made in Marathi in 1948 focusing on Gandhi and the country's freedom struggle. The first was *Bhagya Rekha,* directed by Shantaram Athavale. This Shanta Apte starrer was a commentary on the political and social life in India at the time. Lyricist Shantaram Athavale, who wrote the immortal songs for *Sant Tukaram,* turned director for the first time with this film under the banner of Bharat Chitra Darshan.

This was also one of the first films of P.L. Deshpande, the legendary Maharashtrian writer, actor, director, playwright and performer. The film opens with a scene where the lead character Manik, played by well-known singer-actress Shanta Apte, is seen praying before a statue of Gandhi and taking a pledge to devote her life to working for the freedom of the country.

Vande Mataram, a Marathi film with nationalism as the backdrop, directed by Ram Gabale, was released next. It had an assembly of stalwarts from Marathi cinema. G.D. Madgulkar was the writer and lyricist, and Sudhir Phadke composed the music for the film. P.L. Deshpande and his wife Sunita Deshpande were the lead actors in the film. The themes of patriotism and humanism were woven into the narrative. The film was made under the banner of Nava Jhankar Productions by P.R. Bhide.

Bhide produced a few films, including *Lalat*, which was on the theme of Indian classical music. It featured the renowned singer Hirabai Barodekar and her sister Sarswati Rane, who sang songs based on classical ragas. Later, he also announced a series of topicals based on classical music and shot one featuring Lata Mangeshkar singing a classical song based on the raga Malkans. Bhide wanted to explore the impact of classical musical notes on the human brain!

The film *Vande Mataram* was based on the life of a village ballad singer who gets inspired by Gandhiji's teachings and leads an agitation by singing patriotic songs and organizing pickets. The shooting of the film in early 1948 at Shalini Cinetone in Kolhapur had to be stalled for a month after the assassination of Gandhi on 30 January that year. Even after its completion, the film faced many problems at the hands of the Censor Board. Inexcusably, the Censor Board of independent India took a tough stand and in an irony of sorts, brutally cut many scenes in a film that was based on India's freedom struggle! The change in government, apparently, had no impact on the functioning of the Board. The songs in the film, written by the versatile G.D. Madgulkar and composed by Sudhir Phadke, became instant hits. One song—'*Ved Mantrahun Amha*

Vandya Vande Mataram' (Vande Mataram, the national song, is to be revered more than the mantras of the Vedas)—is popular even today.

After spending a few years in the film industry, Bhide completely changed track and turned spiritual. He founded the Manashakti Ashram in Lonavala near Mumbai and came to be known as Swami Vidnyananand.

One can imagine the extent of the spell cast by the Mahatma, the saint, on this new medium of cinema. Cutting across languages, films brought his teachings to millions of people across the country. And these films were made when he was still alive. Marathi, Tamil, Telugu and Hindi were the languages in which a large number of social films were made in that era. And, given the times, it was natural that Gandhian values dominated as themes in these productions. Actually, the numbers here are not so important as the fact that films were made in all the major languages in India, spreading the ideals dear to the Mahatma.

The imagery of Gandhi both as a saint and Mahatma in the minds of the common people gelled well with the depiction of India's medieval saints in their biopics. It helped filmmakers to infuse the Mahatma's ideas in the popular culture. Not only in the films which captured struggle against colonialism, Gandhian symbolism and philosophy has left a rich legacy in these popular films, with or without direct reference to him.

Some of the films went on to become exceedingly popular, reaching very large population and creating a permanent space for the Mahatma in public consciousness. For a man who did not hold a good opinion about the film industry, it is astonishing that so many filmmakers thought it worthwhile to portray his ideas on screen, and that too during his lifetime.

It tells a lot about this phenomenon that an out-and-out stunt film like *Hero No. 1,* made by Balwant Bhatt in Hindi and released in 1939, had featured a song on Gandhi!

'*Gandhi tu saare desh ka abhimaan ban gaya Jis par nigahen dalin, voh insaan ban gaya.*' (Gandhi has become the pride of the country; whoever he has touched, has become a human being.)

7

Gandhi Sees a Talking Picture

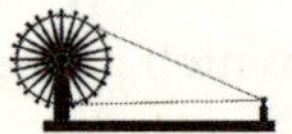

IF A MAN LIKE Gandhi who had openly professed his dislike for cinema decided to watch a feature film, it was considered nothing less than a miracle! At the ripe old age of seventy-five, Gandhi was persuaded to keep aside his deep prejudice for cinema for a while and watch moving images for the first and only time on screen. It was certainly considered a historical moment when he watched the Hindi film *Ram Rajya* (The Rule of Rama) in 1944. It is believed to be the only *Indian* film watched (that too only partly) by the Father of the Nation in his entire life.

The title of the film was a term used often by Gandhi to define a democratic-righteous rule that he envisaged for the country during the Independence struggle. What makes this film truly unique, however, is not merely the human treatment given by Vijay Bhatt, the director, to a mythological tale, but the fact that it was the only Indian film seen by Mahatma Gandhi in his lifetime. Noted actors Prem Adib and Shobhana Samarth played the lead roles in the film.

It was not that Gandhi went to a cinema theatre and watched the film. Even though he had partaken in all kinds of public activities, this was not the one he was willing to do. Therefore, a special screening of *Ram Rajya* was organized for him on 29 May 1944, when he was recuperating after a major illness—later identified as hookworm infection and amoebiasis—in the Juhu suburb of Bombay. His secretary Dr Sushila Nayar had given Vijay Bhatt, the producer-director, only forty minutes of Bapu's time for the film.

But the movie so engrossed him that Gandhi reportedly watched for over ninety minutes, and that too uninterrupted. The original length of the film was 144 minutes. Since it was his Day of Silence, he gave Bhatt a pat on the back after getting up from watching the film to show his appreciation. This remained for Bhatt one of the fondest memories of his life. He never won the prestigious Dadasaheb Phalke award, India's highest award for outstanding contribution to the growth and development of Indian cinema, but Bhatt often used to say, 'The pat on the back by Gandhiji is more precious to me than any award that can be obtained by lobbying the corridors of power.'[1] Three years later, *Ram Rajya* was screened at the prestigious Museum of Modern Art in New York on 5 May 1947. Readers of the well-known film magazine from Madras, *Picturepost*, adjudged it to be the best Hindi film of 1943, and the Bengal Film Journalist's Association selected it as the best film for art direction.

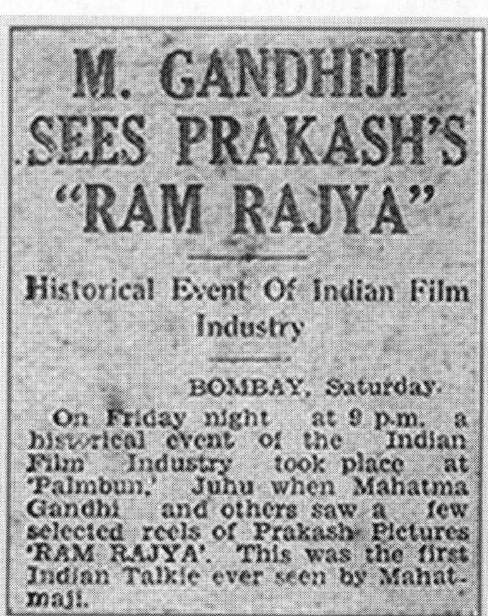
M. GANDHIJI SEES PRAKASH'S "RAM RAJYA"

Historical Event Of Indian Film Industry

BOMBAY, Saturday.

On Friday night at 9 p.m. a historical event of the Indian Film Industry took place at 'Palmbun,' Juhu when Mahatma Gandhi and others saw a few selected reels of Prakash Pictures 'RAM RAJYA'. This was the first Indian Talkie ever seen by Mahatmaji.

But despite all the hype and publicity about Gandhi's viewing of *Ram Rajya,* it was only the first *Indian* film Gandhi had seen, not the *first* film. That honour goes to an English-language film *Mission to Moscow*. This he saw just a few days before he had seen *Ram Rajya,* and this time the screening happened at the insistence of industrialist Shantikumar Morarji, in whose beachside home Gandhi was staying in Juhu, Bombay. Gandhi had neither seen a silent movie nor a talkie film before.

The projector and the reels of the film were brought, and about a hundred people came along too. Gandhi watched the film in a makeshift theatre on 21 May. When Mrs Morarji asked for his opinion about the film, Gandhi replied, 'I didn't like it.' He had not liked the ballroom dancing and the women in scanty dresses in the film; he considered it improper.[2] His grandson Rajmohan Gandhi writes that even though Gandhi was persuaded to watch the film, which was about popularizing America's alliance with the Soviet Union, it did not attract him to Stalin or to communism.[3]

The sensational news of Gandhi watching a Hollywood movie immediately reached America. The New York-based weekly magazine *Motion Picture Herald* headlined their report, 'Gandhi's First'.[4] It said, 'Last week was epochal for India's aged spiritual and nationalist leader Mohandas K. Gandhi. He saw, for the first time, a talking picture. Mr Gandhi released by the British from prison because his health is failing, was shown *Mission to Moscow* and a Mickey Mouse cartoon.' The report also noted that India's newspapers had headlined the event; this they were informed about by a cable sent to the Warner home office from B.N. Nadkarni, their Bombay-based agent. This issue also reported on the screening of *Ram Rajya* for the Mahatma on 29 May 1944. So, for a man who had seen not a single movie in his lifetime, two movies back-to-back in the matter of a few days was binge-watching.

The Madras-based film magazine *Picturpost* also reported the news under the headline 'Mahatmaji sees Mission to Moscow'.[5] It said, 'That Mahatmaji should see a Motion Picture is something unusual when it is known that he had never seen films. The fact that despite his ill-health he saw Mission to Moscow is indicative of his desire to know more about Soviet Russia.' *Mission to Moscow* was produced by Robert Buckner and was prepared for the screen by Howard Koch and directed by Michael Curtiz.

Gandhi's host Shanti Kumar Morarjee, his close associate and chairman of Scindia Steamship Company, was a first-hand witness to the entire event. It was Gandhi's disciple Slade who had persuaded him to watch *Mission to Moscow*. Bamboo poles were erected in the compound of Morarjee's bungalow one day, before arrangements for the electricity connection to show the film were made. The necessary permission for the screening was also obtained from the local authority.

Morarjee recalls that although the film *Mission to Moscow* was based on the memoirs of US ambassador to Russia Joseph Davies, some dancing scenes featuring scantily clad women horrified Gandhi. Gandhi even scolded his colleagues 'for showing such nude dances' to him. After such a distasteful and forgettable experience, it could have been an end of anything to do with cinema for Gandhi. But another close associate of Gandhi, Kanu Desai, a well-known cinema artiste in the Bombay industry, requested him to watch the Hindi film *Ram Rajya* for which Desai had done the art direction. Shanti Kumar had seen the film and was sure Gandhi would not like it. But Gandhi had to yield to Desai's insistence. According to him, Gandhi said, 'I will have to see an Indian film as I have made the mistake of watching an English one.'[6]

From very early on in his public comments, Gandhi made it quite clear, time and again, that he did not think cinema had any value in terms of entertainment or education. He wrote in *Young India,* in its issue of 25 November 1926:

> I have never once been to a cinema and refuse to be enthused about it and waste God-given time in spite of pressure sometimes used by kind friends. They tell me it has an educational value. It is possible that it has. But its corrupting influence obtrudes itself upon me every day. Education, therefore, I seek elsewhere.[7]

This surely was not a cryptic comment. It was followed by his answer in reply to a questionnaire in 1927 to the Indian Cinematograph Committee, headed by T. Rangachariar. The Committee was formed to examine the censorship system in India and suggest measures to encourage the exhibition of films produced within the British empire in general and Indian productions in particular. Gandhi, being one of the popular leaders, was asked to provide his opinion, and his response was,

> Even if I was so minded, I should be unfit to answer your questionnaire, as I have never been to a cinema. But even to an outsider, the evil that it has done and is doing is patent. The good, if it has done any at all, remains to be proved.

His attitude had not changed when he was requested to give a message for the official souvenir brought out on the occasion of the Silver Jubilee of Indian cinema in 1938. Gandhi chose to send the reply through his secretary. 'As a rule, Gandhiji gives messages only on rare occasions and these only for causes whose virtue is ever undoubtful. As for the cinema industry, he has the least interest in it.'[8]

In yet another bizarre take on cinema, Gandhi claimed that cinema is making children ill! In a letter to Sardar Patel written from Jorhat in Assam on 18 April 1934, he is cheerful and begins by saying, 'It is about time for prayers. The birds are singing. It dawns earlier in these parts; twilight appears at five a.m.' and then he turns towards cinema and writes, 'A strange epidemic seems to have attacked children in Ahmedabad. Some say it is due to the cinema. I would not be surprised if it is. Observers say that it imposes a great strain on the brain and the eyes.'[9]

Writing for *Harijan,* he once again made his views very clear:

> If I led a raging campaign against the cinemas, I should lose caste among educationists and reformists. They have often sought to convert me by pleading that cinemas are a fine medium of education and that churches and reformers in the West give them their patronage in an ever-increasing measure. Therefore, if I began to organize picketing, I should lose caste, lose my Mahatma-ship and even lose my head, which of course has very little value at this point of my life. I do not wish to suffer the triple loss.[10]

Gandhi found no reason to change his views towards cinema even as late as in 1947. While answering the question, 'Why do you oppose the growth of industries in our country through machinery?', Gandhi wrote,

> With so much leisure on hand, the people get busy in mischief, for, as the saying is, an idle mind is the devil's workshop. Or they waste their time in cinemas and theatres. Many people argue with me and try to convince me that the cinema has an educative value. But the argument doesn't appeal to me at all. For one thing, sitting in a closed theatre one feels suffocated. I had been in such a theatre only once, when I was a small child. If I had my way, I would see to it that all the cinemas and theatres in India were converted into spinning halls and factories for handicrafts of all kinds.[10]

But Gandhi's disdain for cinema didn't prevent the fledgling Indian film industry from using his name and his values as themes in their productions—directly or indirectly, according to Urwish Kothari, a senior columnist and writer. He wrote, 'One way of doing this was to show a short documentary on Gandhi during the screening of a regular film, as is evident in the following advertisement for the 1933 film *Chintamani*.'[11] Its promotional write-up read:

> Talkie film of a speech Mahatma Gandhi gave at Azad Maidan, which has been exclusively produced by Krishna Company. Also running is the film of his great reception from steamer Pilsna to Mani Bhavan. Do come with family to have the privilege of Mahatmaji's darshan and listen to his clear speech.

It is really intriguing to find Gandhi, who is considered one of the best communicators in the world, would hold such a low opinion about the newest form of art, i.e., cinema. Coincidentally, the growth of the motion picture industry in India happened almost parallel to Gandhi's rise in India's politics, his subsequent leadership of the freedom movement, and his death. Gandhi knew the value and importance of media too well. He was always accessible to the press and gave numerous interviews to Indian and foreign publications time and again. He went on to have very close and cordial relationships with some of the journalists and cameramen who covered him. Despite all this, he took a dim view of cinema. And he did not change his opinion till his last breath.

The power of moving images, even though the newest technological invention, was too strong to be ignored, and one would imagine that it could have been harnessed well for spreading the message of the freedom struggle far more effectively had Gandhi taken an interest in or shown some sympathy towards the industry. It is just that he didn't overcome his initial bias against cinema and no one really tried hard to change his mind either. In the end, it was simply his personal choice to not see films, and he stuck to it.

But one thing was very clear; even though he was averse to the cinema industry in general, he did not really object to or stop motion picture cameramen from filming him. He was not anti-films. One may infer that Gandhi thought he didn't have time to 'waste' on these things for he was far too busy managing the freedom struggle of a country. But at the same time, he did not impose his 'anti-cinema' views on his colleagues. Contrast Gandhi's attitude towards cinema with the way some of his closest colleagues in Congress dealt with the film industry, and the difference is stark!

Sardar Patel was one political leader who realized the importance of cinema as a powerful mode of communication only too well and tried to use it effectively whenever and wherever possible. As the chairman of the organizing committee of the 1938 Haripura Congress in rural Gujarat, he took keen interest in facilitating the making of a short film on the proceedings of the session. He himself appeared on screen, making a short speech about the Congress and explaining its objectives so that his message could reach the masses spread in the far corners of the country. He was aware of the fact that this film, when screened in the interiors of India, would enable the people to not only see its leaders, but also understand the way Congress functioned.

On 23 December 1939, Patel went for the inauguration of Chandulal Shah's *Achhut* at Royal Opera House in Bombay. Shah, the founder of Ranjit Studios, had a special interest in inviting Patel for the show. He explained it at the occasion: 'Entirely unconscious of the cultural work we are doing through our pictures in spite of great handicaps, we are still looked upon as untouchables by people from whom we seek sympathy.' Patel, a pragmatic leader, responded to this concern in his speech by stressing the vital importance of cinema in the life of a nation and underscored the necessity of using the immense potential of film for the welfare of the country. Urging the people to support the Indian film industry with patriotic enthusiasm, Sardar Patel said, 'That if *Achhut* really fulfils the ideals for which it is produced, it will have done a great and noble service to the cause of the Harijans. Untouchability is a blot on Hinduism and on India and must be wiped off as soon as possible. If the picture helps India to remove this cause, it can be said to have helped India to win Swaraj as untouchability is one of the chief obstacles in the road to freedom.' [12]

Patel was also responsible for producing a film on Netaji Subhas Chandra Bose. With the help of Indian Motion Pictures Producers' Association (IMPPA), Patel got real life footage of Bose and Azad Hind Fauj which was included in the film. Patel also recorded a special message against prohibition that was included in Master Vinayak's delightful satire *Brandy ki Botal* in 1939.

Another close colleague of Gandhi, 'Indian Nightingale' Sarojini Naidu, was a natural charmer with a powerful command on language. These qualities were on full display when she appeared on screen during her tour of America in 1928. In her eloquent speech, Naidu, dressed in an exquisite saree, gave a glorious account of the rich heritage of India for Fox Movietone News. She went on to appear on screen on several occasions to spell out the programme of the freedom struggle. While describing the importance of the cinema industry, she said, 'The Cinematic Art is the synthesis of so many arts. And therefore, it is the Art of Arts. Cinema is the most triumphant symbol of modern civilization, a pleasing combination of man and machine for production of human pleasure. The poets, the musicians, the actors, the dress designers, the painters as well as the composers, the photographers, the sound recorders and a host of men and women of intelligence combine to produce a single, composite article. The film industry is consciously or unconsciously, blazoning the trail to superior human culture. If Indian film industry is to justify its existence and fulfil its purpose, it must plan on sound principles and we must all help it do so.'[13]

Cinematic genes were in the family too. Sarojini's sister Sunalini Naidu was a dancer and had acted in a few Hindi films. Sarojini Naidu had also graciously introduced the young M.S. Subbulakshmi in the seminal classic film *Meera* to the Indian audience.

Pandit Nehru, whom Gandhi had anointed as his successor, was instrumental in shaping the Indian film industry after Independence through pragmatic policy initiatives. He set up the Film Enquiry Committee in 1949 to look into the various issues of the industry, including its reforms and development. The report of the Committee, headed by S.K. Patil, a prominent Congressman with V. Shantaram and B.N. Sircar as its members, paved the way for establishment of the Film Finance Corporation (later NFDC), Film Institute of India (later FTII) and other film organizations. The International Film Festival of India (IFFI) was started during his premiership in four cities viz. Bombay, New Delhi, Madras and Calcutta, and that exposed young Indian filmmakers to a new wave of international cinema. While speaking at the inauguration of the first IFFI in its New Delhi edition on 21 February 1952, Nehru said,[14]

> Film has become a powerful influence in people's lives. It can educate them rightly or wrongly … I mean that they should introduce artistic and aesthetic values in life and encourage the appreciation of beauty in all its aspects. I hope that films which are just sensational or melodramatic or such as make capital out of crime, will not be encouraged. If our film industry keeps this ideal before it, it will encourage good taste and help pave its own way in the building of a new India.[15]

Even before Independence, Nehru had shown keen interest in cinema and had reportedly watched Ashok Kumar and Devika Rani starrer *Achhut Kanya* produced by Bombay Talkies, as well as many other movies from time to time. In fact, there was a small one-reeler topical made on Nehru watching this film in September 1936.

Another popular national leader, Netaji Subhash Chandra Bose, had also recognized the power of film as a medium. Bose had a charismatic presonality, therefore it was natural that he featured in many newsreels of the times. His dapper appearance in military uniform definitely helped spread the aura of his personality in the minds of young Indians. In his message recorded for a special film on the Haripura Congress in February 1938, which he famously presided over, Bose said,

> It is a matter of great pleasure and pride for us that Mahatma Gandhi himself was present and bestowed us with His blessings and inspiration. Science has now come to help us in our work, and I hope, that in future we will use film and radio even more for our campaigns.

India's Renaissance Man Rabindranath Tagore, the man who first used the term Mahatma for Gandhi, obviously had artistic clarity on the phenomenon of the moving picture. It is interesting to see what the poet has to say about films:

> The principal element of a motion picture is the 'flux of image'. The beauty and grandeur of this form in motion has to be developed in such a way that it becomes self-sufficient without the use of words. If some other language is needed to explain its own, it amounts to incompetence. If music can achieve profundity without the words of the cadence of a melody, then why should not this motion form, be considered as a distinct aesthetic experience?

This he wrote in 1929 in a letter to Murari Bhaduri, who was the brother of renowned theatre artist Sisir Kumar Bhaduri. Since Tagore was a man of art and letters, he also tried his hand at directing a film.

Natir Puja (The Dancing Girl's Worship), released in 1932, was a recording of his 1926 stage dance-drama of the same name. It was produced by New Theatres' B.N. Sarkar, and part of the cast and crew consisted of students of Shantiniketan, while Nitin Bose, who later became a well-known director, was the cinematographer.

One Congressman who actively tried to use the format of the documentary rather than the feature film as an instrument of propaganda for the nationalist cause was the Tamil leader S. Satyamurthi. He correctly predicted that cinema would play a significant role in a society with such a high rate of illiteracy as India's, and that its influence was destined to be strong. In 1934, Satyamurthi, himself an amateur actor, made a film to reach out to voters before the city elections in Madras and got it screened in several cinema houses. He expressed hope for cooperation between the film producers and directors in India and the leaders of the nation, in a way outlining the importance of cinema in the country's struggle for freedom.

Satyamurthi also went on to become the president of the South Indian Film Chamber of Commerce (SIFCC). It was an umbrella organization for safeguarding the business interests of producers, distributors, studio owners and exhibiters of films. In 1937, before elections to the Provincial Legislature, Satyamurthi produced another propaganda film in Madras. But it failed to get certification. Throughout his life, Satyamurthi supported many film directors and writers working on films encouraging educational and social values.

Even Lokmanya Tilak had realized that cinema was here to stay and could be very useful in propagating the message of the freedom struggle. Tilak was instrumental in facilitating funds for D.G. Phalke while the latter was in desperate need of capital for making movies. The newspaper he edited, *Kesari*, published a review of Phalke's film *Raja Harishchandra* (1913), praising it as the first swadeshi feature film. Tilak also encouraged Baburao Painter, a pioneer in many ways in the nascent Indian cinema industry, and supported the activities of his Kolhapur-based Maharashtra Film Company, where Painter's disciples started their cinema journey by establishing Prabhat Film Company and shifting later to Poona.

As we saw, the beginning of Indian cinema and arrival of Gandhi on Indian political scenario almost coincided with each other. But, right from the beginning, Gandhi somehow could not bring himself to like the medium of cinema. On the other hand, Gandhi would place cinema with other vices like 'race-course, drink-booth and opium-den' as 'enemies of the society'.[16] Even twenty years later, he held the same views. During a conversation with socialist leader Jayaprakash Narayan, Gandhi said, 'If I had my way, I would see to it that all the cinemas and theatres in India were converted into spinning halls and factories of handicrafts of all kind.'[17]

There was another incident where Gandhi decided to express his views on cinema, though in an indirect way. Even though he was present at the 1936 Congress session at Lucknow presided over by Nehru, he did not participate in it. The only exception he made was for the exhibition arranged by the All India Spinners' Association and the All India Village Industries Association. He exhorted one and all present there to visit this exhibition and said, 'When I told you the other day that this exhibition was not a cinema show, I meant more than I said. When you go to a cinema show you meet with things there to captivate in a sensual way your eyes and ears.'

It was not that nobody tried to persuade Gandhi to change his opinion of cinema. And it had to be an insider and a practising filmmaker from the much-maligned industry. In October 1939, K.A. Abbas, a leading journalist, scriptwriter and director, wrote an open letter to Gandhi urging him to reconsider his ideas about the 'evil of cinema'. In a passionate defence and advocation of cinema, he wrote:

> Today I bring for your scrutiny—and approval—a new toy my generation has learned to play with, the CINEMA! You include cinema among evils like gambling, sutta, horse racing, etc. ... Now if these statements had come from any other person, it was not necessary to be worried about them ... But your case is different. In

> view of the great position you hold in this country, and I may say in the world, even the slightest expression of your opinion carries much weight with millions of people. And one of the world's most useful inventions would be allowed to be discarded or what is worse, left alone to be abused by unscrupulous people. You are a great soul, Bapu. In your heart there is no room for prejudice. Give this little toy of ours, the cinema, which is not so useless as it looks, a little of your attention and bless it with a smile of toleration.

Abbas felt that Gandhi has been wrongly advised and said:

> I have no knowledge of how you came to have such a poor opinion of the cinema ... I don't know even if you have ever cared to see a motion picture. I can only imagine that rushing from one political meeting to another, you chanced to catch a glimpse of some lewd cinema posters that disfigure the city walls and concluded that all the films are evil and that the cinema is a playhouse of the devil.[18]

K.A. Abbas went on to direct *Dharti Ke Lal* in 1946, produced by the Indian People Theatres Association (IPTA), and followed it up with brilliant scripts for Raj Kapoor's *Awara, Shree 420* and *Jagte Raho,* and for V. Shantaram's *Dr. Kotnis Ki Amar Kahani*.

Three decades after he wrote this letter to Gandhi, Abbas was to write a script for a film on Gandhi in 1969 as part of latter's birth centenary project. But the project never saw the light of day and we will read about it in another chapter of this book.

Even though Gandhi had strong reservations about cinema as a medium, he professed very different views on music:

> One great stumbling block is that we have neglected music. Music means rhythm, order. Unfortunately, in India, music has been the prerogative of the few. It has never become nationalized. I would make compulsory a proper singing, in company, of national songs. And to that end, I would have great musicians attending every Congress or conference and teaching mass music.[19]

In fact, Gandhi had taken personal interest in arranging for Pandit Narayan Khare to teach music at his Sabarmati Ashram. Pandit Khare, who came from the Satara district of Maharashtra, was one of the main disciples of Pandit Vishnu Digambar Paluskar and belonged to the Gwalior gharana of the Hindustani vocal tradition. After founding the Sabarmati Ashram, Gandhi felt the need to have an expert music teacher and asked Pandit Paluskar for one. Khare then joined the Ashram, where he introduced Ramdhun in the daily prayers and was instrumental in compiling the *Bhajanavali*, a book of prayers in various languages. Pandit Khare was also part of the chosen team of Gandhi's followers for the Dandi March. In one of the letters Gandhi wrote from Yerawada jail in Poona to Pandit Khare on 21 August 1930, he reminisces, 'Your voice as you used to sing at the time of prayers haunts me every day.'[20]

Gandhi did not stop with just having a trained musician at the Ashram. He felt there was a need to propagate music in the entire province of Gujarat. In one of his letters to Pandit Khare, he wrote:

> All Gujaratis are or should be aware of the fact that as compared with Bengal, Maharashtra and the Southern provinces, Gujarat lags far behind in respect of music. Not only are Gujarati men and women less musical but ordinarily even boys and girls cannot sing in tuning even a simple song. It follows then that there can be no difference of opinion on the need for propagation of music.[21]

During his meeting with the great French writer Romain Rolland in Lausanne in 1930, Gandhi had asked him to play the piano, and Rolland played Beethoven's fifth symphony for him.

Gandhi even got political venues designed! At the Lucknow Congress session, he called renowned artist Nandalal Bose from Shantiniketan to set up an exhibition of Indian paintings. He visited every stall at the exhibition and spent considerable time enjoying the works displayed there. Then, during the December 1936 Congress session at Faizpur in rural Maharashtra, Nandalal Bose was once again called by Gandhi to design and decorate the entire village venue, which was named after

Lokmanya Tilak. In his letter to Bose, Gandhi writes, 'A little does not satisfy, the heart demands more.'[22] This time, Gandhi's brief was clear, 'Build the township at Faizpur using only rural material and employing country craftsmen. The conception should be indigenous.'

Pleased by the results at the two previous sessions, Gandhi again entrusted the responsibility of decorating the 1938 Congress session at Haripura in Gujarat to Nandalal Bose. Gandhi's instructions were once again specific: the entire exhibition should be clearly visible to the rural people attending the session. 'Cover the entire area with examples of art,' he said. Bose did 200 paintings to mount at the venue, and two artists from Gujarat, Ravishankar Raval and Kanu Desai, also brought in their work. The same Nandalal Bose was to create an image of Gandhi, with staff in hand, in black-and-white linocut print, which has since turned out to be one of the most iconic images of Gandhi.

There have been many issues on which Gandhi changed his opinion in his lifetime. And while doing so, he clearly stated that his latest view should be treated as his final view. This he did so after careful consideration, and in the light of new facts. Sometimes he did complete turnarounds on crucial issues. But, curiously, in the case of cinema he held on to his views. A man who tried to conquer the bodily senses all his life was not to give in to sensual pleasures of the cinema.

From a very young age, Gandhi believed in controlling the senses. He continually experimented to test his mind and body to win the battle with the senses throughout his life. A man who did not believe in wasting a single minute of his working time must have detested the idea of sitting idle for more than two hours to watch a movie.

The fervent appeal and prayer by K.A. Abbas turned out to be a futile effort. Even though Gandhi managed to watch Vijay Bhatt's *Ram Rajya*, a film more suited to his tastes given its subject, he made his displeasure known in a letter written to his grandson Kanam Gandhi, son of Ramdas Gandhi. On 25 July 1944, two months after he watched the film, he wrote from Panchgani:

> I have had enough of watching the cinema all by myself without my compatriots at Sevagram. When I am out and engaged in some good activity, I would remember all of you. There was no such thing in the present case. Hence, nobody has lost anything by not witnessing the show. On the contrary, I have lost something after having seen the picture. You may ask me what it is.[23]

So, a man—among the most photographed and filmed in the world—remained a non-convert till the end as far as cinema was considered!

8

Mahatma Gandhi, starring Mahatma Gandhi

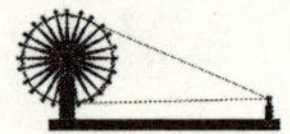

IN A STRANGE STATE of circumstances, the reels of a film starring Mahatma Gandhi in the title role had to be hidden away in temples and other religious places in India for many years. Well, that was what happened with the unique and iconic film *Mahatma Gandhi,* made by A.K. Chettiar, which was released in August 1940 in India. About two and a half hours long, the film was not a feature or fictional film, and neither a documentary nor a newsreel. It was a curious mix of many formats and was something in between.

The film may not have been fictional, but its survival entailed a lot of real-life drama. Due to the charged political atmosphere in India, and with the Gandhi-led struggle for Independence against the British in the final stages, the producers of the film thought it fit to lie low for some time even after the film was released and had a successful run for a few weeks.

There was another film on Gandhi, made after Independence, which also went through a somewhat similar struggle for survival. The unusual length of this documentary film by Vithalbhai Jhaveri, again titled *Mahatma Gandhi,* made its commercial release difficult. Breaking it up into segments to make it watchable would have led to loss of significance over time. So, although it was considered as one of the most authentic documentations on Gandhi's life, it did not get the patronage of either the audience or the government.

Gandhi was a hot topic for the screen, and reel imitated real life! Not knowing any other way to save the film, and fearing its confiscation by the British authorities, the producers of *Mahatma Gandhi* (the one made before Independence) decided to hide the reels of the film in temples, religious mutts and in friends' homes scattered across south India. After a long hiatus of seven years, the film resurfaced at a right time. It was screened one day before India gained independence. On 14 August 1947, *Mahatma Gandhi* had a grand re-release in New Delhi, amidst celebrations of victory against the mighty British who had ruled India for more than 150 years.

The film *Mahatma Gandhi* was a dream come true for the man who had passionately searched and acquired footage on Gandhi from various sources like a possessed devotee. It was while travelling on a ship from New York to Dublin in 1937 that this twenty-six-year-old Indian man, A.K. Chettiar dreamt of making an authentic film on Gandhi's life. Coincidentally, the day happened to be Gandhi's sixty-eighth birthday.

Annamalai Karuppan Chettiar, born on 3 November 1911 in Kottaiyur near Karaikudi in Madras Presidency, had dreamed big, because even though many newsreels had focused on Gandhi, no full-length biographic documentary had been attempted before. Having been trained in photography at the Imperial College of Photography at Tokyo and the New York Institute of Photography in New York, Chettiar had the right credentials for the job. Moreover, he had developed a deep interest in Gandhi and his philosophy. Given all this, it was most appropriate that he thought of taking up such a challenging project.

Chettiar's dream of 1937 finally took shape after three years, in 1940, after a monumental effort on his part, of tracing and acquiring footage from various parts of the world. He travelled almost 1,00,000 miles across four continents to collect footage shot by more than 100 cameramen. The footage he tirelessly collected totalled a staggering 50,000 feet approximately, of which only a fourth could ultimately be used in the film. It would really be any archivist's dream to search for and find the large amount of footage that was edited out of the film. It would surely be a treasure trove of visual documentation of the Father of the Nation. I hope it miraculously surfaces one day!

At the re-release of *Mahatma Gandhi* in 1947, the who's who of Delhi's elite as well as common citizens of newly independent India made for the audience. Leading the huge group of luminaries was Dr Rajendra Prasad, the President of the Constituent Assembly, who attended the show along with his family. There were several important national leaders, Members of Legislatures, ambassadors of foreign countries and representatives of the media in the audience. Indira Gandhi and Devdas Gandhi, one of Gandhi's sons, also attended the screening. A total of twelve reels of the film were screened that day, of which ten were in Tamil and two in Telugu. But language was not a problem for the audience as they knew Gandhi's life story only too well. A year later, the film was released in 1948 with a Hindi commentary.

The two-and-a-half-hour film was initially named the *Life History of Mahatma Gandhi,* which was changed to *Mahatma Gandhi: His Movements and Activities*. When the film was submitted for certification, there were two sympathetic Indian members on the Madras Censor Board—K Srinivasan, then editor of the *Hindu* newspaper and Dr U Krishna Rao, a member of the Madras Corporation. With their positive recommendation, the film was cleared for general release. But these two members had to pay the price for passing the film without any cuts and they were not nominated again to the Censor Board. The film ran successfully for weeks, and one of the prominent national leaders to see it was Rajaji. After watching the film, Rajaji said, 'I never expected it to be so good. It is well done.'[1]

Apart from many other things Chettiar attempted was a short film on Gandhi in colour at Sevagram. Colour film was just being introduced in the industry and it cost Rs 80 for 100 feet of film stock. Moreover, for developing the negative, it had to be sent all the way to London. But the novel experiment failed, as the 100 feet in colour which he had shot turned out to be bad. A few years later, a Russian photographer successfully filmed Gandhi, just few days before his death, in colour.

After the successful run of the film in India, the producers decided to release it worldwide. Gandhi could not just be confined to Indian borders; he belonged to the world. Accordingly, they made an agreement with the American Academy of Asian Studies in San Francisco for the film's release in the USA in 1953. A special screening was organized in Washington on 10 February 1953 by the Indian Ambassador to the USA, Jagan Mehta. It was seen by the US President Eisenhower, General Carlos P. Romulo, the President of the United Nations, and the Russian Ambassador Andrei Gromyko.

Mehta also hosted the premier of the film organized for the diplomats of the United Nations on 28 April 1953 at the Guild Theatre in New York. It was attended by Sir Gladwyn Jebb, British Ambassador to the United Nations; Andrei Y. Vishinsky, Soviet Ambassador to the United Nations; Arthur Lall, Indian Consul General; V.K. Krishna Menon, Indian delegate to the United Nations; and John D. Rockefeller Jr, a noted American philanthropist.

It is a tragedy that the original film is believed to be lost. But in the archiving world nothing is considered lost forever, until found! Proving this maxim true, an abridged version of this English 1953 film was successfully traced by A.R. Venkatachalapathy in 2007. The film, now with the new title *Mahatma Gandhi: Twentieth Century Prophet*, is a re-edited version of forty-five minutes, down from its original length of eighty-one minutes. The American Academy of Asian Studies produced this version. At the start of the film, it is clearly mentioned that the film material was collected by A.K. Chettiar for The Documentary Films Ltd. Madras, India, and acknowledged the cooperation received from

Dr P.V. Pathy, L. Natesan, A. Sambandam, H.A. Kolhatkar, and H.S.L. Polak, among others.

Hollywood's leading film magazine *Variety* reviewed the documentary when it was released in the USA in 1953 and said the best thing about this screen treatment of the Mahatma's life and teachings was not what was seen but what was heard.[2] As the narrator in the film, Quentin Reynolds, a seasoned observer of the world political scene and having just the right vocal qualities for the job, did Gandhi much more justice than the pictorial records. 'Reynolds gives the audience a top-notch run down on Gandhi's life and the meaning of his philosophy which brought independence to India,' said the report in *Variety*.

The different nature of the film prompted the magazine *Educational Screen* to say that the film fell somewhere between newsreel and documentary, without being too much of either.[3] It had the casual immediacy of the former by dint of its content and the planned intention of the documentary as a result of skillful editing, it said. Chettiar himself had clarified that the film was based on the newsreel tradition. The *New York Times* also reviewed the film in its report 'Gandhi's Life Unfolds on Screen', and said: 'This feature-length compilation summarizes the general career, philosophies and practices of a godly politician. In *Mahatma Gandhi: Twentieth Century Prophet*, a cold, merciless camera eye has preserved unquestionable proof that here was a great and a good man.'[4]

Collecting the vast amount of footage that Chettiar did was just half the work done for such a monumental film. The enterprise to collect footages was a costly affair for Chettiar and the British news agencies demanded a pound for every foot of the film. And even that also they refused to provide saying that 'the film on Gandhiji's visit to London had political overtones and that I might use it in a manner prejudicial to the interests of their government.'[5]

There were teething problems when the film went on the editing table. With great difficulty, Chettiar managed to get a team of suitable writers and narrators. The sound recording was done in the studios of

Wadia Movietone in Bombay. T.N. Kumaraswamy, the Tamil writer, wrote the commentary, and it was delivered by four commentators including Serukalathoor Sama, the popular Tamil actor; T.K. Jayarama Iyer, noted violinist who also provided background music on the violin; and V.M. Kothainayagi Ammal, a novelist; and K.S. Ganesan, an actor.

When the film was getting ready, it was reported that the producers hoped to show it to the Mahatma himself and get his approval before its public release. The leading film magazine of the time, *Film India*, reported this and cheekily remarked: 'Will the first film seen by Mahatma Gandhi be 'Mahatma Gandhi' starring Mahatma Gandhi?'![6]

The film starts with a historical perspective, providing background on India's rich history and culture. Images of the graceful but mutilated statue of the Buddha in Taxila are shown, followed by images of the famous Ashoka Pillar, Mughal palaces and other well-known monuments, and finally images of the port of Surat in Gujarat, the state Gandhi hails from. One of the major highlights of the film is the mass-spinning sequence of about 400 feet shot at Tirupur, the hosiery town in Tamil Nadu, which I have described before. It shows about 2,000 women spinning the charkha to the song *Aadu Ratte* (Let the spinning wheel turn), a patriotic poem in Tamil written by Namakkal Ramalingam Pillai and sung by the well-known Carnatic singer D.K. Pattammal.

The entire spinning event, a grand one by any standards, was organized just for this film! K.A. Ayyamuthu, a secretary of the Tamil Nadu Khadi Board and a close friend of Chettiar's, thought such a sequence would help popularize the khadi movement, a cause dear to Gandhi. The women featured in the spinning sequence were suitably compensated in lieu of the loss of their daily wages. Dr Pathy, the cameraman, shot the scene from several angles in view of the technical inadequacies of the equipment of those times.

The advertisement for the film released in the media gave full details of the crew involved in the production, including the names of the singers. It ran like this:

> Mahatma Gandhi; Full length picture in Tamil; Filmed in 4 continents by 100 cameramen from 1912; Produced and Distributed by The Documentary Films Ltd. Madras; Collected & Edited by AK Chettiar; Technical Director Dr PV Pathy; ML Natesan and AK Chettiar, Managing Directors of Documentary Films; Smt VM Kothanayaki Ammal, the lady commentator; Miss Suryakumari and Srimathi DK Pattammal sings background songs.

Since it was a beautiful mix of real footage dealt through the documentary nature of storytelling, the ultimate result is most effective, even though there are not many dramatic elements in the film. The story takes viewers to South Africa, showing the Phoenix Settlement, the Tolstoy Farm and President Krewger's house. Along the way, the audience gets glimpses of many important political leaders, including some of Gandhi's close colleagues. The list is vast—from C.R. Das to Motilal Nehru, from Mohammed Ali to Moulana Abul Kalam Azad, from Vallabhbhai Patel to Khan Abdul Ghaffar Khan, from Jawaharlal Nehru to Subhas Chandra Bose, from Rajendra Babu Prasad to Pattabhi Sitaramayya, and from Sarojini Naidu to Kamaladevi Chattopadhyaya. The film also contained the iconic footage taken by James Mills on board the boat SS Rajaputana.

A delightful scene filmed during Gandhi's stay at Villeneuve as the guest of the French philosopher and writer Romain Rolland shows a group of children coming to offer him flowers. His joy amidst them is a characteristic of his simplicity and love; and when he poses for the camera with the children, he is particular about a charming little boy who stands aloof from the group and is asked by Gandhi to stand next to him. It is this humane nature of the man that comes out so beautifully in some of these sequences. Apart from the mass spinning sequence, there are several shots of the charkha, something Gandhi insisted should be part of the daily life of the people of India. While reviewing the film for Madras-based film magazine Talk A Tone, M.S. Shankaramangalam wrote:

> The credit goes to AK Chettiar who has made a treasure house of evidence to the future historians, which today has emerged as an epic of great endeavour. The credit is also due to Dr PV Pathy who brings first class technical training and a penetrating progressive mind to edit the picture from bins of collected celluloid to a finished story which has a dynamic appeal to every type of film goer, whether he be a patriot or a connoisseur. To every patriot of India this film is a gospel of life. This documentary-biography is a film of 'a man who will live in history and in Heaven with Buddha, Socrates and Jesus'.[7]

Unfortunately, we do not know how working in such close proximity to Gandhi impacted the young filmmaker Chettiar. About that he had only this much to say, 'The most blessed days of my life were those that I spent in Sevagram filming Gandhiji's life!' This was so because unlike other cameramen and filmmakers, Chettiar couldn't bring himself to meet Gandhi in person and engage in a meaningful conversation while filming him. He justified this rather strange behaviour with his own logic:

> Let not anybody think I missed the rare chance of meeting Gandhiji that came my way accidentally, or that I sacrificed my desire to speak with him. I did not utilize the opportunity because my desire to complete the film was stronger than my desire to meet him. If I were to meet him, Gandhiji might ask me what I was doing. Then I would have to say, 'Bapuji, I am producing a documentary on you.' Gandhiji might say, 'Don't do that.' And that would be the final word! I prayed to God that such a situation should not arise due to any reason.[8]

Before embarking on this monumental Gandhi film, Chettiar had some other ambitious dreams. He along with fellow Indian Ramprakash Kohli wanted to start India's own independent newsreel, by and for Indians. Both had graduated from the New York Institute of Photography and visited Hollywood and other production centres of the world to study filming techniques. Their aim was to show the true picture of India which would be free and clear of any British control.

Chettiar and Kohli were photographed and featured prominently in a report titled 'Hindus blame Britons' newsreel coloration' in a leading Hollywood film magazine. 'The only newsreel pictures they saw of India were of elephants, monkeys and snake charmers. There are other things in India besides these,' they said in New York before sailing for London, thence to Bombay. 'It is my belief that much of the vicious propaganda and misinformation about India can be cleared out most effectively by truthful and accurate newsreels from India,'[9] declared Kohli.

Somehow, their plan seems to have not taken off. After Chettiar returned to Chennai from Dublin, he founded a company called Documentary Films Limited in 1937 and set about realizing his other dream of Gandhi film. Film historian S. Theodore Baskaran describes how A.K. Chettiar laboured over the production of this documentary through the years of the Second World War:

> He decided to collect the already existing material on Gandhi from various sources—archives, news agencies, studios and individuals —then shoot contemporary scenes and string these precious visual records together. First, he searched Indian studios and then travelled abroad, to places where Gandhiji had been, to unearth previous footages. In Chennai, he was able to salvage precious footage of 1927 Congress. It showed Srinivasa Ayyangar leading Gandhiji to the dais, followed by Sarojini Naidu and Nehru.[10]

After the release of the film, the popular film magazine *Film India* ran a story under the headline 'Mahatma Gandhi becomes a Film Star!' in March 1940.[11] Even though K.A. Abbas, a noted journalist and filmmaker, wrote the article, the headline was the handiwork of its maverick editor Baburao Patel, and Chettiar didn't like it at all. The news of such a film being made reached USA and *The New York Times* reported that 'A feature length documentary film on the life of Mahatma Gandhi has been prepared ... a short version of it will soon be ready for release abroad. Lowell Thomas will be sought to provide the English commentary.'[12]

The buzz about the film continued to interest Hollywood with a major trade paper, *Motion Picture Herald* published the report 'Gandhi in Film on own Career' on 30 March 1940. It cited a United Press dispatch from Ramgarh, where Gandhi was attending the Indian National Congress session. The report further said the film would be flown to Washington for presentation before President Roosevelt.[13]

The leading newspaper of the world, *The New York Times*, in its issue dated 7 April 1940, carried an article with a headline 'Starring M Gandhi'. Written by K. A. Abbas, it said, 'Mahatma Gandhi, the saint-leader of India, is the subject and principal star of a unique film now in production here (Bombay).' While praising the monumental efforts taken by A. K. Chettiar, the maker of the film, the article said, 'The result is a film which is expected to be more than the screen biography of India's greatest man. It is the story of the Gandhian era in Indian history.' [14]

The film was released first in 1940 with a Tamil commentary, and then dubbed in Telugu. The Telugu version of the film was released in February 1941 in six centres. This version included the AICC meeting held in September 1940 too. The background music for it was provided by V. Nagiah and the songs were sung by B. Rajaratnam, P. Kannamba and Suryakumari. Later, the film was withdrawn from theatres because of the threat of government repression. The Hindi version of the film with eleven reels, and 9950 feet long, was certified by the Bombay Board of Film Censors in April 1948.

Another ingenious touch Chettiar gave to the production was the use of variable density audio track. Normal stock was costlier, and perhaps he decided to make use of this technology as it was cost-effective. This technology was used in non-fiction films during 1940 and 1950s by a few independent filmmakers.

Chettiar was keen to showcase the film around the world. In fact, the plan was afoot to make the film in as many as 21 languages, if the War didn't interfere. Documentary Films Ltd. had offers from most European countries to release this film therein with the separate commentaries to be superimposed in the respective native languages.[15] But the situation changed and accordingly, he re-edited the film in Hollywood with a commentary in English and screened it in the US in 1953, as has been described earlier. It was produced by Edith Martin for the American Academy of Asian Studies and runs for about fifty minutes.

There are two separate title cards giving credit to A.K. Chettiar. One said: 'Film material collected by A.K. Chettiar'. The other called him a 'Technical Adviser'. All those involved in the making of the original Tamil version—especially the lead cinematographer P.V. Pathy—are recognized. The card says: 'Acknowledging the cooperation of … [Pathy and others].' Pathy, who graduated from Sorbonne University, was the technical director of the film.

At the start of the film, the following lines are projected: 'The film you are about to see contains materials collected from four continents and photographed by nearly a hundred different cameramen. Some of the scenes were made many years ago under extremely different conditions. These facts account for certain technical imperfections in some pictures.'

The American Academy of Asian Studies made elaborate arrangements to showcase the film through a vast network of churches, schools, clubs and art theatres across the world. Half of the proceeds from the screenings was to go to the Academy for its work in promoting a better understanding between East and West. The remaining half was to go to Indian National sources for promoting the understanding of Gandhi's philosophy.[16]

Chettiar was fortunate to get an opportunity to film Gandhi from close quarters. And his experience was not very different from those of other cameramen in terms of the difficulty of capturing Gandhi for the screen. He wrote:

> It is very difficult to film Gandhiji. He does not stand for a minute in front of a camera. Generally, he would walk very fast. Moreover, people would be standing around him all the time and would

> stretch their necks towards the camera hoping to get a snapshot with Gandhiji. Most cameramen were not admitted into Gandhiji's cottage (at Wardha). Despite these tremendous odds a few wonderful shots of Gandhiji's life have been recorded.[17]

There is one particular scene in the film which is a real standout, where Gandhi looks innocence personified. During the inaugural function of a museum at Maganwadi near Sevagram, Gandhi is shown sitting on a dais. The function had been organized by the All-India Village Industries Association, of which Gandhi was the founder as well as president. The museum was named after Maganlal Gandhi, his close associate of many years.

During the function, held on 30 December 1938, a small girl comes up on the dais and puts a garland around Gandhi's neck. Gandhi makes her sit near him and then wraps the garland around his and girl's neck so that both are in its embrace. There is a burst of instant laughter from the people present in response to this. Gandhi then removes the garland from his neck and puts it fully around the small girl's neck. The girl is now beaming. And so is the elderly Gandhi with his innocent, toothless smile!

As the function was held in the evening, there was not enough light to capture the action on stage properly. The cameraman Dr Pathy decided to innovate and shot the scene in slow-motion technique. Chettiar said: 'The result was excellent and innumerable people enjoyed seeing it. We owe this splendid shot to Dr Pathy's presence of mind.'[18]

Though the reels of the film had to be hidden away for years to save it from the preying British authorities, Chettiar had taken more than enough precautions before stowing them away. When he got news that officials of the news division of the British government were planning to seize the film material and destroy it, Chettiar prepared six master-positive copies of the film.

Technically, even if a negative is damaged, one can make more negatives from the master-positive film element. It is just that the master-positive film cannot be screened; it is an intermediate element.

Chettiar bought 60,000 feet of master-positive film from Kodak, and after making several copies of the film, sent them to various places in Chennai for safe storage. Chettiar was an enterprising professional, and this precaution showed he also had an archivist's mind.

Arguably, such a biographic documentary in celluloid was never attempted before, and that too one portraying a living man. The closest project of this nature that one can think of was a documentary made on Great Britain's noted political leader David Lloyd George. Again, that project had a mysterious life. *The Life Story of David Lloyd George*, a silent biopic on the British leader, was conceived in 1918 when George was the prime minister. Directed by Maurice Elvey, the film got entangled in legal issues and was not released till 1996.

Against this background, it was certainly an achievement in the history of motion picture in India that the life of a leader whose influence had transcended borders on the strength of his ideas and principles was recorded. Given the fact that the bulk of the material was sourced from scores of film archives and private collections, it indeed was a monumental effort in putting together moving images of the Mahatma from every possible source.

When the film was on the editing table, Chettiar received a strange but pleasant feedback from a correspondent of *Picturpost* magazine, an Englishman. During his meeting with Gandhi in Wardha, the correspondent of the magazine had mentioned Chettiar's film to him and had asked, 'Would you like to see your own film?' Mahatma replied, 'I am eagerly looking forward to see it.' Chettiar was overjoyed on hearing this. In his report on this film in *The New York Times*, K.A. Abbas also wrote, 'After completion the producers expect to show it the Mahatma and get his approval before showing it to the general public.' He further asked, 'Will the first film seen by Gandhi be "Mahatma Gandhi" starring himself?'[19]

Unfortunately, that was not to happen. Mahatma Gandhi did not see *Mahatma Gandhi* starring Mahatma Gandhi. But he would have definitely been amused had he seen the film, and particularly one scene. Chettiar finalized the last scene to highlight the greatness of Gandhi. It had a photograph of a postal cover, supplied by his friend Trivedi on which an unusual address is written. The envelope was sent from abroad bearing the address:

Mahatma Gandhi
The King of India
New Delhi

Five and a Half Hours of the 'Mahatma'

How does one compress the extraordinary life of Gandhi into two or three hours, the normal duration of a feature film? Almost every filmmaker who has taken on such a challenging project has faced this dilemma. The dramatic elements in Gandhi's life are far too many, and to show each and every important event of his life in a single film would make it extraordinarily long. Richard Attenborough realized to his horror it when the first treatment note for his *Gandhi* film ran five-and-a-half hours long!

For a documentary filmmaker, though, this was not such a big concern. Filmmaker Vithalbhai Jhaveri, a staunch Gandhian, tried to accommodate as much from Gandhi's life as possible without any concern as to his film's length. In the process, his film turned out to be an epic five-and-a-half-hour long documentary *Mahatma: Life of Gandhi, 1869–1948*, one of the longest documentaries in the world.

Released during the birth centenary celebrations of Gandhi in 1969, it is arguably one of the most authentic biographies of Gandhi in film. Produced by The Gandhi National Memorial Fund in cooperation with the Films Division of the government of India, it consists of thirty-three film reels and can safely be considered as a near-complete documentation of Gandhi's eventful life. Similar in tone and structure to A.K. Chettiar's film, *Mahatma* was yet another monumental effort by an equally passionate man, Vithalbhai K. Jhaveri.

It took nearly seven years for Jhaveri to compile and put together animation, photographs, voice recordings and newsreel footage depicting the life of Gandhi from his early years till his death. Jhaveri, a photographer and a freedom fighter, not only scripted and directed the film but also wrote its commentary. The focus was to tell the life story of Gandhi and also to highlight his incessant search for Truth. The story is narrated using mostly Gandhi's own words to cover most of the important events from his life—the Dandi March, the Swadeshi Movement, his village programmes and the Noakhali March.

Several versions of the film were made to cater to different audiences. There is the five-and-a-half-hour version in English, the longest; there is a shorter version that runs for two hours and sixteen minutes and an even shorter version that runs for an hour. A Hindi version too exists, running for two hours and twenty minutes, and a German version of one hour and forty-four minutes. The English commentary, written by Jhaveri himself, was rendered effectively by Romesh Thapar, while the Hindi commentary was written by veteran Gandhian Usha Mehta and rendered by Brij Bhushan. Vishnudass Shirali composed the music for the film, with liberal use of the popular tunes of Gandhi's favourite bhajans. Shirali had studied music with V.D. Paluskar and Allauddin Khan. From 1931 to 1944, he was part of Uday Shankar's troupe and had composed music for his seminal film *Kalpana* in 1948.

Jhaveri had an illustrious partner in writer and filmmaker D.G Tendulkar in conceptualizing and making this documentary. Tendulkar is mostly known for his critically acclaimed eight-volume biography of Gandhi, *Mahatma*. This book project had the blessings of Gandhi himself, since he supervised the editing of the draft in the initial stages. It is to Tendulkar's credit that Gandhi, who never blessed any biography project on him, actively encouraged the former to go ahead. 'Since Bapu knew that I was not a Gandhian, therefore he could trust me,' was Tendulkar's tongue-in-cheek answer when asked about Gandhi's faith in him.[20] The idea of the Gandhi biography was conceived in October 1944 by Tendulkar and Jhaveri.

Born in Ratnagiri in Maharashtra, Tendulkar went on to study film in Germany and Moscow and was trained under the iconic filmmaker Sergei Eisenstein in the 1930s. While studying mathematics in Berlin,

Tendulkar had read an article on Eisenstein's and Pudovkin's filmmaking methods written by Marie Seton, a film critic who had taken a liking for Indian culture. She was later instrumental in conceiving many pathbreaking initiatives in popularizing film culture in India. Tendulkar managed to get her referral to go and study cinema in Moscow, where he came across material on Gandhi and got fascinated by him. After specializing in sound, he came back to India and started working in the Bombay film industry.

But, after having worked in studios like Sagar Film Company for some time, he soon got disillusioned and left to pursue other interests. While Tendulkar focused his energies on the Gandhi book, he also assisted Jhaveri in putting together the documentary. It was not smooth sailing, though. The young filmmakers faced challenges of doubt and uncertainty about the magnitude of the project they had undertaken. There were also ups and downs in their personal relationship while working together, but ultimately the importance of the subject prevailed and the monumental work was completed.

It is this documentary which later became the visual window for generations of students in school and colleges in India, through which they were introduced to Gandhi. For many years, and even today, this piece of documentation continues to be one of the most authentic films on Gandhi. Jhaveri, a photographer himself, collected a huge number of photographs from different sources, particularly from Gandhi's early years, and used them liberally in this documentary.

What comes across prominently in this film and one watches with amazement is the action in Gandhi's daily life; Gandhi is constantly on the move; never a still moment for him. He is walking, talking, touring, making speeches—'action' is the operative word here. In effect, Gandhi comes 'alive' through these scenes, as he leads the freedom movement of India. The footage also focuses on his private chores besides his public persona. When being filmed, Gandhi seems to take no notice of the camera, and in that sense he is the most natural actor the world has ever seen! He is busy doing whatever he is doing while the camera silently records his actions.

While putting together such a challenging film, Jhaveri faced great financial difficulty. A situation came when he had to resort to selling his personal possessions, including the camera and the projector, to pay off the loans he had taken. Moreover, he went through a lot of physical and mental fatigue in securing the material from various sources. Against all these odds, the film on completion proved to be a rich documentation of that period in India, about which not much visual reference is available.

It also showcases vividly the changes in Gandhi's appearance and personality as the years go by. From a fully clothed man wearing either Indian and Western attire to wearing only a loincloth, and from a man with all his teeth and a head full of hair to one with a toothless smile and bald head, Gandhi's full transformation is wonderfully traced for the audience.

But what makes the film even richer is the way it delves deeply into the mind of the man. While quoting liberally from his speeches and writings, the philosophy and principles of Gandhi are brought forth succinctly with accompanying visuals. Only a few photographs are available from the early part of his life, and this film had to make use of these stills to take forward the storyline. It is the narration, then, that keeps the viewers engaged.

Even though the narration is slow, it provides the audience an opportunity to imbibe the personality of Gandhi in whole. The fact that government-owned Films Division was a collaborator in the project helped the film in reaching audiences far and wide. Due to the dedicated slot for Films Division newsreels in the cinema halls, the film—its shorter version, though—was screened across India from time to time.

But it's the longer version which made it difficult to release the film commercially. Notwithstanding its long duration, the screening was attempted in a few cinema centres. One such screening happened in early February 1969 and the response was very good. At Bombay's Liberty Cinema, the hall was almost full for the initial few screenings. The show started at 6.30 p.m. and ended ten minutes past midnight, with three intervals. The viewers sat glued to the film, missing their dinner in the process.

Not only in Bombay, but in Ahmedabad too the film turned out to be popular. The length of the documentary did not deter the film enthusiasts, and the film grossed more than Rs 30,000 in one week at a single theatre (two shows daily) in Bombay, while it raked in Rs 20,000 in Ahmedabad during the same period. In Bombay, the film ran for a continuous four weeks in different theatres, including Liberty, Swastik, Aurora and Shanmukhananda Hall, which was quite an achievement.[21] Several state governments arranged for the film to be screened in schools on special occasions.

Despite this excellent response, there were early troubles in ensuring smooth and wider exhibition of the film. Due to its inordinate length, it was difficult to screen for the general public in a single show. Therefore, the thirty-three-reel film was split into fourteen short films in chronological order and then screened one after another, according to convenience. It was also dubbed in seven languages—English, Hindi, Bengali, Tamil, Telugu, Kannada and Malayalam. But the screenings were held up initially because the existing rules mandated showing approved films of only 2,000 feet in theatres. Some of the short films in the series exceeded this length, and this led to poor response from exhibitors. Despite the monumental efforts of Jhaveri in creating such a film, the rules and regulations of the time prevented it from being shown like other regular films.

When the editor of *Screen* magazine, S.S. Pillai, met with Jhaveri in October 1969, the latter was in tears as he could find no way to release all segments of the film on a countrywide scale that year. Till then, only one segment was being shown everywhere. In a sad commentary on how quickly our political leaders had forgotten the man who led the country's freedom struggle, it was also reported that very few Parliamentarians showed interest in attending a special screening of the film in Goa organized to commemorate Gandhi's birth centenary.[22]

Apart from the sporadic screenings at educational institutions and other organizations, the long documentary film had a permanent screening slot at the country's premier film school, Film & Television Institute of India (FTII) in Poona. Amit Tyagi, an FTII alumnus and a former dean (films) there, fondly remembers watching the film in his student days in the late 1970s. 'On every 2 October, the screening would start by 10 a.m., and as it's a 330-minute film divided into fourteen chapters, it would be six in the evening by the time it ended, with a lunch break in between,' he said.[23]

Gandhi and his values seem to have had little place in the consciousness of the then student community, at least the ones in creative fields. Tyagi recalled:

> By the 1970s, Mahatma Gandhi was not the popular flavour with youth like me; we only understood the rituals associated with him by the then governments, not the 'real' Mahatma as one now knows [with age]. But I came from a khadi-wearing family with a tradition of being freedom fighters, so anecdotes about Mahatma Gandhi were stuff that I had grown up with. So, I went to watch Jhaveri's film to see what the Mahatma was really all about. The film is slow moving, encyclopaedic in its scope, full of still photos and movie footage that is rarely seen.

Jhaveri's epic *Mahatma* tried to capture as much as possible from all archival material available then. But it was not merely a compilation of sourced footage. Apart from it being a record for posterity to witness the life of one of the greatest men on the earth, it was a labour of love. The entire tone of the film, therefore, is reverential, because the subject is a revered one. It does not try to discuss or analyse Gandhi's life, and the narrator throughout the film guides the viewer very subtly. Tyagi sums up his experience of watching the film,

> I loved watching the film for what I learned about the Dandi March and the Quit India Movement and everything else. But at the end of it all, Vithalbhai's film is like a bottle of medicine, you watch it because everything says it is good for you, but it's not an enjoyable experience.

Due to its authentic documentation values, watching this documentary has constituted a much-required learning curve for future directors and actors. Many filmmakers have seen it so they can understand the man before embarking on their own film projects on Gandhi. For actors, it is all here, to learn and imbibe the spirit of Gandhi through his innumerable photographs and moving images. And for the common audience, it is a visual history of the man whom they call Father of the Nation.

9

God Needs No Sleep

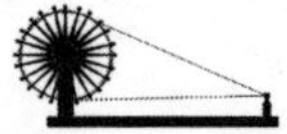

GANDHI'S TRAVELS ARE LEGENDARY. After coming back to India from South Africa in 1915, he consciously decided to travel in the third-class coach of Indian railways. It was his own way of identifying with the common man of the country. He was one among them, and they knew it. Therefore, it was obvious that Gandhi was filmed a lot while he travelled by rail. In many of the newsreels of the time, he is seen either boarding the train or alighting at many little-known stations in the hinterland.

He was deeply conscious of the connection he had established with the masses. While speaking in Bombay at a Congress session in 1942, he said, 'I have travelled all over India as perhaps nobody in the present age has. The voiceless millions of the land saw in me their friend and representative, and I identified myself with them to the extent it was possible for a human being to do.'

In many topical films capturing Gandhi's train journeys, a recurring visual is that of thousands of people waiting on the platforms to catch a glimpse of the travelling Mahatma. Madeline Slade (aka Mirabehn), a constant companion of Gandhi's on these travels crisscrossing rural India, described the irony of these visuals in moving words in a letter to her spiritual father Romain Rolland,

> Father, how strange that on those cemented platforms along the railway tracks that disappear in the dusty Indian courtyards, I kept seeing a painting that hangs in London's National Gallery! Have you seen Sebastiano del Piambo's 'The Raising of Lazarus', the faces looking up at Christ in expressions combining different proportions of awe, wonder and adoration? Those are the faces I saw on the platforms.[1]

There are several accounts which describe scenes where, despite the poor means of communication in those days, the villagers would know the exact time of arrival of the train in which Gandhi was travelling and would insist on seeing Gandhi by stopping the train. For them, 'Gandhi Darshan' was the most important thing—a moment to cherish their entire lives. So, even if Gandhi was resting or sleeping, he would be woken up by the loud cheers and incessant chanting of his name when his train stopped. Many times, the train had to make an unscheduled stop on the insistence of villagers on the way. No reasoning would work. For the people, Gandhi was like God, and God does not need sleep!

This universal feeling among common Indians towards Gandhi was most evident during his 'Harijan Yatra' (Harijan Tour) undertaken during 1933–34. The special tour was a continuation of his epic fast in Yerawada jail in Poona in 1932 to oppose separate electorates for untouchables. Many motion picture cameras were stationed at the gaol in Pune to cover that event. Pathe News produced a topical film titled *Gandhi's Fast Brings New India Crisis*. In its editor's note, it described the situation clearly: 'These pictures show the frail Hindu leader whose self-imposed hunger strike has stirred millions. Upon his actions hinges the peace of far-off India.' Gandhi's fast was for the cause of untouchables, as part of his objective of full inclusion of them in a united India.

Hearst Metrotone News made a topical film on the epic event titled *Mahatma Gandhi begins death fast.* A line in introduction said: 'India's leader in prison goes on hunger strike as a protest against British vote plan.' The narrator described Gandhi as a sixty-three-year-old leader of 300 million people and added that he was willing to sacrifice his life for the cause. After describing his physical condition, viewers were reminded of his Geneva speech a few months back where he had described himself as a soldier of peace. The visuals in the topical, in fact, were old and did not show any pictures of Gandhi actually at his fast.

Gandhi toured many states for about nine months as part of his 'Harijan Yatra' to spread the message against untouchability. Many film companies shot these tours in the Orissa, Bengal, Assam and Bihar provinces, apart from south India. One particular footage is titled *Mahatmaji's South Indian Tour and Harijan Yatra.* It was produced by Madras-based Projection of India Pictures. It starts with visuals of the steam engine of the Gandhi Special train decorated with flags, flowers, the tricolour and his portrait.

The train was special in the sense that Gandhi was provided with an exclusive saloon that had a platform with arrangements for a loudspeaker. At various places, Gandhi appears outside the railway coach for darshan and the one sequence showing his arrival at Trichinopoly Junction is especially memorable as he makes an impromptu speech in front of an assembled crowd near the station.

There is a beautiful visual of Gandhi watching a mass spinning demonstration by villagers on the Manapparai railway platform. The film also has footage of Gandhi visiting the ancient temple of Sri Meenakshi at Madurai on 3 February 1946. It was a return of a triumphant Gandhi for darshan at the temple since it had been thrown open to the untouchables following the temple entry movement that had his blessings. Despite the huge gathering of people during Gandhi's visit to the temple at Palani, the narrator of the film says his visit earned Gandhi praise for the disciplined behaviour of the crowd. At both these temples, he had entered the holy precincts with the Harijans.

The highlight of this leg of his trip in the film is the visual of a huge gathering standing in the shallow waters of the Arasalar river near Kumbakonam for his darshan. He obliged them and spoke from the specially erected platform attached to his saloon. He literally stuck his hand out of the train window to accept coins, donated in various denominations, for the Harijan Fund. The happy faces of the people donating money to the cause dear to Gandhi dominate the visuals.

Paramount News produced a topical film showing his tour of Calcutta in 1934 as part of Harijan Yatra. It was titled *Flashes from Everywhere* and the inter-title card added, 'Mahatma Gandhi hailed on tour of India!' The narrator said, 'Now sixty-five, Hindu leader presses war on oppressive caste system.' The visuals showed Gandhi, his upper body bare, arriving by car and then proceeding to address a huge gathering. Another shot taken during the Harijan Yatra showed him in a running train, engaged in writing. Visuals taken from onboard the train showed a huge crowd assembled beside the tracks in anticipation of a darshan of Gandhi.

On the subject of Gandhi's train journeys, one instantly recalls a vivid scene from Richard Attenborough's *Gandhi* (1982). A steam locomotive enters a station where a huge crowd is gathered. Perplexed, the British police officer asks his colleague what is going on. 'He is coming', is the answer! 'Who the hell is he?' is the next question. Though this incident took place in the very early period of Gandhi's arrival in India, people who had gathered there knew who he was!

The same film shows Gandhi's initial familiarization train journey into the interiors of India in a long, poignant sequence. Gandhi had decided to travel third class with his wife Kasturba by his side. The train travels through the different terrains and contours of rural India while very beautiful sitar and sarod music plays in the background. This music was composed by the sitar maestro Pandit Ravi Shankar.

As celebrations in honour of Gandhi's 150th birth anniversary were being planned across the world, I received a phone call in August 2019 from my Mumbai-based source Jayaraj Punatar informing about some reels that had been found. Punatar, descendent of Sardar Chandulal

Shah, a prominent producer and filmmaker, had been one of my regular collaborators in hunting down obscure films. I immediately rushed to his small warehouse located in what now remains of the erstwhile Ranjit Studios in central Mumbai. To my surprise, many film cans with 'Gandhi' written on them were lying there. After getting them transported to Pune immediately, I sat for weeks together on the flatbed machine at NFAI looking at the grainy visuals on the small monitor. Little by little, the fascinating story of Gandhi unfolded on the screen as my colleague Kiran Dhiwar, film preservation officer at NFAI, loaded the reels on the Steenbeck machine.

My eyes popped up when I saw one metal can with 'Haripura Congress' written on it. Shot by Dr P.V. Pathy, considered the father of the documentary movement in India, the short film was believed to be lost. Both Pathy and J.B.H. Wadia of Wadia Movietone had said that during the Quit India Movement in 1942, the British government had seized the negatives and other material of this film, along with several other topicals.

While underlining the importance of this significant footage, documentary historian Jag Mohan wrote:

> When Wadia Movietone took up the assignment to film it, it was Dr Pathy to whom it was entrusted. In the course of filming what was meant to be a small topical, it soon became a finished documentary of three reels. In the opinion of many knowledgeable persons, this film remains the best documentary of the Indian National Congress to date. It is sad to reflect that this grand pioneering effort in the genre of the documentary is lost forever,' Wadia had said.[2]

The newly discovered film contained many unedited shots of the historic Haripura Congress session presided over by Netaji Subhash Chandra Bose. The credit roll listed Nanik Motwane as the producer, under his banner The Chicago Telephone & Radio Co. The credit scenes in the film showed the charkha as the background incorporating the Indian Screen Gazette while it was released by Wadia Movietone and exclusively distributed by Bombay-based MB Billimoria. Few scenes were edited in such a way that viewers could see and understand how Congress sessions were held and organized. The film had the blessings of Sardar Patel. As the head of the organizing committee of the session held in his backyard in rural Gujarat, Patel was very clear that this film was intended to reach out to lakhs of people across India.

At the start of the film, Patel appears on screen and explains the motive behind the filming of the proceedings, which was that people who could not attend it would be able to view for themselves the Congress session. The camera then takes the viewers to the venue showcasing the telegraph office specially set up for the session, the huts in which Gandhi and Patel were staying, and the dining and sanitation facilities. The narration provides general information. The arrival of the president of the session, Subhash Chandra Bose, by train and his reception by Sardar Patel is shown.

A grand welcome procession consisting of fifty-one bulls and a bullock cart bearing Bose to the venue is the highlight of the film. Gandhi's arrival by train for the session, amidst chants of '*Mahatma Gandhiji ki Jai*' (Victory to Mahatma Gandhiji) from the huge crowd present there, is filmed. For good measure, Gandhi is looking into the motion picture camera as he arrives.

The British government was not sitting idle during this time and its all-powerful Boards of Censors at five locations were busy cutting scenes or words, and sometimes the whole newsreels, which they thought were against their interests. These Boards were headed by the Police Commissioner of the place where they were located including Bombay, Calcutta, Madras, Rangoon and Lahore, and they controlled the certification as well as exhibition of films. The Journal of the Motion Pictures Society of India lists as many as fourteen newsreels/documentaries that featured Gandhi released in 1937, some of which were banned 1930 onwards.[3]

In early 1946, Gandhi visited Madras in connection with the silver jubilee celebrations of Dakshin Bharat Hindi Prachar Sabha. The organization was established by Gandhi himself to promote Hindi in the southern states of India. The organization celebrated its centenary recently. Gandhi's son Devdas had been its first pracharak, while Gandhi remained the president of the Sabha till his death. Gandhi's entire visit was filmed by Projection of India Pictures Company. This included the silver jubilee celebrations as well as Gandhi's south India tour. The short film is titled *Gandhi in Madras City; January-February 1946*.

The film starts with scenes of Gandhi's arrival at the gates of the venue, which was named Hindustani Nagar. A huge crowd waited to greet Gandhi who was coming from Ambattur railway station to the Sabha premises, named as Gandhi Nagar and consisted of thatched huts. Gandhi was accompanied by C. Rajagopalachari. At the convocation ceremony, Gandhi was filmed presenting sanads (certificates) to the graduates who had passed the Hindi examination. He then visited the Sevagram Constructive Programme Exhibition and went on to tour various stalls displaying handmade products.

The highlight of the film was Gandhi donning the role of a mason. He laid the foundation stone for the Harijan Industrial School in true mason style! He also held a prayer meeting where verses from the Upanishads, Gita and Quran were recited. One can see a huge crowd gathered for the meeting, as well as a separate group of women volunteers in white khadi sarees.

While going through this vast amount of unedited footage on Gandhi, I came across a very private documentation of Gandhi. He had clearly been filmed from very close quarters at the Sevagram Ashram, and I discovered this footage had been shot by Kanu Gandhi, his grand-nephew. The shots have a certain warmth, showing Gandhi's humane side while he is engaged in routine work. What strikes one the most is his depiction as a family man, far away from his political role. Kanu had filmed him leading a quiet life at the Ashram with his family and colleagues, and there is a certain intimacy and candidness evident in these shots, thanks to the close access Kanu Gandhi had to his grand-uncle.

Kanu Gandhi, born in 1917, had joined Sevagram Ashram at the age of nineteen and developed an interest in photography. He expressed a keen desire in photographing the activities at the Ashram, but Gandhi turned him down initially. Later he relented and asked his industrialist friend G.D. Birla to help Kanu acquire a camera. Thus started, in 1939, Kanu's journey of documenting some of the best moments of the last decade of Gandhi's life.

Gandhi laid down three conditions for allowing Kanu to photograph: no use of flash, no posing for the camera and no funding from the Ashram. Even while away from the Ashram, Gandhi always kept a close tab on the activities at Sevagram, which centred on the community and constructive work. 'My true body is the Ashram. If the Ashram is nothing, I am nothing,' was how he felt about the place.[4]

There are several scenes shot by Kanu capturing the simple and idyllic life at the Sevagram Ashram in central India. One scene shows Gandhi's hut and the interiors of his room, while in another Gandhi is filmed taking a walk with Kasturba. Always known as a public person, here, in these scenes, Gandhi is a private man. He would put his hands on his wife's shoulders while he walked in the Ashram premises. Moreover, he allowed it to be filmed!

Though the Hindi title-card of the topical film says, '*Sevagram mein Bapu*' (Bapu in Sevagram), in these visuals Gandhi is not alone; Kasturba Gandhi is extensively filmed, for a change, at her usual household chores. Even though Kasturba had been around Gandhi most of the time, theirs was an unspoken and silent companionship. The visuals of the couple filmed together at the Ashram do capture that innate understanding and faith of long years of togetherness. Like a scene straight from any household in India, Gandhi can be seen sitting on a raised platform while Kasturba is busy serving him food and fanning him! There is nobody else around, and the lunch is in an open veranda. No words are being exchanged between these two old people, but viewers can get a feel of the eternal bond between them.

Each of these visuals has inter-title cards in Hindi with an aesthetically done handmade drawing accompanying it. In a short clip titled *Gau-Seva* (Service to the Cow), Kasturba, wearing a white khadi saree, feeds a cow at the Ashram. In another clip, Gandhi goes to the field in the

Ashram and keenly watches a demonstration of agricultural equipment. For those who believe that Gandhi was against machines, this footage will compel them to change their opinion. Gandhi is also seen planting trees in the Ashram.

Another exceptional visual in the film is of Gandhi attending to Shri Parchure Shastri, a Maharashtrian Sanskrit scholar who was affected by leprosy. It shows Gandhi tending to Shastri with his own hands. Shastri had become a close follower of Gandhi since the time they were together in Yerawada jail in Pune. The love and affection between the two can be gauged from the fact that when Gandhi broke his fast way back in 1932 while in jail at Poona, he wanted Parchure Shastri to give him his first sip of fruit juice, despite knowing that Shastri had leprosy. The bond between them continued to grow, and during the last stages of his illness, Shastri requested Gandhi to permit him to stay at Sevagram Ashram. Gandhi readily agreed and took upon himself the task of attending to Shastri daily and supervising his health.

Gandhi's trusted secretary Pyarelal also featured in these visuals. The title-card of one visual says, '*Pyarelal ke Satyagrah ke din*' (Days of Pyarelal's Satyagrah). The footage also has shots of Gandhi's visit to Shantiniketan in February 1940, titled '*Shantiniketan me Gurudev se bhet*' (Meeting with Gurudev at Shantiniketan). The two great sons of India, Tagore and Gandhi, are seen exchanging ideas, and it turned out to be their last meeting before Tagore passed away the next year. Another film sequence from the Kanu Gandhi collection has visuals of Gandhi's visit to Malikanda, a small village in Bengal. He was participating in a meeting of Gandhi Seva Sangh, an organization for constructive development, in February 1940. The title-card says, '*Malikanda ke dehat me*' (at Malikanda village).

Gandhi's visit to Peshawar and Ramgarh is covered in another unedited footage in which Gandhi is seen walking with Khan Abdul Ghaffar Khan. It is titled *Peshawar Aur Ramgardh ki Kuch Smriti* (Some memories from Peshawar and Ramgarh). Few scenes show Gandhi visiting Ramgarh in Jharkhand to attend the Congress session of 1940.

Visuals of a convocation ceremony held at Delhi showing Gandhi distributing certificates to Harijan graduates are also part of this footage.

Kanu Gandhi and James Mills were the two fortunate cameramen who got the rare opportunity to film Gandhi extensively over a period of time. In the process, both developed a close rapport with Gandhi, and that gave them unrestricted access to film the man. But not everyone was as lucky as these two. Given his natural reluctance to be photographed and his objection to the use of flashbulbs, it was always a very difficult task for cameramen who wanted to shoot Gandhi. Maurice Lancaster, a British representative of *March of Time,* a news magazine in video format, and its director of production and cameraman Robert Nabarro, were to face the heat one day from Gandhi.

On their assignment in India in 1941, Lancaster and Nabarro crisscrossed India for eight months shooting about 26,000 feet of film. *March of Time* being a video news magazine, it differed from the prevalent newsreels in the sense that it delved deeper into the subject being dealt with. The *March of Time* series produced two films of twenty minutes' duration each focusing on India. They were titled *India in Crisis* and *India at War.* These films, in general, were supportive of India's freedom struggle and described Gandhi as the 'personification of the only unity India has ever known'.

When Lancaster and Nabarro reached Wardha Ashram in central India on their first visit, Gandhi flatly refused to have them film him at his activities. When introduced to the crew, Gandhi listened patiently and asked what he could do for them. 'We explained the purpose of our mission, sought his advice and suggestions. He listened most politely and turned us down flat,' Lancaster recalled. Gandhi told them, 'You can have everything in Sevagram but me.' The team protested, but without avail, and told him they would visit later.

During their next visit, Gandhi allowed them, that too after endless persuasion, to bring the camera close to him to take some visuals. There was a special Congress meeting held in Wardha after the release of its leaders in 1942, and the *March of Time* crew were the only European press people at the venue to capture those moments. In order to get enough exposure, cameraman Robert put some photofloods above the place where Gandhi was to speak. This was immediately noticed, and Gandhi asked them to be removed. When Gandhi started speaking and the cameras were clicking, one Indian still photographer jumped up all of a sudden and let off a flashbulb. This was too much for Gandhi and he stopped his speech. The photographer was removed from the scene and Gandhi made his annoyance clear that if he heard so much as the noise of another camera, he would leave the meeting![5]

Despite the rebuke from the venerable old man, the remaining shooting was done by Lancaster and his associates without any disturbance. Finally, when the film was completed, the editor of *March of Time* chose to showcase the shots taken at Wardha Ashram to end the film. The content and focus of the film, coming at a crucial time in the freedom struggle showcased to the world the fact that only Gandhi, the leader, and his actions were to lead the future course for India!

10

Walking for Peace

AS INDIA'S BATTLE FOR freedom entered its final lap, the focus of the motion picture cameras on Gandhi became more pronounced. The key event, of course, was the Quit India Movement of 1942. The historic Congress session of 1942 held at Gowalia Tank in Bombay saw many film companies send their cameras to the venue where Gandhi gave the clarion call 'Quit India'. Nanak Motwani of The Chicago Radio and Telephone Company of Bombay filmed this entire session of the Congress. About 8,000 feet of footage of the proceedings was shot, but when Gandhi was arrested by the police, all these film rolls were also seized. All of it was reportedly burnt by the police to destroy the visual records of one of the most crucial events of the freedom movement in India.

But time throws out surprises that defy the draconian acts of imperialists. Somehow, somewhere, things remain in the dark for years. That is what happened to these important visuals. Some of the footage taken of this historic session has miraculously survived and has been discovered. In one of them, Gandhi is seen arriving for the crucial meeting in Bombay by train. He looks frail and young Congress volunteers offer him a hand to help him disembark at the station.

Gandhi was also filmed leaving the house, where he was staying in Bombay, for the meeting by car. The visuals captured on 7 August show a huge crowd assembled for the meeting and the British police force having a difficult time controlling it. Gandhi arrives to a rapturous welcome, and he too has difficulty in reaching the venue through the jostling crowd, which chants '*Mahatma Gandhi ki Jai*'. The visuals show a few of the volunteers throwing a cordon around him to provide him smooth passage to the venue. After the speeches by Congress leaders Azad, Nehru and Patel, it is the turn of Gandhi, and he speaks for no less than two hours while seated on the platform. Soon afterwards, Gandhi is arrested and sent to the Aga Khan Palace in Poona. There is a scene where his women followers smear vermilion on his forehead as an auspicious gesture.

British Movietone News made a short topical film the next month, mostly providing the point of view of the British government. It said India had managed to check riots as the arrest of Gandhi and the Congress working committee members had helped to quell the Civil Disobedience campaign. Ironically, the report, mostly a propaganda film, went on to say that Congress did not represent the spirit of India! It said the Indian forces fighting the Second World War at various places across the world represented the true spirit of India. The report also said the Congress mobs were swayed by the eloquence of their leaders into falsely believing that an India without England would be India for the Indians. It is pungent irony that all this was said while the visuals showed the huge demonstrations across India by Congress supporters!

Fox Movietone News, in comparison, was more sympathetic in its coverage and provided an accurate account of the activities as they had happened in its topical film made on 9 August 1942. The topical had an editor's note describing the first pictures received from Fox Movietone newsmen sent to India on the outbreak of the great national revolution against England. The narrator said, 'Here, 300,000 natives are shown parading streets of Bombay in advocacy of boycott. Great masses of people express their patriotism but observe non-violence counsel of Gandhi in jail.'

In the same month, Fox Movietone News came out with another topical, *Movietone News visits scene of rioting in India's revolt.* It said, 'We bring you sound pictures made on the spot at Bombay in the heart of Hindu trouble.' The visuals showed the huge demonstrations that had happened in the central part of Bombay. One man in the crowd pulled down the Union Jack, which was captured on camera. The inter-title card described women joining the demonstrators, whose parades entirely paralysed business in the city. The demonstrations were peaceful as a big queue of protesters walked on the road in formation while crowds stood on either side cheering them. The demonstrations at Wadala Salt Pan were also filmed, and local police were seen charging at the protesters.

But one visual of the demonstration stood out and showcased the fearless character of the Gandhi-led Indian freedom movement. A brave khadi-clad young volunteer is seen holding the Congress flag firm despite being beaten repeatedly by British policemen in Bombay. The narrator in the newsreel had only this much to comment, 'This is a true Gandhi follower!'

A special Congress meeting held at Wardha at the start of 1942 was also well covered by many film studios. There were some interesting visuals shot during this meeting. One shows Gandhi standing while a national song is being sung by a group of women volunteers, one of them holding a tanpura in hand. Another visual shows prominent Congress leaders like Sarojini Naidu and Pandit Nehru looking on while Gandhi, seated on a chair, speaks. Gandhi could not stand for very long while speaking, so he preferred to sit while making his public speeches. Curiously, the president of the session, Maulana Azad, is seen smoking even in the presence of Gandhi!

Is It a Machine Gun?

During the visuals shot when the Cripps Mission came to India in March 1942, again Gandhi was the focus. Though the visuals captured the bonhomie between Gandhi and Stafford Cripps, their meeting resulted in no fruitful outcome. A funny incident happened during the filming of these crucial talks. Veteran cameraman Ezra Mir was heading the film crew of the government production team. Having placed the camera equipment at various vantage positions, the crew waited for action. Mir recalled what happened that day:

> I had fixed all the lighting and camera equipment much in advance. Behind me were a host of foreign and Indian newsreel cameramen. I suddenly espied Sir Stafford entering the main hall with Gandhiji. Then to the surprise of all I stepped forward, hauled my camera into the hall and took the shots even as Gandhiji was chiding me and questioning, 'Kya yeh machine gun hai?' (Is it a machine gun?).[1]

Paramount Sound News made a short topical film called *Gandhi's Revolt* in July 1942. The visuals show Gandhi in discussions with his colleagues. His wife Kasturba also features in the visuals. Gandhi is shown leaving after the talks with Cripps and waving his hands in disapproval, all the while smiling.

During his detainment at the Aga Khan palace in Poona in 1942, Gandhi lost two of his closest allies. Mahadev Desai, his secretary and man Friday for more than twenty years, passed away in August 1942. It was a sudden and shocking loss for Gandhi. Desai was like a shadow around Gandhi and he featured in many of the newsreels focusing on his boss. Gandhi's wife and lifelong companion Kasturba too suffered heart attacks and died in February 1944. It was a double blow for Gandhi, who suddenly felt all alone.

Kanu Gandhi, who had been capturing many of his activities on camera, both private and public, was around in Poona, but Gandhi prevented him from taking moving images of anything related to either event, as they were too personal. Therefore, we do not have much visual documentation of Gandhi from those days, but there are a few still photographs that show the poignancy of those moments. Gandhi was photographed sitting in a pensive mood in a corner of a room with Kasturba's body lying at his side.

Soon afterwards, Gandhi himself developed health issues and was released from detention. The Indian News Parade, India's own newsreel service, had started in 1943, with its initial focus on war propaganda. Despite being backed by the British government and mostly putting forth the imperialist point of view, it did the unthinkable and dared to produce a topical on Gandhi's release. The visuals showed the Aga Khan Palace in Poona where Gandhi was under arrest, and a huge crowd rushing in after hearing the news of Gandhi's release. The narrator said, 'Once again the familiar third-class carriage, once again the familiar figure!' The visuals showed a frail Gandhi, who had to be supported by both his aides while alighting from the train.

Clearly, the loss of Kasturba and Mahadev Desai had affected his health badly, which was visible in the pictures taken on the occasion. The narrator of the newsreel added, 'But he has lost none of his cheerful kindliness that has endeared him to his followers.' Another topical film covered his stay at Juhu, where he was recuperating after his release. People followed him on Juhu beach, where almost every evening he addressed them. The topical showed people coming for Gandhi's meetings and greeting him. He was filmed sitting on a small platform on the seashore—the leader was back among his followers.

During the latter half of that year, Gandhi's sole attention was focused on the issue of communal harmony. He made efforts to reach out to many stakeholders in the society to solve the problem and reach a solution. His meetings with Jinnah, leader of the Muslim league, were covered by most of the newsreel companies. The visuals showed the starkly contrasting figures of Jinnah, always dapper, dressed in a suit in the hot and humid weather of Bombay, welcoming Gandhi, who was half-clad as usual. While entering Jinnah's palatial house, Gandhi greeted him warmly, and in a gesture of friendliness put his hand around Jinnah's shoulders. After hectic parleys with Jinnah, Gandhi preferred to walk back to Birla House; the visuals showed him refusing the car.

Gandhi's seventy-fifth birthday was a special occasion and the world celebrated it with many activities. Wishes poured in from across the world. At Sevagram Ashram, it was a joyous affair, with a lot of festivities and singing and dancing, which was filmed. In the film, Gandhi, for a change, appears to be enjoying it all.

In 1945, there was a crucial meeting at Simla called by Viceroy Lord Wavell and attended by prominent political leaders from all parties. Several newsreel companies thronged the hill city with their cameramen to report on the discussions focused on exploring a self-government formula for India. One of the topicals on that event was *Mahatma Gandhi at All-India Parleys*. Pandit Nehru was filmed climbing on to a balcony to address people who had gathered in large numbers. For a change, Gandhi was seen travelling in a cart pulled by men. He had resented this practice, but perhaps due to ill-health and advancing age he made a compromise at that time.

Another newsreel made by British Movietone News was titled *Simla offers new hope to India*. Apart from showing visuals of several leading leaders who had assembled on the lawns of the Viceregal Lodge, the newsreel also showed a large crowd waiting for a glimpse of Gandhi. The Indian News Parade also filmed what unfolded after the crucial conference got over. It had images of Gandhi leaving the city by foot, surrounded by followers. Gaumont British News also joined other film companies in making a topical. It was titled *Conference at Simla*. It too showed visuals of Gandhi arriving at the venue, the narrator saying, 'the excitement of the crowd rose at a fever pitch at the arrival of Gandhi.' He joined his hands together in acknowledgement of their love and affection.

There was another attempt at resolving the key issues relating to the way ahead for India's freedom, and the Cabinet Mission visited India in 1946 to hold further discussions with leaders of key political parties. The British Movietone News made a topical captioned *Congress Party in Conclave*, which showed Gandhi and key Congress leaders studying the proposals of Cabinet Mission. Gandhi was filmed while arriving for the meeting. He had a cloth over his bald head to protect it from the mid-summer heat of Delhi.

Another topical film made on the event described Gandhi as the symbol of liberty for millions of people. Here, Gandhi was filmed while walking in for the meeting. He had a smile on his face and acknowledged people in his usual way. Another visual showed him at a prayer meeting where Abdul Ghaffar Khan, known as Frontier Gandhi, was sitting beside him.

A private moment was also part of the footage. Here, Gandhi was lying on the floor while his colleagues Pandit Nehru and Sarojini Naidu sat on chairs in front of him. Gandhi must have been getting his favourite mud-pack treatment, but it was quite unusual that he permitted its filming. Even though he looked unwell, there was that famous toothless smile on his lips. After resting, Gandhi went for evening prayers, and the visuals showed him sitting on a raised platform addressing hundreds of people in the colony of Bhangis (scavenger community).

As freedom for India loomed on the horizon, tensions between two main religious communities in the country took a turn for the worse in October 1946. The Muslim League called for a Direct Action Day, and riots took place far and wide in Bengal province. Gandhi rushed to Kolkata to assuage the situation. As usual, the newsreel companies sent their crews to report on the events. One topical from this event was called *Turmoil in India* and showed in detail Gandhi's efforts in Calcutta to calm the political and religious turmoil there.

Tension in India was the topical made by Paramount Sound News on the situation, and it said a crisis meeting was called following the riots. It showed visuals of refugee camps full of people who had fled their homes after the riots. The topical referred to Gandhi's visit as a 'Peace Mission' and showed him boarding a train to tour the riot-affected areas. On the way, crowds thronged the railway stations to catch a glimpse of him. The topical also speculated that he might begin a fast to bring the situation under control.

Gandhi travelled by boat to visit the interior areas of Bengal after getting down from the third-class compartment of his train. He then addressed huge crowds consisting of people from both faiths and appealed for harmony with folded hands. British Movietone News also followed Gandhi on the tour and made a topical named *Gandhi visits riot-stricken Calcutta* in November 1946. There were some exclusive images of Gandhi discussing the situation with Sir Frederick John Burrows, the Governor of Bengal in Calcutta, before leaving for the interior areas in East Bengal.

Another topical showed crowds waiting for Gandhi, who was to tour their area. The narrator referred to Gandhi as a 'great soul' and underlined the importance of his mission. The topical showed him travelling on a train and then in a boat on the river Padma, where crowds thronged along both banks of the river to catch a glimpse of him and hear him. In all these visuals, he looked grim and sullen. The painful situation had obviously saddened him, and he seemed to be looking inward even while he was surrounded by crowds.

In the midst of this gloom came an occasion for celebration. It was 2 October 1947, Gandhi's seventy-eighth birthday. It was a special occasion because it was Gandhi's first birthday in free and independent India. There were celebrations all across the country and a special event was held in Delhi, attended by the prime minister, Pandit Nehru, and the Congress president, Kriplani. V. Parkash, a veteran cameraman, filmed the entire event for British Paramount News. The result was a two-reel topical with the title *Gandhi, 78, Acclaimed by All*, showing Gandhi's arrival at Gandhi Ground in the capital and his acknowledging the greetings of the citizens of Delhi.

Ekla Chalo Re (Walking Alone)

Gandhi's peace mission in Noakhali in the eastern parts of Bengal, the epicentre of communal violence at the time, is now a part of folklore. A man of seventy-seven trudged the riot-stricken area to apply his balm; a balm of love, peace and non-violence. For four months during November 1946 till February 1947, he walked the areas of Noakhali to wipe the tears of the refugees and remove distrust among the clashing faiths. 'The earth of Noakhali is like velvet and the green grass is a magnificent carpet to walk on. It reminds me of the soft grass I had noticed in England,' he said.[2]

It was not only the press that sent photographers to cover the peace mission, but the motion picture companies too realized its importance and sent their cameramen to film Gandhi's tour of riot-hit Bengal. Noakhali tour film was one such short documentary on Gandhi's tour of the riot-affected area. It was made by two staff photographers belonging to *Hindustan Standard* and *Anand Bazar Patrika*. The film, about 1,000 feet in length, was shown to Pandit Nehru by Suresh Chandra Mazumdar, the managing director of these two newspapers.

Extensive footage was shot of Gandhi's stay and travels in the Noakhali area. Again, some of the most intimate footage of Gandhi in this peace march was filmed by his grand-nephew Kanu Gandhi. One recurring visual from this footage shows Gandhi in Noakhali walking ... walking, walking and walking with his bamboo staff in hand. There was a small group accompanying him on these travels, consisting of men and women, children and some aged persons; the entourage also consisted of Hindus, Muslims, Sikhs and others.

Gandhi travelled in small and big boats and also used steamers. Along the way, he crossed many makeshift bamboo bridges. He walked through bare fields. Sometimes, the road was so narrow that he walked alone, while his group followed in a single file. Most of the time there was no road at all. Even then he trudged on to his next destination.

The visuals show him jumping to avoid puddles. He had great difficulty in boarding a roofed boat, as Kanu Gandhi's visuals show. Gandhi was extensively filmed as he walked through the terrain of Noakhali—a tiny figure with water bodies and forests providing the backdrop for the frame. One image captured him being carried in a hand-driven carriage or palanquin. When Gandhi travelled by boat, people could be seen walking on both sides of the water body. At seventy-seven, Gandhi needed support, and there was always someone younger he leaned on. Freedom was yet to come, but many shots from that time show some policemen in khaki uniform who could not resist saluting him! One newsreel report described him as a holy man, a vegetarian, who eats only rice, fruits and nuts and was on a physical trial.

Gandhi walked like a possessed man on this tour of peace. The moving images of his captured on this march make it seem as if he was walking in a trance. The white cloth he had wrapped around his body accentuated this impression. His bald head was mostly bowed low while he walked. He walked barefoot, and some close-up shots reveal the weary feet of the old man. He looks sideways only when people join him and greet him. Most of the time, he was filmed from a distance and viewers get to see the tiny figure of Gandhi walking against the backdrop of vast grasslands in many of the visuals.

His usual smile, that famous toothless ear-to-ear grin, was almost absent. He looked grim and pensive. Whenever he stopped and sat for prayer meetings, the mood was sombre. He stayed in huts and mostly kept to himself. This was a very different march that he had undertaken from the one at Dandi almost a quarter of a century ago. Then he was fitter, and the fight was against a foreign power. Here in Noakhali, he had aged considerably and looked frail. Moreover, he was fighting the demons of religious distrust among his own people. A cause that he had pursued lifelong was at stake. And he was in no mood to forsake it towards the end of his life. So, he put his own life at stake. In many ways, the visual of Gandhi crossing the numerous bridges on the wetlands of Noakhali was symbolic; he was trying to bridge the communal distrust between people as freedom loomed on the horizon.

Amid this gloomy atmosphere came a silver lining. A short folk dance sequence was organized in the courtyard of Gandhi's hut in one of the villages where he had stayed on this tour. Of this a little bit of film footage is available. A group of Bengali women dressed in simple traditional sarees danced in a circle as the Mahatma watched them from the doorstep of his hut. It is a moving and poignant scene, reminiscent of devotees dancing before a deity in a temple. The silent visuals show women moving around in simple yet elegant dance steps that manage to delight the old man. Given the turbulent times, this surely was the highlight of the film footage shot on Gandhi's Noakhali peace tour.

Finally, peace prevailed. It was nothing short of a miracle. The British Movietone News, usually guarded in praising the cause of the nationalist freedom struggle, decided to give the man his due this time and titled their topical film *The Miracle of Gandhi*! The newsreel, shot by an Indian cameraman Pat Mohan, started with visuals of the house where Gandhi stayed in Calcutta during his visit, where he had undertaken his fast against the communal violence. People came out in large numbers on the streets to appeal to Gandhi to break his fast.

It took just seventy-three hours for the situation in the city to become normal. Gandhi came out of the house to cheers from the crowd gathered there. Though he looked pensive, the attendants, aides and followers around him wore happy faces. The visuals showed Gandhi addressing a huge meeting; it was a thanksgiving speech to the people who had listened to his fervent appeals for peace.

His mission successful, Gandhi returned to Delhi and plunged into the hectic political action around the handover of power by the British to the Indians. Though he was not part of the formal talks initiated by the new Viceroy, Lord Mountbatten, the latter wanted Gandhi to mediate at the talks. The moral authority of the man was too important to be ignored, and Mountbatten invited Gandhi and discussed with him the future course of action. Gandhi thus figured in several newsreels flanked by Mountbatten and his wife Edwina.

These visuals were, in a way, a very good public relations exercise for the new Viceroy. In fact, as we read earlier, Mountbatten arranged for a special newsreel man to fly down from London to India to film the various activities that were conducted in the run-up to the transfer of power. Here Gandhi was seen sharing a laugh with the Mountbatten couple on the lawns of the Presidential Palace. But most of the time, the newsreel companies trained their cameras on his prayer meeting held daily in the capital.

The occasion demanded solemness, and Gandhi, now seventy-eight, could be seen at what he did best. His role now was mostly that of a saint, less of a politician. The people of India had realized it long back and they flocked to his prayer meetings. Listening to him was obviously on their minds, but for most people his 'darshan' was enough. On the appointed day of transfer of power, 15 August 1947, Gandhi was back in Calcutta. Away from ceremonies, he preferred to be alone, and despite requests from newsreel companies, including BBC, he did not allow them to film him. So, unfortunately, we do not have any moving images of Gandhi on the auspicious day for which he had led his people for more than thirty years.

What had happened in Calcutta, Bihar and Bengal was, unfortunately, repeated in the capital city of Delhi. Freedom had come at a price—in the form of Partition, and it was too heavy a price. One of the greatest human tragedies in the world struck India, and the saviour was back in the thick of action trying to douse the fire fuelled by communal disharmony. Gandhi appealed to people gone mad with hatred. Once again, his prayer meetings were the meeting points for minds gone astray. His words, filled with love, were the balm for a populace struck by wild emotions.

In the cold winter of early January 1948, Gandhi again had to resort to fasting, his last one. He lay energy-less on a bed in Birla House, covered in warm clothes, while people queued up to have a 'darshan' of their saint. His act of fasting was like a much-required cleansing in the tense atmosphere, and sanity returned. People thronged the streets in procession to request their leader to break his fast. Only after 200,000 petitions were signed pledging communal harmony did the man relent. This time it took five days. Paramount Sound News reported the breaking of his fast, screening their film snippets as the first pictures from India on this event for their worldwide audience.

If Gandhi's walking tour in Noakhali was the greatest test of the values and principles he had espoused for years, then his fasting for religious harmony in Delhi proved to be the much-needed balm for bruised minds. The moving images, now available, of his walking tour and peace mission in Noakhali are a true testimony of the character of the man in the toughest of times.

11

Hollywood Loves Gandhi

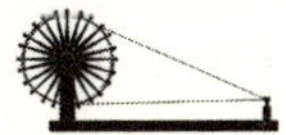

TWO LITTLE GIRLS FROM the United States of America had a unique mission on their minds when they boarded a ship at New York in October 1931. Mariam and Lilabati Ghose were travelling with a plan to meet Gandhi and to request him to visit America. Gandhi then was attending the Second Round Table Conference across the Atlantic in London. Trust the American film studios for their sense of drama and spotting news value as Paramount Sound News produced a special newsreel reporting on this bold, unusual mission.

Will You, Mr Gandhi? is the title of their short topical film with two-and-a-half minutes' duration. These two girls of Indian origin were interviewed and filmed onboard their ship in the New York harbour. The inter-title card of the newsreel said, '"Come to America!", Mariam and Lilabati Ghose, daughters of U.S. Hindu leader, sail to invite Mahatma here, October 1931.'

The film opens with a scene where a reporter from Paramount Sound News is seen on the deck of a ship in New York harbour. With a microphone in hand, the reporter interviews these girls on their unique mission on 14 October 1931. The two little girls, daughters of Sailendra Nath Ghose, president of the Indian National Congress of America, are well covered for protection from the cold. The elder, Mariam, aged seven, was studying in a public school at the time in Brooklyn.

Both sisters looked confident and had no trace of nervousness while facing the motion picture camera; rather, they seemed to enjoy all the attention. Naturally, they were excited and jubilant at the prospect of seeing the Indian leader. It was Mariam, the elder girl, who answered all the questions. These are some of the interview highlights.

> Reporter: Young lady, I understand you are going alone to Europe to see Gandhi.
>
> Mariam: Yes, and I am going to bring him back to America with us.
>
> Reporter: And you are going to tell him something?
>
> Mariam: Yes, I have a message from all Americans.

At this stage, the reporter asks her, 'Suppose, you broadcast that.' Then Mariam Ghose reads her message out from a paper:

> Children, I am very happy to tell you, my sister Lila who is four years old and I are sailing for London. We are going to visit Mahatma Gandhi in London. When we meet him, we are going to tell him … all American children are so happy to have him visit our country.

While the younger Lilabati is busy munching something and looking into the camera, her elder sister continues to read the message. '[W]e have a lot of presents for Mahatma Gandhi. But I wonder what he will give us in return.' Lilabati, on her part, also chips in with a murmur that is not audible in the available video. But this small clip is such a delight to watch. It also shows the earnest desire among the Indian population in America to have Gandhi visit the country. The children were carrying official messages from various societies and Gandhi sympathizers in

Boston, Chicago, New York, Pittsburgh and Baltimore. The *New York Times* reported next day that the children travelled in third-class on the liner Europa of the North German Lloyd line, in keeping with the spirit of their mission to see the ascetic Indian leader.[1]

For the record, Gandhi never visited the United States of America. He found no time to visit that country because he was fully committed to the Indian freedom struggle. In fact, he left the Indian shores only a few times after returning from South Africa in 1915. While coming back from the Second Round Table conference, he stopped over in Paris in France, Rome in Italy and Geneva in Switzerland apart from visiting Sri Lanka once. Thereafter, his attention and energies were solely focused on gaining freedom for India. Like these little girls, several American people and organizations at various points in time requested Gandhi to visit America. But the much-anticipated visit did not happen.

When James Mills asked Gandhi during his first-ever talkie interview in 1931, taken on behalf of the American film studio Fox Movietone News, about the possibility of his visiting America, Gandhi answered, 'Much as I should like to be able to give you the time, I have absolutely no notion except this—that I would not like to visit America till the experiment in India has become demonstrably successful.' In the same vein, he acknowledged, 'I appreciate all the interest and sympathy America has shown in our struggle, and I hope we shall be able to retain the friendship and goodwill of the American people to the end of our struggle.'[2]

One of the oldest democracies in the world has had a very strange fascination for Gandhi. Despite his never having set foot on American soil, Gandhi has captivated the imagination of American minds. In his first talkie interview, Gandhi was told that there was a great deal of interest and sympathy in the United States for India's struggle for independence, because America itself had a similar struggle for liberation 150 years ago. Individuals and institutions from America have devoted their lives to the cause of Gandhian principles and philosophy. Gandhi's name and news about the work he was engaged in had, however, reached America much before Mills' famous newsreel brought his moving images before the nation.

Gandhi's activities in South Africa were reported in the American press frequently. As early as May 1897, *The Nation* reported about the work Gandhi was doing among the east Indian community and the racial discrimination they were facing from the British regime there. Then in 1921, John Haynes Holmes, a prominent American church leader, put Gandhi on an equal pedestal with Christ and called him the greatest man in the world. A number of prominent political and religious leaders in America were getting attracted to the values and principles being propounded by Gandhi.

The newsreel companies, many of them based out of America, got a whiff of Gandhi's increasing popularity there and started focusing on him. As early as in 1922, Universal News produced a newsreel on Gandhi's agitation in India. They titled it *Exclusive Views of Mysterious India*! Announcing it, the studio said, 'The first of these pictures clearing up the Mysteries of India appears in International News No. 60 and shows tremendous demonstrations by the followers of the patriot Gandhi, at present imprisoned, against the domination of white civilisation.' It further said, 'These exclusive pictures were taken at great personal risk by Captain Ariel Varges.'

Then came the real scoop that turned heads and created history in the motion picture industry—Fox Movietone News's filming of Gandhi's interview by AP correspondent James Mills. Given Gandhi's dislike of machines in general and cinema in particular, it was considered a significant accomplishment. The questions ranged from India's freedom struggle to prohibition, the forthcoming Round Table Conference in London and also the likelihood of Gandhi making a visit to the USA after that.

New York-based *Motion Picture Herald*, a leading film trade magazine in America, devoted two full pages, that too in colour, to highlight the importance of Gandhi's first talkie interview. A graphic display of newspaper headlines that highlighted the uniqueness of the event filled these two pages. A glance at these headlines reveals why the American publication decided to splash two whole pages in colour with Gandhi's name all over.[3] 'Gandhi Surprises India By Appearing in Talkie', 'Gandhi Breaks Vow By Posing for Talkies', 'Gandhi in Talkie Role, Break 25 Years' Rule; Set All India Babbling', 'Gandhi Astounds All India by "Staring" in U.S. Film', 'Little Indian Idol Poses and Talks of Trip to US for Newsreel Men', 'Gandhi Talkie Amazing to India', 'India Gasping Over The Movie Debut of Gandhi', 'Gandhi Persuaded to Pose and Talk For News Cameras', 'First Motion Picture Interview Granted by Mahatma Gandhi', 'Gandhi Talkie Debut Amazes Followers', 'India Is Surprised by Actor Gandhi', 'Gandhi As "Star" In American Talking Picture Upsets Hindus', 'Gandhi Film Ends with Dinner Call', 'Gandhi Gives First Movie Interview', 'Gandhi Makes Debut in American Talkies', 'Gandhi Discusses Several Topics in Movie Interview'. One is really amazed at the lengths to which the magazine went to publicize that rare event in the history of the motion picture industry.

At that time, Fox Movietone News and their newsreels were being shown in thirty-seven countries and had a massive reach of 10,00,00,000! Fox, Paramount, Hearst Metrotone, and Universal, four major American film companies, continued to make many newsreels on the developments in India and also filmed Gandhi extensively throughout the national movement for independence.

Another American reporter, William Shirer, the one who had persuaded Gandhi to get him a ticket on the train from Marseilles to London, also developed a close working relationship with Gandhi. The *Chicago Tribune*, for which Shirer reported, was one of the first newspapers from America to specially deploy a reporter in India to cover the freedom struggle. When asked by Shirer about his intentions to visit the USA, Gandhi replied,

> I long to visit your great country. I have had the most tempting invitations to do so. But I must deny myself that luxury until my task of achieving independence is finished. I would like to carry my message of non-violence and love to America. But I cannot do so until I have been able to show the American people that such a

> doctrine has triumphed in India, and it offers the whole world a new instrument for winning the rights of man peacefully and insuring the brotherhood of all nations.[4]

While in London to attend the Second Round Table Conference, Gandhi recorded a special message for the people of America, which was broadcast live in that country. This radio talk by Gandhi in 1931 is considered to be one of the most memorable events in the initial years of international broadcasting. Like the historic first-ever talkie interview he gave for the newsreel few months before, Gandhi spoke into a microphone for the first time! Again, there is an interesting story behind how he had to be chased and persuaded to agree to do this radio talk. In his memoir *Hello America*, Cesar Saerchinger, a pioneer in transatlantic radio broadcasting, provides a detailed account of the efforts that went into convincing Gandhi to give the talk.

A few months before Gandhi's London visit, Saerchinger, who was tasked to arrange an interview with Gandhi, got some nice advice on the dos and don'ts involved in achieving the desired result: State clearly the objective of the proposed address; Make no appeal to his vanity, as he has none; On no account offer him money; Do not try to impress him; and spell his name correctly. Meanwhile, the office of Columbia Broadcasting System (CBS) in New York, for whom Saerchinger was working, tried to get in touch with Gandhi through Indian Congress representatives in America, but with no luck.

Their competitor radio network, National Broadcasting Company (NBC), acted smartly and sent a personal emissary to meet Gandhi, which worked. He agreed to the broadcast but had no knowledge about the other large radio network in America, CBS. Not one to lose heart, Saerchinger got in touch with Muriel Lester's sister and secured permission to install the special telephone lines and other equipment at Kingsley Hall, Gandhi's residence in London. Luckily, he also managed to get consent from Sir Samuel Hoare, the Secretary of State for India, for going ahead with Gandhi's radio broadcast. It was a sensitive matter, since Gandhi talking directly to the American public from British soil could have been embarrassing for the British government.

Finally, the day Gandhi arrived in London, Saerchinger managed to secure an audience with him and made his proposal. 'He listened to my explanation of the American broadcasting system and the existence of the two major competitive "chains". He said he was not willing to make two broadcasts, but would like one to be shared by all … He proposed a miniature "round table conference" with the two American competitors and himself.'[5] When the idea was presented before the rival broadcasting company, they agreed to the proposal. 'Hurrah! America is at peace. That's splendid,' was Gandhi's reaction. Despite their assurances given before the Mahatma, the rival companies engaged in one-upmanship to proclaim their own broadcast as 'exclusive' and announced it as much to the press.

On the day of the broadcast, NBC applied for a separate telephone line, which was impossible due to shortage of time. Columbia had already installed their own line, and Saerchinger, a pioneer in transatlantic radio broadcasting, agreed to allow NBC to use it 'provided they are not used earlier than our broadcast'. Gandhi was blissfully unaware of all these ongoing machinations behind the scene, and, uncharacteristically, got late for the recording. The reason … he was busy eating! 'Calm and unconcerned, he was finishing his meal of fruit and goat's milk upstairs.'[6] After Ms Lester introduced Gandhi, he arrived in the hall.

Apparently, he had never seen a microphone before. With no knowledge that he was already live on air, Gandhi inquired, 'Do I talk into this thing?'[7]—and that was heard by millions of people live in America. With no prepared manuscript for this all-important radio talk, Gandhi sat opposite a statuette of Saint Francis, folded his hands, and closed his eyes for a few seconds. Then he spoke without taking any pause in his simple yet beautiful English, explaining the cause of the Indian struggle to millions of American people.

Saerchinger, the man responsible for arranging the broadcast, described the way Gandhi spoke:

> For nearly half an hour he went on, slowly and every word distinct, his thin, high-pitched voice automatically lowered through transmission, but clear and unwavering, explaining his 'non-violent' revolution: 'I feel in the innermost recesses of my heart that the world is sick unto death of blood-spilling. The world is seeking a way out, and I flatter myself with the belief that perhaps it will be privilege of the ancient land of India to show that way out to the hungering world.'[8]

Like in the beginning, after his address ended, Gandhi remarked without knowing that he had to stop, 'Well, that's over!' These words also were heard by the listeners. The talk was heard live by millions and printed in full the next day in newspapers across three continents. Few months later, Columbia Broadcast System ran this all-important broadcast again as 'Mahatma Gandhi, India's man of destiny, explains the political plight in an American re-broadcast from London.' Saerchinger knew the full import of this talk and said, 'Nothing Gandhi ever said reached so many people; it was the largest audience he had ever had.' [9]

Just the next month, *Radio Digest*, brought out by National Broadcast Authority from New York, carried a special story, 'India on the Air', focusing on Gandhi's radio broadcast. With the voice of Gandhi sweeping across the country, America suddenly became conscious of India as never before. Among the listeners was Helen Spring, a famous American actress, in her apartment on Long Island, who had toured India just a year before and had come back as an ardent admirer of Gandhi.

After listening to Gandhi's talk, Spring wrote,

> Acquiring leadership in India is one thing and holding a critical American audience is another ...In my opinion the three outstanding points of his speech were: First, his admission that India is not perfect, that it has many shortcomings. This required courage. Second, his public acknowledgement of the participation of the women of India in this struggle for freedom, and the psychological

as well as the practical effect of their splendid assistance. The third point and the one which endeared Gandhi to my heart even deeper was the fact that during his entire broadcast he never condemned the country against which he is struggling.[10]

Even though she couldn't meet Gandhi during her India visit since he was lodged in jail, she said she felt 'I knew him well, for the pulse of India beats through Gandhi. Everywhere there seemed to be a sense of him.'[11]

Columbia Records brought out gramophone records of this Gandhi radio talk, and it sold like hot cakes in America and India. A leading New York–based magazine The Phonograph Monthly Review in March 1932 rightly termed the record as 'a most unusual recording, and one that will be of great historic value.' If this was not enough, then the management of an internationally famous hotel invited Gandhi to America and offered to set apart an entire floor for him and his team, free of cost. Moreover, they were ready to hoist the Indian flag for the period Gandhi stayed in their hotel, an honour reserved only for heads of states! Such was the charm he held for the American people and his popularity among them that hordes of invitations were sent to him to visit the USA.

A.K. Chettiar, the man who made a significant film on Gandhi, has written about an incident that would indicate the eagerness of the American people for a glimpse of the old man. Chettiar was in a film archive in Rome searching for film footage on Gandhi, but unfortunately there was no trace of Gandhi in the reels he was shown. While he was at it, one particular reel with the title *Signor Grandi Arrives at New York* was shown to Chettiar. Dino Grandi was at that time the Italian minister for foreign affairs and this footage was shot when he disembarked at New York harbour in November 1931. Chettiar wrote:

When Grandi arrived at the New York harbour, thousands had assembled to welcome him. He was astonished on seeing the crowd, but no one showed any sign of excitement on seeing

> him. Grandi could understand the reason only after reading the evening newspapers. People had mistaken Grandi for Gandhi and had thronged the harbour to catch a glimpse of the latter. The newspapers reported that the crowd had been very disappointed.[12]

A minor difference of one syllable in their names had created this misunderstanding, but this case of mistaken identity revealed the popularity Gandhi enjoyed among Americans.

In 1927, three American students from University of Oregon decided to go on a world debating tour including India, and they also met Gandhi in Madras and filmed him. The 42nd session of the Indian National Congress was being held there and the team comprising of Walter Hempstead, Benoit McCroskey and Avery Thompson, heard that Gandhi was there. They managed to secure an audience with him, and Hempstead wrote about the experience.

> As press representatives we proceeded to interview Mahatma Gandhi in his temporary home. He was observing a day of silence and could not speak to us, so he wrote on a piece of brown scratch paper. He did let us come into his room while he read an English paper. In the remote hope that it would be successful, we filmed the great Non-Cooperationist.[13]

The American love affair with Gandhi was not always rosy. There was an attempt in 1935 to make fun of Gandhi, and it was not at all in good taste. RKO studio, a major Hollywood production house, came out with a two-reeler comedy film *Everybody Likes Music*, in which a character closely resembling Gandhi was shown as a drunk and dancing with a white woman. A lot of noise and protest followed, compelling the production house to cut the objectionable scene before release of the film in India. Even though care was taken to not name the character as Gandhi, the portrayal was a cheap gimmick to garner some laughs at the expense of the old man.

Four years later, another RKO film, *Gunga Din*, directed by George Stevens, also had a character closely resembling Gandhi. With a similar physique and wearing a loincloth for dress, the villainous character of a guru in the film was clearly an attempt to challenge the nationalist narrative of Gandhi in various Indian films of the time. It seemed a deliberate case of caricaturing of Gandhi. Author Prem Chowdhry wrote, 'the film, therefore, portrayed Gandhi (a real-life Vaishnavite and follower of Bhakti), as a worshipper of Kali, the goddess of violence, believing in the cult of violence and murder, to achieve his surreptitious agenda.'[14] RKO created one of the largest film location camps in the Alabama Range near California to make it a 'Hindu city'. A lot of planning and preparation went into making of the film.

> Although many of the extras were genuine Hindus, some, of course, were not. In order to save time in making up the large number of extras, the company erected a 55-gallon drum of brown make-up paint, connected the tank with a spray gun, put six extras at a time on a wooden turntable, and sprayed them under pressure until they could hardly tell themselves that they were not actually Hindus![15]

Once again, there was a vehement protest against the film, which was loosely based on Rudyard Kipling's 1890 poem of the same name, that led to the banning of the film in India. India's leading film magazine *Film India* led the protest, with K.A. Abbas terming the film as a 'scandalously anti-Indian picture' in which Indians were portrayed as sadistic barbarians.[16] Notwithstanding such odd incidents, the American movie industry for years has generally had a positive fascination for the Eastern world and its mysticism.

The citizens of the land of riches strived to look for peace, which they believed could be found in the ancient Indian scriptures, the eastern philosophy and its proponents. Right from Swami Vivekanand, who captured the imagination of the American mind in 1896 at the Congress of World Religions, to J. Krishnamurti, who made the USA his base, Indian yogis and philosophers have been sought out by Americans for answers to their life questions. This reflected in their films too. As early as in 1902, Thomas Edison had made a three-minute silent film *Hindoo*

Fakir, filming the magical acts of an Indian yogi. Made as a 'trick film', it showed the magician making his assistant disappear and reappear!

American film trade publications always featured Gandhi in some context or the other. It was also a fact that he was considered a major newsreel star right from the early 1930s. An amusing comparison in this regard was reported in Chicago-based *Motion Picture* magazine in their April 1932 issue. A photograph of Gandhi was prominently published with an article that discussed why certain men were considered newsreel stars. 'Mahatma Gandhi is Lionel Barrymore of the talking newspapers—the great character actor of world affairs,' said the piece.[17] Barrymore was a great American actor who had won the Academy Award for best actor for his role in *A Free Soul* in 1931.

While discussing several eminent people of the era, the magazine rated the Mahatma of higher camera appeal than Queen Marie of Romania, whom the magazine described as a show-woman. 'She is probably the most fascinating of all newsreel subjects, with the exception of the colourful, but humble Mahatma Gandhi. Knowing the value of publicity and loving the limelight, the Balkan queen can always be depended upon for a spectacular appearance,' said the article.[18]

There were several Hollywood stars who were mesmerized by the simplicity of Gandhi. New York-based *New Movie Magazine* did a cover story on the suppressed desires of Hollywood stars in September 1931. Bela Lugosi, who became popular by portraying Count Dracula in 1931, was one among the stars featured. When this Hungarian-born actor was asked what his suppressed desire was, he said he wanted to trade all his success for the simplicity and mental greatness of a Gandhi. He said,

> What a man, this Gandhi! He sits with worldly greats – with viceroys and diplomats bedecked in glittering uniforms. His raiment a cotton loin-cloth, but possessed of a mentality that sways millions. That's greatness! … Gandhi wins his way by virtue of simplicity. He dares to be himself – to force recognition by his mental equipment, not an outward showing of power.[19]

Yet another popular Broadway star, Eddie Cantor, wanted to have the very unlikely combination of Gandhi and Greta Garbo as guests for a private dinner! When Hollywood-based *Picture Play* film magazine asked some stars to name celebrities whom they would like to meet for dinner, the famous comedian and performer said, 'Well, Mahatma Gandhi first, because he doesn't eat much—he brings his own dinner along, you know. But seriously, I would be thrilled to be listening to one of the greatest of all beings—a fellow who embodies so much unselfishness.' And about his other choice, 'the ever mysterious Garbo', Cantor said, 'In all my time in Hollywood I didn't even *see* her. Yes, I would want her there to see if I could break up that Sphinx-like attitude.' [20]

Another Hollywood beauty and screen idol, Rita Hayworth, had certainly heard Gandhi's name and knew about him. When asked about her choice of men whom she would like to take to a desert isle, Rita's tongue-in-cheek answer was, 'But I am afraid I couldn't get by with a single male!' She then named her imaginary list and added, 'I hope you won't mind the fact that they all hail from Hollywood.' Her reasoning for not including others was that she had not met likes of Sir Anthony Eden, Toscanini, etc., and she added Mahatma Gandhi to this list, 'I am not in a position to judge very well,' she said.[21]

This fascination with Gandhi and his scant way of dressing, sometimes, led to funny incidents. A very popular comedian Eddie Cantor starred in a musical film *Kid Millions* produced by Samuel Goldwyn. The fantasy drama turned out to be a huge success at the box office with film's plot focused on Egyptian setting. Otto Hoffman, in a strange casting plays the character which is Gandhi-like.

With a shaved head, round spectacles and white shawl wrapped around, the character is given an umbrella instead of a bamboo staff! But the fun part was, as per a Hollywood custom, a player could buy his wardrobe for half the price on completion of the picture. It was reported that Hoffman wanted to buy his cotton cloth so that Goldwyn production department charged him two bits![22]

Even though the experiments to introduce colour in filmmaking had started as soon as moving images were invented, the results were slow in coming. The transition from black and white to colour had major technological, economic and aesthetic issues. The invention of the Technicolor process in 1915 was a breakthrough. The decade of the 1930s saw Hollywood studios making increasing use of colour in filmmaking. During the same decade, an American social philanthropist, Adelaide Pearson, embarked on a world tour with a 16 mm camera and went on to film many major events and important personalities. In 1936, she filmed Mahatma Gandhi in colour while he was at the Sevagram Ashram in Wardha. Arguably, this made for the earliest colour footage of Gandhi.

The Great Depression of the 1930s propelled America to look for solace somewhere, and this probably led them to look to Gandhi among others for answers. He was not only preaching but also himself living his ideals. Baburao Patel, editor of India's premier film magazine *Film India* travelled to the USA in 1939, and after meeting several Hollywood artistes and studio executives, he wrote in his editorial,

> Americans know Mahatma Gandhi more than they know India. His mysticism puzzles them, perhaps because such spiritual grandeur is denied to the average dollar-crazy Americans. They asked a thousand questions about our patriot saint and while giving them all the news about him, I had to tell my grievance about the anti-Indian films.[23]

Incidentally, the magazine cover for that month prominently featured Gandhi with the caption 'Leading the nation'. Gandhi's having not travelled to America probably enhanced his mystic persona even more for the people there. Americans of different faiths and belonging to different professions then chose to travel to India to meet Gandhi in person and explore his teachings deeply. The USA, incidentally, was only the second country in the world after India to issue a stamp in 1961 honouring Mahatma Gandhi. The stamp hailed him as 'apostle of non-violence' and 'champion of liberty'.

The American fascination for Gandhi continued even in the new millennium. Gandhi and America's favourite sport of baseball certainly made for a very potent and dramatic combination for the screen. So, even though Gandhi had nothing to do with baseball, a newsreel having him in the lead role in a game, though a mock one, was made in USA. *Gandhi at the BAT* is the title of a mock newsreel made in 2006, based on a short story by Chet Williamson which had appeared in the prestigious *New Yorker* magazine in 1983.

In this fictional story, Gandhi had secretly visited the United States in 1933. At President Roosevelt's request, all contemporary accounts of this top-secret visit were suppressed, and no records have ever been found. Noted writer Salman Rushdie praised the story as one of the funniest he had ever read in the magazine. The film, written and directed by Stephanie Argy and Alec Boehm, was shot in Bakersfield, California, and the makers used visual effects stunningly to make the field look like one from 1933. The movie, a fictional newsreel, actually, was made by Silvertone News (History as it happens) and the inter-title card says, 'Visitor from exotic East charms baseball's Bronx Bombers and confounds Connie Mack's Philadelphia Athletics.'

The narrator of the film makes an announcement that a little brown man in a loincloth has arrived at the stadium with a baseball bat in hand. The opposing team is completely baffled at the sight of him. Delfin Labao starred as Mohandas K. 'Mo' Gandhi in the film, and goes on to pinch-hit for his team, New York Yankees. This 'Mo' Gandhi had met the mayor of the city before the start of the game and had also mingled with the who's who of baseball in the locker room. While he is seated in the mayor's box to watch the game, a vendor offers him a hot-dog, which he politely refuses. The mayor then offers him crackers. While watching the game attentively, Gandhi sheepishly tells the mayor that he wants to play the game!

A quick meeting is held with the referees on the side lines to discuss this unique request and they decide to allow him in. Yankees' fellow players offer him some tips before he goes onto the field. The crowd erupts in joy to see him on the ground. 'It is a very big field and a very small ball!,' he says with a chuckle. He assumes a traditional cricket guard before batting, and a colleague quickly comes up to correct his stance and body posture. After missing a few balls, he connects and hits the ball hard. He then runs and runs while the opposite team misfields and overthrows the ball.

The commentator describes Gandhi as a sixty-three-year-old white-robed saint who is a vegetarian when he takes an energetic shuttle. While running, Gandhi blows a small mouth organ with a child's innocence. He then offers the ball to the opposition player with a smile and does a namaste. The runs are added and Gandhi's team wins! The team carry him on their shoulders in a victory celebration. The manager comes up to him and offers him a permanent position on the team. With folded hands, Gandhi says there is only one team for which he would play, and that is India!

The match over, Gandhi leaves by train, and then the audience is shown a few delightful comments made by fellow team members on Gandhi. The mayor says, 'I don't think there is another one like him in the world.' Gandhi also offers his own comments, 'Oh, I am sure, this will be the first and last time. I have much work to do at home.' An inter-title card then appears on screen. It says, 'Over the next 15 years, Mohandas K. Gandhi used non-violent methods to end British rule in India and bring independence to 350 million people. He never played professional baseball again.'

For good measure, the short comedy film makes a tongue-in-cheek comment that for decades, historians have searched for material on Mohandas K. Gandhi's top-secret visit to the United States in 1933 ... until film historians unearthed this never-before-seen newsreel footage of Gandhi's legendary visit to Yankee Stadium. To make it look like an authentic footage, a careful preservation process by which the film was 'restored' is also shown.

The mock newsreel went on to win an award for filmmaking excellence at the Baseball Hall of Fame Film Festival! The film had history and it had baseball, all in the USA. The filmmakers added Gandhi to it, and the film turned out to be a humorous take on Gandhi's US trip that never happened. Gandhi had nothing much to do with sports in general. He was too busy leading India's freedom movement.

Therefore, there was no question of Gandhi wielding any bat, let alone a baseball bat. This was made possible only in a fictional newsreel.

The American cinematic encounter with Gandhi has been a long one. While Gandhi was in prison at Yerawada jail in Pune, an American cameraman, Cornelius Vanderbilt Jr, was going around the world asking some great men about their movie tastes. The list consisted of the who's who of world politics and leadership, including the Duke and Duchess of Windsor, Adolf Hitler, Josef Stalin, Emperor Hirohito of Japan, Mussolini and General Franco. Vanderbilt also approached Gandhi in jail. Obviously, Gandhi had no idea about motion pictures. Vanderbilt recorded his experience and said:

> To all questions submitted, Gandhi, Hindu mystic, remained silent. It began to look as if the eighty-five-hundred-mile trip had been made in vain; then, just as I was about to leave him, the interpreter said that India's great man wanted to ask me a question. I listened attentively to the almost inaudible sing-song of his voice. Finally, the interpreter spoke forth: 'I know little about America, sire,' said he, 'except from what I see from the occasional motion pictures I attend. To what class there, sire, do you belong?' My first impulse was to tell him that, as far as I knew, America had no classes. But instead, I decided to ask him first to clarify his statement. 'Well, sire,' came back that even-leveled, age-old voice, 'are you a gangster, gentleman or cowboy?' Amusing? Yes—and perfectly understandable, too, when you think of the type of film foreign exhibitors choose from our home producers.[24]

Either Vanderbilt got all this completely wrong or Gandhi was in a jolly good mood to pull the American's leg, because Gandhi had hardly seen any films to form an opinion on them. But he was well-read enough to know about American society to ask questions about class there!

The same year, there was a spotlight on two very different Indians in a Hollywood magazine. The story featured Sabu, the wonder boy from India, who had gained immense popularity through his film

Elephant Boy. He was interviewed, paraded, and showcased as a miracle boy. When he visited Madame Tussaud's, the famous wax museum in London, he recognized only three figures he knew; Charlie Chaplin, King Edward VIII and Mahatma Gandhi![25]

Gandhi's dislike for cinema was known, and some of his followers were concerned that he had arrived at such an opinion and held on to it without even having seen movies. One such follower, Bellur Shivaram, made a public appeal to Walt Disney, creator of the Mickey Mouse cartoon phenomenon, to send an emissary to Gandhi in the form of an autographed caricature of Mickey Mouse! This, he thought, would induce Gandhi to have a look at the silver screen.[26] Funnily enough, twelve years later, Gandhi was reported to have seen a picture of Mickey Mouse along with a Hollywood film *Mission to Moscow*!

The visit of the two little brave Ghose girls from the US to the UK was not just a publicity gimmick for the newsreel cameras. A lot of planning had gone into undertaking their journey. The girls were initially supposed to sail on the liner President Roosevelt, and to be accompanied by Ranlal Bajbai, secretary of the Indian Nationalist Association in America. The latter failed to get re-entry permit in time, so Mrs Salandra Ghose, the girls' mother, decided to go with her children at the last moment. They indeed landed up in London with their mother in tow and secured an audience with the man they were keen to invite to the USA.

The children visited Gandhi in his Kingsley Hall home on his birthday, 2 October 1931. Gandhi was impressed by their motivation and patted their heads. But he had to decline their sweet invitation. 'Naturally, I am pleased to receive the invitations, but I do not believe America is ready to receive my message,' Gandhi said, smiling. 'I hope they understand. Nonetheless, you are very determined representatives,' were his parting words of appreciation.[27]

If a postcard was sent to Gandhi from abroad with only 'King of India' written on the address line, and it got delivered, then anything was possible when it came to Gandhi. Noted American actor Martin Sheen had watched newsreels featuring Gandhi as a school boy. He later went on to play the crucial role of journalist Walker (a combination of many correspondents including James Mills) in Richard Attenborough's *Gandhi*.

Gandhi's name had really caught imagination in the show business in America. This fascination reached to such a level that his name meant honesty and dedication. Oscar Kafer who was a successful showman in North Carolina, realized it to his great delight. Kafer took over the management of 677-seater Masonic Theatre in New Bern city in 1917 and ran it well for more than 28 years. To honour Kafer's stupendous feat, his friends and customers aptly called him 'Mahatma Gandhi'![28]

Gandhi was so well-known that even though he never visited the USA, he was assigned ownership of a cinema theatre there! *Motion Picture Herald*, a leading American film magazine, reported this strange but amusing happening in 1933.[29]

A film exhibitor from Salt Lake in the USA, on learning that his bank was about to foreclose his loan, assigned ownership of the theatre, of all the person, to King George, Benito Mussolini and Mahatma Gandhi. Obviously, under the law the bank had to sue the assignees. We do not know what happened ultimately in this case. Imagine a man who disliked the cinema getting sued for the very reason of owning a cinema theatre in the USA. The pucca bania that he was, Gandhi would have surely gone on to become the owner of a chain of cinema theatres in the USA!

12

Champagne Glass Dance for Gandhi

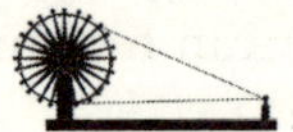

INDIA GAINED FREEDOM ON 15 August 1947. The next year, Gandhi attained martyrdom. The new nation started taking slow but steady steps to build its path, based on the agenda of development. Under the leadership of Pandit Nehru, the first prime minister of India, the country tried to make rapid strides to provide food, clothing, shelter, and health and education, to millions. The domestic film industry too took up the theme of nation-building, to tell the stories of new India on screen. It was not the village economy, the dream of Gandhi, that was the focus though; modern industrial development was the mantra.

Was Gandhi being forgotten too early? Had the film industry, which had been so very eager to portray Gandhian values and principles in a large number of their productions, decided to dump his ideas suddenly? Did filmmakers feel these ideas had nothing to offer in the context of the new vision of modern India? Did the nationalistic hangover disappear so very soon, or was there still some of that fervour left? Were there not even a few filmmakers still inspired by the vision of the Mahatma?

The decades of the 1950s and 1960s provided a mix of answers to these questions. Even on the seminal occasion of the birth centenary of Gandhi, only lip service was paid him by the film industry. Nothing worthwhile and memorable came out in film to commemorate the event, and no serious attempt was made in Indian cinema industry to examine Gandhi's life and ideas or to analyse the many layers of his personality.

Immediately after his death, though, there had been a spurt of films on him. Within a year of Gandhi demise, a Tamil film, *Geetha Gandhi,* was made by K. Subrahmanyam. This was the filmmaker, a staunch follower of Gandhi, who had made the trilogy of *Balayogini, Seva Sadan* and *Thyagabhoomi* before Independence. These films had highlighted social issues with an emphasis on Gandhian values and were critically acclaimed. Subrahmanyam felt that these very values were being forgotten soon after Independence. So he came up with a story that combined the principles of the sacred Bhagavad Gita and the teachings of the Mahatma.

Geetha Gandhi, made under the banner of Madras United Artistes Corporation, was released in March 1949, just a year after the death of Gandhi. While the story, screenplay, dialogues and direction were by K. Subrahmanyam himself, the music was composed by his wife Meenakshi Subrahmanyam. Able orchestration was provided by Pandurangan, a leading music director in the south Indian film industry, and Brother Lakshmanan.

The film starts with '*Manmohan Das Gandhi*', a song in homage to Gandhi, as the credits roll on screen. Portraying the relevance of the Gita and Gandhi in everyday life of an Indian, a song in the film shows children taking an oath with the Bhagvad Gita placed on their heads, in front of a bust of Gandhi. It signifies that they will live amicably sharing their happiness and sorrows. Gandhi is referred to as Ahimsamurthy. The film told the tale of a large family, whose head Subbaiyer is a living Gandhian. His four sons go their different ways, their paths occasionally crossing, and there is a granddaughter, a university student, who gets caught in a situation that is not of her making.

Gandhi and his wife Kasturba feature throughout the film, either in the form of a bust or photograph. The dialogues refer to Gandhi frequently. The motif of the joint family and its analogy to the nation, where different languages are spoken, are depicted beautifully in the film. The character of the grandfather is clearly modelled on Gandhi, and when he is dying, the entire family comes together in the end to take an oath to stay together, as if to symbolize the country's people taking an oath to stay united. Incidentally, Subrahmanyam had opposed the reorganization of Indian states along linguistic lines.

Subramanyam was a staunch Gandhian and a hardcore Congressman. Gandhi had famously wished to disband the Congress after Independence, and, paying heed to his call for dissolving the Congress, Subramanyam had resigned. He focused his energies on two principles: *dev bhakti* (devotion to God) and *desh bhakti* (devotion to Nation). His daughter Padma Subrahmanyam, the renowned Bharatanatyam dancer, told me that Pandit Nehru had invited him to become the minister of information in the first cabinet, but he refused. He believed in serving the country in the field of culture and not through politics.

The filmmaker's daughter, 'Baby' Padma, was a major attraction in the movie, playing the part of the pet granddaughter. She even sang two songs, one on the Mahatma and the other about her ambitions to become a famous dancer who stages a dance recital in America. In a significant line, she sings '*Nam naattu naattiyathai America medayiley aadi pugazh adikkaporen…!*' (I will perform our country's dance and earn fame on American stage). Fortuitously, it all came true, for 'Baby' Padma later rose to prominence as the legendary Bharatanatyam dancer Padma Subrahmanyam. She recalled her father as a true taskmaster who believed in taking realistic shots.[1] In one particular scene, the five-year-old girl had to be pushed off a balcony. Being the daughter of the producer-director, no one from the unit was ready to do it. Finally, Subrahmanyam himself had to do it.

Bhakta Vidur (1921): A silent era sensation, with Gandhi-like role on screen, it became the first feature film to be banned under the new censorship system in India.

Balayogini (1936): A saga of the struggle of a Brahmin widow in a caste-ridden society, this was the first film of the trilogy (*Seva Sadanam* and *Thyagabhoomi*) by K. Subramanyam.

Malapilla (1938): Tackling the issue of untouchability, this social drama focused on temple entry movement inspired by Gandhi.

Seva Sadanam (1938): Based on Premchand's Hindi novel, the film highlights Gandhian ideals in critiquing conservative social practices with a woman protagonist leading the reforms.

Brandichi Batli (1939): A brilliant narrative on the evils of alcoholism, delivered in a hilarious manner, that advocated the need for prohibition.

Narsinh Mehta (1940): A tale of popular Gujarati saint–poet, it contained Gandhi's favourite bhajan *Vaishnav Jana To …*

Ram Rajya (1943): The only *Indian* film watched by Gandhi, depicting the story of Ramayana.

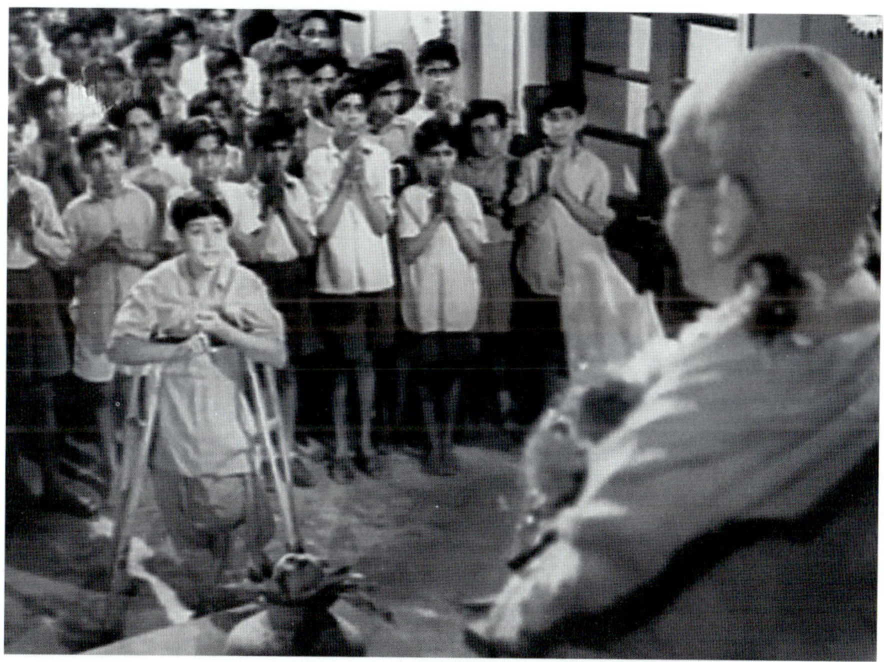

Jagriti (1954): Showcasing a kaleidoscopic vision of newly independent India, with a focus on value education.

Padandi Munduku (1962): With Dandi March as a backdrop, it portrayed struggle against the British economic monopoly.

Bapu Ne Kaha Tha (1962): A film for younger audience with focus on Gandhi's philosophy of truth.

Sachaai (1969): Two friends on the roads of honesty and crime end up meeting in front of a Gandhi statue.

Uttarayanam (1974): A critical yet poignant look at the crumbling values in post-Independence India showcasing conflict between a Gandhian father and his rebellious son.

Sardar (1994): Story of Gandhi's trusted lieutenant, instrumental in the unification of the country after Independence.

Gandhi Se Mahatma Tak (1996): A poignant story of the transformation of a young man into a leader of the masses.

Veer Savarkar (2001): Depicting the life story of a freedom fighter, it vividly portrays the personal hardships and the variance in ideology between Savarkar and Gandhi.

Maine Gandhi Ko Nahin Maara (2005): An intriguing narrative of a retired professor bringing up social and political aspects of Gandhi's assassination in contemporary context.

Lage Raho Munna Bhai (2006): A potent yet hilarious combination of Gandhi and a local Don making Gandhi cool again for younger generations.

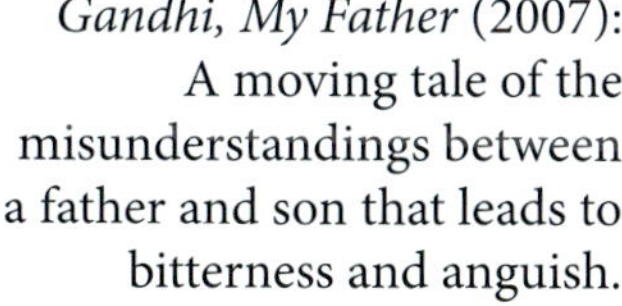

Gandhi, My Father (2007): A moving tale of the misunderstandings between a father and son that leads to bitterness and anguish.

Road to Sangam (2010): With a fictional account about transportation of Gandhi's ashes, it focuses on contemporary political scenes and conflict of identity.

Kurmavatara (2013): A film within a film, it underlines the importance of Gandhian values for sustainable development of the planet.

Images courtesy of NFAI

For good measure, a dance sequence by Lalitha and Padmini of famous Travancore Sisters in the film, was an added attraction. The film had three songs specifically referring to Gandhi; '*Manmohan Das Gandhi*', '*Gandhi Thatha*' (Gandhi, the grandfather) and '*Sonnarodi Gandhi Mahatma*' (Mahatma Gandhi said), written by Meenakshi Subrahmanyam, the filmmaker's wife. In one particular song, '*Parinile Seerongum Naadu Nam India*' (In the world, India's glory will rise), Subramanyam is prophetic in warning the Congress party that merely donning the Gandhi cap and wearing khadi would not get them votes. It had to do real welfare work to win the trust of the people! Despite the strong story and fine performances, the film did not do well … perhaps a sign of the changing times and values.

In the same year, a Bengali film, *42/Biyalish,* based on the Quit India Movement, was released. Directed by Hemen Gupta, the plot was set in Midnapore district during the time of the Movement and focused on Gandhi's peaceful demonstrations. People are stirred into action through a signed communiqué by the local leader conveying Gandhi's clarion call for large-scale participation. The director, Hemen Gupta, had been actively involved in the freedom struggle and had been jailed for five years. A close associate of Subhash Chandra Bose, Gupta had also served as his secretary.

But the film encountered problems with the Censor Board in various states because of a few realistic scenes of violence and cruelty. The government had changed, but not the character of governance. Even in independent India, a film tackling one of the most important chapters of the country's freedom movement had to face the ignominy of a ban. Though it was cleared for screening by the Bombay Censor Board, it could be released in other states only in 1951 after incorporating some changes. Gupta later went on to make an all-time classic, *Kabuliwala*, in 1961.

Gandhi's Non-Cooperation Movement, the agitation at Bardoli and the Quit India Movement featured prominently in the Hindi film *Andolan* in 1951. Veteran filmmaker Phani Mazumdar directed this stridently nationalistic story of India's freedom struggle, covering the major events of the struggle. Produced by Motwane Studios, the film saw the legendary singer-actor Kishore Kumar play a militant hero. Incidentally, it was his first lead role.

Motwane was one of the major newsreel producers in India, and their Chicago Radio System, providing public address facilities, was a constant feature at Congress mass meetings, as also at Gandhi's public rallies. Several old documentary clips of the freedom movement, including a shot of Rabindranath Tagore singing his composition '*Jan Gan Man*', featured in the film. The national song '*Vande Mataram*', rendered by Manna Dey and Sudha Ghosh in the film, still remains in the memory of music lovers.

Two years later, a Marathi film, *Shyamchi Aai* (Shyam's Mother), featuring a Gandhian theme, won the President's Gold Medal for the best film in India. Made in 1953 by a leading Marathi writer and playwright P.K. Atre, the film was based on the well-known Maharashtrian social reformer and writer Sane Guruji's novel of the same name. In the film, the woman (Shyam's mother) is an incarnation of ahimsa. Gandhi had once admitted that he learnt his methods of satyagraha from his mother and wife, and he put it into practice as a major strategy to rebel against the exploitation of India by the British.

The writer Sane Guruji was heavily influenced by Gandhi as well as his staunch disciple Vinoba Bhave and was jailed many times during the Quit India Movement. The fictional novel was a tribute to motherhood, with a touch of earthy philosophy, and also evoked nationalist sentiments. The plot consists of a series of stories told by a young boy about his mother—who was a deeply religious person—and her teachings. The renowned actress Vanamala played the title role of the mother, and the film turned out to be a timeless classic.

Even though various members of Gandhi's family actively took part in the freedom movement, it was Devdas, his fourth and youngest son, who had been constantly present around his father during his private and public activities. Devdas, therefore, featured prominently at his father's side in many newsreels. There were many intimate visuals shot by James Mills on board the SS Rajaputana, that showed a young Devdas massaging Gandhi's weary feet. Apart from taking an active part in the freedom movement as well as being a key member in Gandhi's Hindi propagation programme, Devdas later served as editor of the prominent English newspaper *Hindustan Times*.

When filmmakers, both Indian and foreign, decided to film Gandhi or make a film on him, it was Devdas to whom they turned for advice and guidance. Having been closely involved in his father's activities, he had the mind and material for such projects, and many filmmakers sought him out for help. Unlike his father, Devdas Gandhi knew the importance of cinema very well and had himself produced an hour-long documentary *The Voice of India*, a black-and-white film with commentary in English by Mira Behn (Miss Slade), Pyarelal and himself.

While the film depicted Gandhi as a political leader and presented the human angle of his personality, it also emphasized his greater role as a spiritual teacher. The background music included Western, Indian and Middle-Eastern tunes, and the legendary singer, Gandhi's favourite M.S. Subbulakshmi, lent her voice for the Ramdhun and the bhajans. The Middle-Eastern music included an Egyptian boatman's song. The film was a vivid portrayal of two of the most eventful years of Gandhiji's life, and it has fascinating shots of Gandhi, both at his activities and speaking. The precise period covered by the film was December 1929 to January 1932. There are also a few glimpses from 1947–48. The larger part of the film covers Gandhi's visit to Europe and England in connection with the Second Round Table Conference. The Telugu version of the film was called *Bharat-Vani,* and the Hindi version *Bharat ki Vani.*

Speaking about the film on All India Radio, Devdas Gandhi had said,

> While the film is made up entirely of newsreel material and just a few stills, there are in it several highlights showing Gandhiji speaking. One striking piece is an interview which an enterprising American correspondent had with him in 1931 at Borsad (Gujarat). The correspondent carried his recording equipment to the village on a bullockcart. His plan to interview Gandhiji and to have him filmed at the same time was a creditable success. You see Gandhiji and his

> interviewer, you hear the dialogue and to overcome possible defects in the sound, you also read the talk on the screen in synchronisation with the voice.

Devdas Gandhi also produced two more short films featuring his father. As chairman of The Gandhi Films Committee of the Gandhi National Memorial Trust of India, he made a 400-feet film, *Seaside Prayers,* in 16 mm format, depicting Gandhi's prayer meeting in 1944 at Juhu Beach. The other short, also of 400 feet, was titled *Noakhali. Educational Screen* magazine, in its issue of December 1952, reported these developments and said that these films were the first of a series of documentaries being made by the Committee.

India's freedom had come with a very heavy price of Partition. *Nastik,* a Hindi film made in 1953 by maverick filmmaker I.S. Johar, was based on the bloody Partition and the communal riots that had spread across the north-western parts of India. The protagonist Ajit's parents are killed in sectarian violence, which leads him to lose faith in God. The film makes use of documentary footage of the refugees of Partition to project a realistic environment. The famous song from the film on riots, Partition and Gandhi's relevance, '*Dekh tere sansar ki haalat kya ho gayi Bhagwan, kitna badal gaya insaan*' (Look at the condition of your world O God, the humans have changed so much), written and sung by noted poet Pradeep, appear strikingly pertinent even today.

One of the finest tributes to Gandhi on the silver screen after India attained freedom has been *Mahatma,* which was released in 1953. Simultaneously made in three languages, Marathi, Hindi and English, the film told the poignant story of a Gandhian follower and freedom fighter. Datta Dharmadhikari, who directed this film, had started as a doorkeeper in Prabhat Film Company and went on to become an assistant to V. Shantaram. His ambitious project focusing on Gandhian values had major contributions from Maharashtrian stalwarts like P.L. Deshpande, who wrote the story, and G.D. Madgulkar, who penned the songs.

The film starred veteran actor Gajanan Jagirdar and David Abraham as protagonists. Jagirdar, who later became the first principal of Film Institute of India in 1960, enacted the role of Shidba, a junk-paper buyer who helps to nab a thief. It turns out that the thief had stolen a cycle to pay the medical bills for his pregnant wife. She dies and he is jailed for the petty crime. Shidba repents his act and adopts the thief's daughter. Meanwhile, he wins a crossword puzzle and gets substantial prize money. He donates some money for the destitute and then decides to donate the rest amount to a women's hospital for the cause of free and safe deliveries. But destiny has other plans, and he is fatally wounded by the same thief. He dies with 'Hey Ram' on his lips. The doctor at the hospital has a defining comment on his life when he says, 'From Christ to Gandhi, people like him suffer the same fate!'

The same year, Hearst Metrotone News Studio made a fifty-two-minute documentary, *Mahatma: The Great Soul,* as part of their series 'Perspective on Greatness'. Produced and directed by veteran Canadian filmmaker Harry Rasky, the film starts with a song which says that although Gandhi is gone, his spirit is still everywhere, in the water and the air; Gandhi is immortal. The film with a brilliant narration by noted American actor Sam Jaffe, explored the man and his philosophy in great detail. The footage used is mostly moving images of the time concerning India's freedom movement with major events involving Gandhi as the main focus.

One of the most popular child-centric Hindi films, Satyen Bose's *Jagriti* showcased a kaleidoscopic vision of India with a focus on value education. The story of a rich, spoilt boy crisscrosses with that of a special child. The latter's sacrifice opens the eyes of the rich boy, and he excels in academics and sports. Closely associated with the moral project of nation-building launched by the leaders of newly independent India, the film also highlighted the teachings of Gandhi and celebrated the diversity of the nation. Released in 1954, the film had songs with direct reference to Gandhi, '*Sabarmati Ke Sant Tune Kar Diya Kamal, De Di Hame Azadi bina Khadag bina Dhaal*' (Hey Saint of Sabarmati, you did a miracle, brought freedom without a spear and shield), and '*Aao*

Bachhe Tumhe Dikhaye Jhanki Hindustan Ki' (Come, let us have a look into the rich culture of India), which became very popular, and is now part of cinematic folklore.

The impact of Gandhian values was not only related to mainstream cinema. Few strains of such influence were also visible in languages where the production was relatively less. Therefore, *Piyoli Phukan*, an Assamese film released in 1955, focused on a fictional narrative on the life of Piyoli Phukan, the son of Badan Borphukan, who was chief of Ahom forces from Assam. This great Assamese patriotic leader was among the first to organize an uprising after the Treaty of Yandabo (1926), which ceded Assam to the British empire. The film, directed by Phani Sharma, blended Assamese aspirations with a pan-Indian impulse. Piyoli's characterization presented an example of Gandhian influence in Indian popular cinema.

Gandhi's ideas of love and compassion found one of the best cinematic representations in a 1957 Hindi film, *Do Ankhen Barah Haath* (Two Eyes, Twelve Hands). Master director V. Shantaram's reformist social film focused on the moral empowerment of a band of dreaded prisoners. It was an innovative experiment of an open prison started in the princely state of Aundh in south Maharashtra that caught the attention of Shantaram, who then conceived the idea for this film.

The novel experiment of an open jail was based on the idea that no force should be used while administering the inmates. Shantaram himself played the lead character of an idealistic jailor, Adinath, who takes with him six hardened criminals and tries to transform them through love and compassion. His trust in the ethos of love, truth and moral honesty readily reminded viewers of the Gandhian way of life, where mutual benevolence can bring change to the soul and life of human beings.

Shantaram made effective use of visual language to showcase this transformation cinematically. He shot the film in the 1:1.66 ratio to get the effect of a wide screen and chose the black-and-white medium instead of colour for a more realistic effect. The film, deservedly, got a special Golden Bear at the Berlin International Film Festival, apart from winning many national and international awards. Another special prize the film received was from the International Catholic Bureau, awarded to films depicting humanitarian values, where Charlie Chaplin was one of the members of the jury.

The classic theme of inter-caste romance, once championed by films like *Achhut Kanya* (1936), got a new interpretation in Bimal Roy's 1959 film *Sujata*. The film subtly brought out the Buddhist mythological tale of Chandalika, Gandhi's idea of Harijan politics and Dr B.R. Ambedkar's struggle against casteism in Indian society. Written by Nabendu Ghosh, the film's focus was the practice of caste as one of the major challenges before the newly independent nation.

In 1960, Raj Kapoor, known for the classics *Awara* and *Shree 420*, came up with a film that was largely influenced by the ideals and principles of Gandhi and his disciple Vinoba Bhave. The film, *Jis Desh Mein Ganga Behti Hai* (The country in which the Ganges flows), was directed by Raj Kapoor's cameraman Radhu Karmakar. It chronicled the story of a wandering innocent who reformed a gang of bandits by making them abhor the path of violence. Set on the banks of the holy river Ganga, the main lead, played by Raj Kapoor, convinces the dacoits to lay down their arms and surrender before the law. The songs, '*Hontho pe Sachhai Rehti Hain*' (When there is truth on the lips), '*Aa ab laut chalen*' (Come, let us return), play a critical role in the film, bringing out the principles and ideology, based on truth and love, propagated by Gandhi.

Padandi Munduku, released in 1962 in Telugu, brought back vivid memories of Gandhi's historic Dandi Salt March. Directed by V. Madhusudhana Rao, this film showcased people's participation in the struggle against British economic monopoly. Valorizing Gandhi's leadership in the nationalist struggles, the film also underscored the aspect of Gandhian self-dependence as a fundamental prerequisite for freedom. Inspired by Dilip Kumar's Hindi film *Shaheed* (1948), which was based on India's freedom movement, the veteran Telugu actor Rao decided to make a similar film in Telugu. P. Chengaih wrote the story, which is about a family of freedom fighters that was strongly associated with Gandhi's Salt Satyagraha.

Children always had a very special place in Gandhi's heart. Despite his hectic schedule, he always found time to engage with them by becoming one among them. Therefore, the Children's Film Society of India (CFSI), the government body devoted to making films for younger audiences, decided to produce a film based on Gandhi's teaching. *Bapu Ne Kaha Tha*, a film directed by Vijay Bhatt, was thus released in 1962. It was based on the Gandhian philosophy of truth. It narrated an interesting tale of a village boy Raju, who takes up '*Satyamev Jayate*' as the principle of his life. Written by Krishan Chander, the movie starred veteran character actor Nana Palshikar in the lead role, with Kesari and Narmada Shankar in other roles.

Village development was an agenda dear to Gandhi. He believed in 'Gram Swaraj' (Village Republic) in which the needs of a village would be fulfilled using locally-available resources. A 1964 Kannada film, *Chandavalliya Thota* (Chandavalli Plantation), directed by T.V. Singh Thakore, focused on the problems of rural poverty in India. Based on a novel of the same name by T.R. Subba Rao, the film starring the popular star Raj Kumar turned out to be a landmark one in Kannada cinema. T.R. Subba Rao had participated in the freedom movement and was one of the pioneers of the Navya Movement in Kannada literature.

Hrishikesh Mukherjee was one of the major filmmakers who traversed middle-of-the-road cinema in Hindi industry. He adapted Narayan Sanyal's novel *Satyakam* that presented a saga of human conscience and morality in the midst of corruption, unemployment and increasing violence in post-Independence society. The climax of this film, released in Gandhi's birth centenary year of 1969, shows the grand patriarch, played brilliantly by Ashok Kumar, publicly acknowledging that despite spending his whole life pursuing religion and practising many rituals, he still had much to learn about the nature of truth. He thus passes on a humanist message, much like Gandhi's teaching.

A major Tamil star Sivaji Ganesan's *Bharatha Vilas*, although a drama, was based on the themes of religious unity, secularism and brotherhood, important aspects of patriotism, instilled by Gandhi back then. This Tamil film was a huge success when released in 1973. G. Aravindan, the maestro filmmaker who went on to carve a special place in Indian cinema history, announced his arrival with the debut Malayalam film *Uttarayanam* (Throne of Capricorn) in 1974. It focused on the struggles, both internal as well as spiritual, and decline of ideals in post-Independence India.

Set against the backdrop of the Indian independence struggle, *Uttarayanam* showed the ideological conflict between a Gandhian freedom fighter father and his rebellious son. The 1960s and 1970s were a period of turbulence as the older generation found its hopes dashed and the youth were facing joblessness and insecurity. Based on a story by the playwright Thikkodiyan, the film portrayed the encounters of a young man in search of a job. He meets a series of people, and his journey ends mystically when he meets a godman.

The same year, a short film that took a critical look at the lip service being paid to Gandhi's values by society was produced. Ismail Merchant, in his first directorial venture *Mahatma and the Mad Boy,* used sarcasm most effectively to portray India's class-conscious society. Shot in just five days on Bombay's Juhu Beach in 1973 with a budget of $25,000, the twenty-seven-minute film was produced by Merchant Ivory Productions. The story idea was by the lead actor Sajid Khan, who played a young boy, and it was developed into a script by Tanveer Farooqi. In the time frame of a single day, between dawn and dusk, the film captured the wanderings of a boy who sleeps on the beach and scavenges for food with his monkey. All this while, he engages in conversations with a statue of Mahatma Gandhi on the beach.

Thanks to brilliant camera work by the renowned cinematographer Subrata Mitra, cameraman for many a memorable Satyajit Ray films, who captured Gandhi's statue from several angles to suggest different reactions on Gandhi's part to the banter of the boy. By afternoon, a little ceremony is held at the beach to celebrate Gandhi's concepts of love and brotherhood. A Gandhian speaker delivers a sermon on 'Godly love', but when the little boy comes too close, he is shooed away by a guard, in a pungent travesty of Gandhi's ideas. The film also featured one of the most well-known 'silent' film stars, Sulochana (Ruby Myers), who played the character of a woman who feeds dogs on the beach. The music for the film was composed by Suman Raj, and it featured a sarangi performance by the maestro Ram Narain.[2]

Filmmakers across the country tried to explore in their own regional languages the various principles and ideas professed by Gandhi in their works. After his demise, many cinematic ventures kept the memory of Gandhi alive. Some of these films chose to traverse known paths without taking too much of a cinematic risk. A few them decided to embark on unknown journeys, thereby exploring new idioms of cinema. Some told their stories in an interesting way while some found new ways of telling their stories. One thing was common to all these themes; Gandhi and his ideas. These films also showcased many real-life stories of people inspired by Gandhi and his principles. If cinema is a mirror of the life around, then these stories on the screen kept the memory of Gandhi alive.

* * *

Gandhi had famously wished to live to 125 years of age. But he did not. Had he lived to 125, Gandhi would have been alive in 1994 too! It also meant he would have been present for the celebration of his hundredth birthday in 1969. In India, obviously, his birth centenary was a special occasion and there were several cultural events organized in memory of the Father of the Nation. But, apart from some sporadic films, the domestic film industry did not show much enthusiasm to pay cinematic tribute to the man. Hardly any major film was released that year commemorating Gandhi on screen.

It was the government-owned Films Division that came out with four special short films and documentaries during the year focusing on some specific contributions of Gandhi. A two-reeler film *Porbandar-48 Nayak ni Pol* featured the birthplace of Gandhi. The other three films were on the Harijan problem, women's issues and Gandhiji and the youth. One of them, *India of My Dreams*, was a real stand-out effort.

Directed by Promod Pati, it was a novel documentary showcasing multiple dimensions of Gandhi's personality. The thirteen-and-a-half-minute film did not have any commentary, and not a single image of Gandhi was shown.

The film was a unique visual experience where, 'the three films, projected simultaneously with inter-locking device to ensure frame to frame synchronisation, finally emerging as one with a difference,' according to Ashok Sagar, the cinematographer for the film. Of the three films projected simultaneously, the middle film was shot using a wide-screen process and colour, with a squeeze ratio of 2:1 and an aspect ratio of 1:2.66, which is wider than Cinema Screen. This screen was supported by two side screens on the left and right, these two films being shot in black and white using academic aperture, that is, 0.825 inches by 0.600 inches, with an aspect ratio of 1:1.33.

Despite the limited time and budget at the disposal of the filmmaker, the effort was to maintain consistency in all three films to obtain rhythm and balance. This film was edited by Kalyan Ray. Shot in Ooty in Tamil Nadu, and in Gujarat and Orissa, among other locations, a special auditorium had to be erected in Delhi for its screening. Apart from the selective use of colour, many special techniques like multiple focus and rhythmic zoom were used in the film. In 1927, Abel Gance's silent film *Napoleon* had used for the first time the Polyvision widescreen format spectacularly.

Veteran Marathi producer-director Vasant Joglekar planned his Hindi film *Prarthana* to be made in Gandhi's birth centenary year as a tribute to the Mahatma. Based on Gandhian ideals, particularly on the issue of untouchability, the film starred newcomers Rajnish (Aziz Mirza) and Kanan Kaushal in the lead roles, apart from veterans like Nana Palshikar and Dhumal. Noted writer and playwright Vijay Tendulkar wrote his first screenplay for this film.

The main plot revolved around the evil of untouchability, which persisted even after India's own Constitution was established in the new Republic. Even though the attempt to present the issue was a bold one, the weak manner in which it was dealt with made the film unimpressive.

Pandit Hridaynath Mangeshkar debuted as a composer in the Hindi film industry with this film. (Coincidently, it was also a Vasant Joglekar film, *Aap Ki Sewa Mein* in 1946, in which the singing legend Lata Mangeshkar had started her musical career.)

So, apart from *At Five Past Five* (about which I write in detail in the next chapter) and the two noteworthy films mentioned above, there were no major feature films released during Gandhi's birth centenary that tried to explore Gandhi's life in a realistic manner. Many activities did take place in other art and cultural forums to mark the occasion, but the Indian film industry paid only lip service to Gandhi.

Contrast this with the celebrations of the birth centenary of the Soviet leader Vladimir Lenin, a contemporary of Gandhi and younger by only a few months. The Soviet government not only planned and organized screenings of films focusing on Lenin across the world, but also got many documentary films made afresh. One such screening was held at Strand Cinema in Bombay in 1970, where *The Sixth of July* was shown. It was based on an event in 1918, when forces opposed to Lenin surrounded the Kremlin and tried to overthrow him immediately after he had established the Soviet State. Other films on Lenin shown around the country included *Pages from Lenin* and *The Mother's Devotion*.

While Gandhi disliked movies and overlooked its value, Lenin understood the importance of cinema as a mass medium. Therefore, immediately after the great October Revolution, Lenin issued two decrees, one of which concerned the nationalization of cinema in the Soviet Union. According to writer and filmmaker K.A. Abbas, 'Lenin foresaw the great potentiality of the film as a medium of art. Under the State's patronage, the Soviet cinema flowered, and films made by Sergei Eisenstein and Pudovkin and many others are considered classics in world cinema.'

Lenin was an avid follower of cinema and used to watch films regularly. He had a sound understanding of the methods of cinema as an art and its potential in the cultural space. In all, about thirty-eight films were made on Lenin during his lifetime. Like Vithalbhai Jhaveri's *Mahatma*, a compilation of film footage on Lenin was undertaken in the Soviet Union, out of which a film *Lenin, Ever Living,* was made, directed by Mikhail Romm and Maria Slavinskaya. The first version of it was released in 1948. Auteur Sergei Eisenstein used his theory of montage very effectively in dramatizing the Russian Revolution in *October* (1928), projecting Lenin.

In a major coincidence, the birth centenary of Gandhi was celebrated almost at the same time as not only Lenin's, but also D.G. Phalke's, known as the Father of Indian Cinema.

Even though Gandhi's life is full of drama with many ups and downs in both his personal and public journey, it was his actions after he came back from South Africa to India that have received maximum attention from filmmakers. But much before Shyam Benegal thought about depicting the transformation of Mohandas Gandhi into a Mahatma, it was K.A. Abbas who had first conceived such an idea in 1969. Abbas, a leading writer and filmmaker, who had famously written an open letter to Gandhi in 1939 urging him to change his opinion of cinema, focused his energies on telling the story of Gandhi's evolution in South Africa in a film as a mark of tribute to the great man.

Weaponless Warrior was the tentative title of the motion picture script on the early life of Gandhi in South Africa that Abbas wrote, in collaboration with the Gujarati author and playwright Pragji Dossa. The film was to be made for the Mahatma Gandhi Centenary Charitable Trust founded by Champaklal Dadhawala, a Gujarati industrialist. Both writers carried out extensive research and worked on the script for almost eight months. The plan was to release the film in the Gandhi centenary year, 1969, but unfortunately, nothing came of it.

Even though the film could not be made, a play on the same theme with a different title, *Barrister-at-Law*, by Abbas and Dossa was staged in 1977. Since the original script was for a film, even the play had all the qualities of a screenplay. Thus, it had four acts and sixty-one scenes. Each scene was written as if for a film frame and was short for better impact. The writers even provided detailed instructions for the lighting, costumes and sets.

It was an honest effort to present Gandhi as a man whose views were forming on issues like discrimination based on race, caste and colour, and on untouchability and imperialism. The play ends with Gandhi's return to India. That was only the beginning of Gandhi's story in India, of course. Abbas wrote:

> And so ends the tale of the struggle in South Africa, a war fought by a Weaponless Warrior, a Barrister-at-law, who chose to be an advocate of his people. But this is not the end. It is the beginning of the end of a non-violent revolution that was to follow in India for the liberty of a nation whose aspiration and growth was strangled by Imperialism. He was not a man but a Mahatma, a great soul who dedicated his life, sacrificed himself to hold aloft the banner of humanity, of love and truth, and the freedom of man![3]

For the Indian maestro Satyajit Ray, the birth and phenomenal growth of cinema was one of the most important events of the nineteenth century. Ray was instrumental in putting Indian cinema firmly on the world map through his Apu Trilogy—*Pather Panchali* (1955), *Aparajito* (1956) and *Apur Sansar* (1959)—and other notable films. Naturally, people expected him, an auteur, to bring Gandhi's life on screen. Gandhi's birth centenary year was an appropriate time, many thought, for Ray to embark on such a project.

But the great filmmaker was not convinced at all about such a project. It was not that Ray was against making biopics. He had already made a documentary depicting the life of the poet-philosopher Rabindranath Tagore in 1961, and later made one on the Bharatanatyam dancer Bala Saraswati in 1976. But about a film on Gandhi, his reasoning was very clear and rational. When asked specifically about such an idea at the special screening of his film *Goopy Gayen Bagha Bayan* at the British Film Institute in London in July 1969, Ray turned down all such suggestions. 'No actor could play the part of Gandhi,' he said in London.[4]

Ray felt that Gandhi's presence was so deep in the Indian consciousness and his imagery so firmly entrenched in the psyche of the Indian people that no actor could ever do justice to even attempt to convey his aura for the silver screen. Therefore, even though the idea of making a biopic on Gandhi was very good, Satyajit Ray said he was not at all interested in making one.

Lenin was lucky to have Sergei Eisenstein, who fictionalized his image cinematically, forcefully and effectively. Even though the circumstances and contexts in India and Russia are different, one can say that Gandhi has not found any filmmaker to do full justice to his enigmatic mystique.

The celebrations of Gandhi's birth centenary were not limited to India only. British Broadcasting Corporation (BBC), a public service broadcaster from Britain and a leading television network in the world, decided to revisit Gandhi's life for the screen. Accordingly, a five-member team of the BBC, led by producer Jonathan Stedall, made a fifty-five-minute television film, *Gandhi's India,* on the influence of Gandhi's philosophy on Indian life. The crew, consisting of cameraman John McGlashan, sound recordist Dave Brinicombe and camera assistant Cyrus Bharucha, went around visiting various parts of India on their six-week-long shooting schedule.

Stedall was very clear in his brief: the film was not only to tell Gandhi's story but also analyse how Gandhi's ideas have survived even twenty years and more after his death. He actively collaborated with the renowned economist E.F. Schumacher and co-scripted the film with Hallam Tennyson. The film, a co-production of BBC, National Educational Television of the United States and the Canadian and Australian Broadcasting Corporations, was shown on television in the four countries simultaneously in October 1969.[5]

German television networks also explored Gandhi's life in specially commissioned documentaries to mark the occasion. Surprisingly, they chose a young Indian filmmaker, George T. Paruvanani, to write and direct the short films. Paruvanani was born in Kerala and had studied in West Germany, where he wrote his Ph.D. thesis on the German film industry. *Das Erbe Gandhis* (Gandhi's Legacy) was a thirty-minute documentary in German, focusing on Gandhi's legacy in post-Independence India. It was produced by Zweites Deutsches Fernsehen (ZDF) and released in 1970. Another short film, *Vergessen–Verehrt–Ein Inder Rauf Gandhis Spuren* (Forgotten–Revered–An Indian in Gandhi's Footsteps), written and directed by Paruvanani, was released on 21 September 1969 on Westdeutscher Rundfunk (WDR) television network in Germany.

It is hard to imagine the two Hindi film stars Shammi Kapoor and Sanjiv Kumar with their contrasting styles of acting coming together in a film, and that too one claiming to propagate Gandhi's message. But a veteran south Indian director, K. Shankar, did bring them together in a film, *Sachaai,* in Hindi. It was released on Gandhi's birth centenary year. The film showcased a curious journey of two friends going through various challenges in life.

The road of honesty and morality meets with the road of crime with the chance meeting of the protagonists after many years. Kapoor and Kumar portray these two friends who meet after many years in front of a statue of a smiling Gandhi. The stone bearing the statue has the sentence '*Jhooth ke lakho raaste, sachaai ki ek dagar*' (The lie has a million ways but truth has only one path) written on it.

But the filmmaker was not confident that the combined stardom of Kapoor and Kumar would be enough to spread the message of Gandhi. So the popular dancer-actress Helen was brought in to add oomph to sell the idea. Accordingly, a sizzling 'champagne bottle dance' number was conceived to attract audiences. Advertised as a special attraction of the movie, Helen, along with twelve semi-clad dancers, danced in specially made life-sized glasses.

To make these twelve huge glass bottles, the production house called for a tender, which was won by a Bombay-based firm. The song, '*Kab Se Bhari Hai Saaqi, Botal Sharaab Ki' (The cupbearer has long since filled the bottle with wine),* was written by well-known lyricist Rajendra Krishan. Ironically, Krishan had penned one of the most popular songs on the virtues of Gandhi, '*Suno Suno Aye Duniya Walo Bapu Ki Ye Amar Kahani*' (O People of the World, Lend an ear to Bapu's immortal Story), just few months after Gandhi had passed away in 1948. A young twenty-four-year-old Mohammad Rafi had sung it to the tune of the renowned composer pair Husnlal–Bhagatram and it became a huge hit.

More than 500 workers toiled hard for seventy days to make these huge champagne glasses. The glasses were then transported from Bombay to a Madras studio where the dance sequence was shot. Helen wore four different dresses for the song. As part of the dance sequence, she had to keep her feet splashing about in the fake liquor at the bottom of the bottle. The film's publicity campaign featured these large champagne bottles prominently, with the Gandhian message from the film relegated to the background.

'World's greatest and costliest dance on the screen!' declared the film poster proudly. Call it a travesty or a sheer lack of empathy on the part of the film industry that the Gandhian values had to be promoted in India in a film with a champagne bottle dance, and that too in his birth centenary year!

13

Three Shots to Eternity

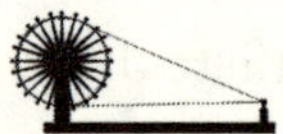

THREE SHOTS FIRED FROM close range ended the life of Gandhi. The incident had all the ingredients of intrigue and suspense. A dramatic death, and that too of a famous person, is readymade material for the screen any day. Even so, it took many years after his death for filmmakers to look back at the tragic incident. Perhaps the dangerous mix of ideology and passion that led to Gandhi's murder was too sensitive a subject to take artistic liberties with. Opinions were sharply divided on both sides, and it would have been difficult to depict the episode dispassionately and, given the circumstances, too risky to portray his death at all.

But two films, both made in English, did attempt to explore the theme of Gandhi's assassination cinematically. Even though the focus of these two films was the same, their interpretation and treatment were vastly different. One was an Indian film, and the other a joint US-UK production. Some of the well-known artistes from both India and the USA were part of these two films, which had strong technical teams for support.

Even years after his death, Gandhi as a subject for the screen was a hot potato and the filmmakers soon realized it. It was not only their interpretation but also the very subject that perhaps spelled doom for these two films. The foreign film, a production of 20th Century Fox, was banned by the Indian government while the Indian film went into the wilderness, never to be seen.

The first film to release was the foreign production *Nine Hours to Rama,* in 1963. Fifteen years after Gandhi was assassinated, veteran Hollywood director Mark Robson decided to make a film to look at the tragic incident in a fresh light. Based on well-known author Stanley Wolpert's novel of the same name, this 125-minute English film is a fictionalized account of Gandhi's assassination, told from his killer's point of view.

Wolpert, a professor of history, had focused on Gandhi's assassin Nathuram Godse and had dwelt on the nine crucial hours before the killing. Nelson Gidding wrote the script and the characters of Godse and Gandhi were played by Horst Bucholtz and an Indian actor J.S. Casshyap, respectively. The publicity material for the film advertised it as 'Nine terror-filled hours of running, hiding, waiting to commit the murder that would change the lives of millions!'[1]

Months after Wolpert's book was published in London, the government of India decided to ban it. According to a report in *Times of India*, no reason had been cited as to why the book had been banned, but the paper mentioned that Godse's portrayal in the book was 'in wrong perspective and that some portions were liable to hurt the feelings of various sections'. Even though the critics had said the book was in poor taste, the ban, which happened in 1963, generated curiosity about as well as publicity for it. The author Wolpert, who was a prolific Indologist, criticized the ban and appealed to the Nehru government to lift it. Years later, in 2001, he went on to write a biography of Gandhi. Incidentally, he also wrote a biography of M.A. Jinnah, a political adversary of Gandhi.

Even before the book was published, the Academy Award-nominated director Mark Robson had purchased its screen rights. He had planned to make a film on it with the title, *Day of Darkness*, but changed it later to *Nine Hours to Rama*. Robson possibly knew the pitfalls of the project and was quick in planning the production. In fact, he had obtained the necessary permissions from Indian government authorities well before the book was banned in India.

He showed the same efficiency in shooting too—lived in India for three months and managed to complete it at various locations, including Delhi, Bombay, Poona and Nashik. The Delhi locations included Yusuf Sarai, the actual Birla Garden and Ladu-ki-Sarai villages, besides Red Fort and Chandni Chowk. In fact, the Delhi schedule was completed in two months, over November and December 1961.[2] Another report claimed that Robson managed to shoot some scenes from overhead by means of a helicopter. 'It was the first-time scenes have ever been permitted to be filmed from the air, just as this is the first picture ever made about the character of Gandhi.'[3]

In an irony of sorts, even though the entire focus of the film was on Gandhi's assassin Godse and his activities, the film opens with a quote by Gandhi on the screen:

> 'It is impossible for us to realise the perfect truth as long as we are imprisoned in this mortal frame. We can visualise it in our imagination. That is why in the last resort we must depend on faith - Mahatma Gandhi.'

It is followed by a disclaimer: 'Except for certain actual events, places and people, what you are about to see is historical fiction.' It was a clever ruse by the filmmaker to avoid any controversies the film might encounter by making it plain and clear that it was a fictionalized account of one of the most important and tragic events in India's history.

As the credit starts rolling with a piece of background music that is distinctly Indian instrumental, a clock is shown ticking with the time. The music was composed and conducted by Malcolm Arnold, who had won the Academy award for the David Lean epic *The Bridge on the River Kwai* in 1957. Academy Award-nominated cinematographer, Arthur Ibbetson, was the director of photography. He was later nominated for best cinematography at BAFTA for *Nine Hours to Rama*. The screenplay of the film was written by American screenwriter Nelson Gidding, yet another artist on the team who had received a nomination for an Academy Award. It was a strong Hollywood team of competent professionals that had come together for the project.

The opening scene shows a train speeding fast towards Delhi on 30 January 1948, the fateful day of Gandhi's assassination. A goat is stranded on the tracks, and a shepherd boy rescues it just in time before it comes under the train. It is an ominous sign of things to happen on that day. At the other end of Delhi, a police team has swung into action after a tip-off about a possible attack on Gandhi. As the senior police officer reaches the railway station, a man is lying in his room, deep in thought. While the clock strikes, he takes out a pistol hidden below his pillow. There is another accomplice in the room, and they wait for the train to arrive, bearing the third colleague who will join them.

The police party catches him at the railway station and his interrogation begins. An astrologer is consulted by the Police as to when the attempt is going be made because the fanatic secret society to which the men belong believes in auspicious timings. He replies, 'There is no auspicious day or time to kill a saintly man but to kill an evil man, it is today before sundown.' So, it is established that Gandhi was an evil man in the minds of his murderers.

The action shifts to Birla House, where Gandhi is sitting and doing what he loves the most—spinning the charkha. A minister and a police officer arrive there and apprise him about the impending attack. G.D. Birla, the industrialist-owner of the house, played by veteran Indian actor P. Jairaj, informs Gandhi about the sinister plot. Gandhi responds with his typical wry humour: 'Birla, do not bend over me so much as if I am a stone image in a temple!' When they try to caution him about the imminent danger to his life, Gandhi replies, 'But it has always been so, my child! If they want to destroy me, it is for my sins, not for their own. If I am killed violently, it is because I have failed.'

This scene is a vivid portrayal of Gandhi's principles that he had espoused in his entire life and how he chose to adhere to them till his last breath. Eventually, he doesn't permit the police officer to carry a gun and protect him at the prayer meeting, simply because it was against his values. 'I will not save my life by surrendering to the gun this late in my day' is his logic.

Even though Robson managed to shoot the film discreetly in India, he encountered many problems during the production. As it is, there was growing unrest in the Indian film industry about the liberal policy of the Nehru government in welcoming Western directors to shoot in India. Several requests by Hollywood filmmakers to make biopics on Gandhi had received approval from the Indian government, and this was resented by the local industry.

The scandal Italian maestro Roberto Rossellini caused in India in 1957 had further angered Indian filmmakers. The red-carpet welcome Rossellini received from the Indian government, when he famously came on the special invitation of Prime Minister Nehru to make a film on India, and his subsequent association with a married Indian actress who eloped with him, created ripples in Indian society in general and the film industry in particular.

With questions being asked about the permissions granted for Robson's controversial Gandhi film, the government decided to tread cautiously. Accordingly, in May 1962, the minister of information and broadcasting, B. Gopala Reddi, announced that Robson had entered into 'a gentleman's agreement' with the government of India that he would not exhibit the film even outside India without first showing it to Indian official representatives and obtaining their approval.[4]

Thus, a special screening of the film was held for Prime Minister Nehru and his cabinet colleagues on 2 January 1963 at Rashtrapati Bhavan in New Delhi. *Times of India* reported that the President of India Dr S. Radhakrishnan had already seen the film the previous day.[5] But the uproar over the scurrilous nature of the film had not died down and many members of Parliament raised the issue next month. While answering to various questions, Dr Reddi, the minister of information and broadcasting, told the Lok Sabha on 27 February 1963 that permission of the government was not necessary for shooting a film in

India. The government, however, did not raise any objection for this particular film being shot in India.[6]

The minister, then informed that the government has decided not to approve the exhibition of the film (Nine Hours to Rama) in India. 'Government feels that the film has failed to bring out the personality of Gandhiji in its true light and that the film, as made, is likely to cause resentment to many people in India,' the minister announced.[7] To a specific question about whether the script was seen by the Ministry before the shooting commenced, Dr Reddi said, 'It was seen by the Ministry, but there were various deviations from the main script in the course of shooting of the film.'[8]

When asked about the course of action the government wants to take as the film was being shown outside India, the Minister clarified, 'When we approved the script or when we said "no objection", this did not carry any approval of the government. We take no responsibility of the picture being made … but as we cannot enforce our decision outside, we have kept quiet.'[9]

Not satisfied with these answers, another member asked whether the government would take up this issue with other governments. This time, it was Prime Minister Nehru who intervened and gave a detailed answer:

> I do not think it is correct to call it (the film) scurrilous. It is very mistakenly made and the ideas of the maker of the film, I feel sure, were not in any way deliberately to defame Gandhiji or anything in India. Of course, their thinking is different and the whole concept of the film is based on other reasons.

He further said:

> In the film itself, Gandhiji comes very little and the person who is supposed to represent Gandhiji, well, lacks dignity, lacks all that is required. They probably got someone who was physically resembling Gandhiji but who is otherwise completely different from one's conception of Gandhiji.[10]

What Nehru observed was true, as Gandhi comes in only in the last few pages in the original book, so in a way the focus is entirely on Godse and his viewpoint rather than on Gandhi and his ideology. Thus, the actual screen presence of Gandhi is only for about ten minutes in a more than two hours long film.

Veteran Film Society activist and filmmaker Vijaya Mulay found the film full of myths and clichés and said,

> Godse's character in this film is given more prominence than that of Gandhi. I have no quarrel with Godse being made a central figure, except that the film does not explore the complexity of the opposition to Gandhi's ideas and actions; it merely repeats imperial and postcolonial myths and clichés and spends considerable footage depicting the improbable involvement of Godse with a young white woman. What is worse, this film trivializes India's struggle for independence.[11]

The American press, though, was not swayed by the emotions in India and gave mostly positive reviews to the film, praising it as conforming to the original book on which it was based. *Daily Express* in its review said, 'The film smells of the heat and dust of Delhi.' A review in *Daily Mail* said, 'The film, embracing the whole paradox of the Indian scene, is pictorial triumph ... unforgettably tense and touching.' [12] The *Box Office* reported on the premiere held in London and said the performance of J.S. Casshyap as Gandhi was a piece of stupendous character acting. Hollywood-based *Film Bulletin* commented, 'Despite some slow-moving sequences, the film emerges a fascinating canvas of political intrigues, suspense and exotic sights and sounds.'

The Indian character actor J.S. Casshyap, who played the small role of Gandhi in the film, was a veteran artiste from Bombay Talkies, a major production house in India in the 1930s and 1940s. Casshyap had also played a major role with celebrated star Devika Rani in *Jawani ki Hawa,* which was directed by Franz Osten in 1935. Starting as a writer, Casshyap went on to write songs for many films.

Mark Robson had searched for artistes to play Gandhi's role by putting out an advertisement in Indian newspapers. Casshyap was aware of his uncanny resemblance to Gandhi and sent in his application. When Robson saw his photograph, with makeup on, he knew Casshyap was his man as Gandhi. In a small role that had a screen time of only about ten minutes, Casshyap tried his best to portray Gandhi with his sober mannerisms and dialogue delivery.

During the climax, the film shows Gandhi forgiving Godse for the 'crime' he had committed before succumbing to the bullets. In a Christ-like gesture, Gandhi says, 'I forgive you, my brother. I bless you. Hey Ram!' Godse is shown shocked at Gandhi's words and kneels before the body, touching Gandhi's feet while murmuring and crying, 'I killed him, and he blessed me!' While he is dragged away from Gandhi, he moans, 'Bapuji!' Was this meant to be an act of repentance on Godse's part? Even if the film is a work of fiction, it was historically wrong, because Godse never really repented his act.

If cinema is an art of make-believe, this film failed miserably in achieving it. That the makers were not clued into the culture of India was clearly evident in a scene where they had a Bharatanatyam dance sequence, a south Indian classical dance performance, in a marriage ceremony happening in the heartland of Maharashtra in western India. Though the film is technically strong in most departments, the foreign accents of the major characters cannot be brushed away, and it is jarring to hear their dialogues.

The only credible character was that of the police superintendent Gopal Das, played convincingly by Jose Ferrer, à la Balraj Sahni. A Puerto Rican actor, Jose Ferrer had already won the Academy Award for best actor in 1950 for the adventure film *Cyrano de Bergerac*. The Indian character actor David Abraham played a junior police staff in the film.

One has to admit that the film did try to present an alternative viewpoint, represented by Godse, which had not been attempted on screen before. Since the focus was Gandhi's assassin, there are hardly any scenes in which Gandhi appears in the film, and the narrative gives short shrift to his ideology of love, peace and non-violence. Until then, the film industry had portrayed Gandhi in a positive light only and had not really attempted to explore alternative viewpoints different from his. Therefore, the film could have been a welcome change, in so far as exploration and understanding another point of view goes. But, in the end, that was the only novelty in the film.

One major flaw of the film was the casting of foreign actors of various nationalities in a totally Indian setting. Why on earth this was done, and that too for such an important film, one cannot understand. It made the whole exercise inauthentic and unbelievable. Putting brown paint on white faces and making them act as Indians was a laughable idea. By this logic, can anyone imagine an Indian film about the murder of American President J.F. Kennedy without white actors featuring in it?

The film, much anticipated elsewhere but banned in India, was released in the USA, UK, and some countries in Europe in 1963. A major publicity drive was launched for the film, with producer-director Robson touring America's key cities from coast to coast, giving interviews on radio and appearing on television. 20th Century Fox planned an arrangement with publisher Random House on Wolpert's novel so that both, the book and film, could receive maximum benefit from each other.

Full page advertisements in the book review sections of the New York Times and Chicago Tribune were planned that discussed the book as well as its screen version. 'It is expected by 20th Fox that the book will reach the top of the charts and remain there through the premier of the film in the fall, thus exploiting the name of the property continuously before the public,'[13] said one media report.

All these efforts didn't help, and the film failed miserably at the box office. Years later, it premiered on Hungarian television in 1978. With the advent of digital technology, the film is now available on YouTube. Though banned in India long back, about 50,000 people had seen it, at the time of writing this book, after it was uploaded on the platform in 2016.

At Five Past Five

A team of four conspirators is on a mission to kill an old man, the Mahatma. Hours before the incident, one of them develops cold feet and is uncertain about killing an individual instead of simply opposing his thoughts. The other three then decide to hold a mock trial to win back the dissenter. A flurry of accusations is hurled at an invisible Gandhi and a very strong defence is made before the audience present in court, which represents the citizens of India. This was a brave and innovative approach to explore such a sensitive but evocative topic on screen. An experimental film made in English titled *At Five Past Five* explored such a bold approach and was timely released in 1969, to mark Gandhi's birth centenary year.

The film starts with a unique opening sequence. For the first few minutes, the screen is blank, with only instrumental music being played, featuring tabla, flute and sitar. Only audio in the beginning is a bold start. One is inclined to believe that the black screen was intended as a cinematic tribute to Gandhi. Renowned composer Vasant Desai aptly scored the opening tune of '*Vaishnav Jan To*', Gandhi's favourite bhajan, as the credit titles rolled.

The audio start is followed by a few tense moments with images of grim-looking surroundings. A clock indicates the time is 3.30 p.m. A man is juggling with a pistol in his hand as the clock ticks away. He is tense and in deep thought, and his movements are uneasy. It is clear to the audience he is the man who is supposed to fire at Gandhi. There is nervousness writ large on his face. Even though there is intent and resolve on his part, the final moments before the crime are unnerving, even for a committed assassin.

Suddenly, a loud voice is heard: 'You will be executed in public!' The intentions of the plot are revealed with a bang. There is turmoil in the air and fast-paced visuals follow, enhancing the tension. Desai makes use of effective background sounds to make it more dramatic. There is no direct reference to Gandhi in the film, but the victim is identified as someone born in Porbandar.

Based on the Hindi play *Hatya Ek Akar Ki* written by Lalit Sehgal, the film was directed by Kumar Vasudev, a student of the first batch at Film and Television Institute of India (FTII). (Kumar Vasudev later directed the iconic television serial *Hum Log* for the public broadcaster Doordarshan in 1984–85.) The story was adapted for the screen in English by the well-known actor and filmmaker Zul Vellani. The original play was written in 1967 for the Gandhi Centenary Celebrations Committee and was staged in Delhi and Calcutta to wide critical acclaim.

Initially, it was planned to have the film made in Hindi too, titled *Hatya Ek Akar Ki*. And the original title of the English version was *The Verdict*. New Dimension Enterprises had presented a powerful defence of Gandhian ideology in this seven-reeler courtroom drama. Vimal Ahuja produced the film and also played a major role in it. The film featured veteran actors Zul Vellani, David and Iftikhar. 'Ever since we first saw the play,' Ahuja pointed out, 'Kumar Vasudev and I both dreamed of making a film out of it.' [14]

The characters portrayed in the film are symbolic and represent the assassin (Vimal Ahuja), the brain behind the conspiracy (Iftikhar), the means that actuated it (David), and the conscience of the man to be killed as well as defence counsel (Zul Vellani). Another FTII alumni, Amar Bose, edited the film. Bose had edited Mani Kaul's pathbreaking film *Uski Roti*. A close associate of Hrishikesh Mukherjee, Bose had also edited Bimal Roy's *Sujata* (1959) and *Parakh* (1960), and Merchant Ivory's *Shakespeare Wallah* (1965).

Yet another Bimal Roy colleague, Kumar Bose, who had shot most of Roy's iconic movies, including *Sujata, Bandini, Parinita, Do Bigha Zamin*, and *Devdas,* helmed the camera. The film was shot, starting from 22 June 1969, on a single set at Rajkamal Studios in Bombay, where an imaginary courtroom in the basement of a building was created. The studio owner, the legendary filmmaker V. Shantaram, reportedly visited the set and complimented the young team for their novel approach.

Before leaving for their mission to kill Gandhi, four persons are shown engaged in an argument. In fact, there are five people party to this dastardly act, and we come to know that the fifth has just been arrested. Then one among them, clad in a simple khadi kurta and pyjamas, played by Zul Vellani, refuses to accompany them and questions the very act, a heinous one, that they are going to commit. He says: 'Is it right? A peaceful demonstration will be better.' This angers the other three conspirators and they accuse him of being a coward. His response is calm and measured, 'We don't hate him personally.' The other three are unmoved. According to them, this was the last chance they had on that particular day. 'Let's go without him,' is their response, as everything had been planned. Still, the group, now jittery, wants to make a last-minute effort to win over the dissenter. 'We must make him reconsider.'

They decide that the best way to break the deadlock is to hold a mock trial. Gandhi, not present physically, is charged with various accusations, with history acting as the prosecutor. Iftikhar's character stands in the witness box and claims he is the definitive history of Indian Independence. He starts by saying, 'I am proud of his (Gandhi the accused) period in South Africa', but then goes on to make one accusation after another against Gandhi. The first accusation is that Gandhi abused all political revolutionaries. There are people in the audience representing the common masses from all corners of the country. They shout, 'Shame! Shame!' Gandhi's character has his response ready, 'Violence is always wrong. Moreover, my speech has been misreported.'

The second accusation follows, 'Then why did he oppose them (the revolutionaries who believed in armed struggle)?' The third accusation is to do with Gandhi's differences with his colleagues like Netaji Subhash Chandra Bose. The fourth questions his stance on the Second World War. The doubting one among them defends Gandhi, referring to his real quotes and speeches. It is a spirited defence. 'My ideology is not personal. Our aims must be noble as well as [our] means,' he says. The people present in the court support Gandhi's character. Since the people are on Gandhi's side, the conspirators are in a fix and the court has to be adjourned. Another allegation is about the Khilafat Movement, and Gandhi's response, and the actual facts, are supplied. Again, there is unanimous support for Gandhi's character from the audience in the courtroom.

The rest of the three conspirators are now nervous. Their plan has gone haywire. The aggressive man with the pistol says, in a resigned tone, 'I won't have the energy to pull the trigger. Ask for a compromise.' The usual allegation about Gandhi's purported concession to minorities is hurled. Again, a defence is offered with facts. Now, the three conspirators become edgy. They have exhausted their list of allegations, all of which were based on half-truths and hearsay only.

History is based on facts and a judge needs to be impartial and neutral, but here it is made clear that they are not what they should be. The courtroom trial is just a ploy to somehow justify the ultimate ghastly act they have planned to commit. Left with no option, they decide, 'We must find him guilty.' And the judge pronounces his verdict, 'You will be executed in public.' Then the clock strikes; it is 5 p.m.

The voice-over gives the audience a complete historical perspective. Right from the crucifixion of Christ to the American Civil War and Abraham Lincoln, it has happened again and again, it says. In the end, the three conspirators leave the court and three loud pistol shots are heard in the background, and a feeble voice saying 'Hey Ram!' The last and final sentence heard on screen tells the attacker and viewers in no uncertain words, 'You fool, you have killed only the body, not his principles!'

It is Zul Vellani whose steadfast defence of Gandhian ideology stands out as the performance to watch out for in the film. Vellani was known for his unique voice, an integral element of some of the best-known documentaries made by Films Division. He also directed a few critically acclaimed documentaries: *Khajuraho* and *Man in search of Man*. In this film, he effortlessly portrays the character who defends Gandhi and his values. While doing so, he gradually gets transformed into a staunch follower of Gandhi, and one can feel the spirit of Gandhi in his character. Vellani was born in Mombasa and went on to obtain a diploma in direction from a London polytechnic. He acted in various short and feature films, including Conrad Rook's *Siddhartha* with Shashi Kapoor. He also lent his voice for the commentary for a seminal album by Lata Mangeshkar, named 'Lata recites Bhagwat Geeta and Dnyaneshwari', brought out by The Gramophone Company of India.

Vellani, who wore different hats as an actor, director, scriptwriter, and commentator, was also a keen follower of Gandhi. In fact, there was a deep personal connection he had with the Father of the Nation. When Gandhi was assassinated, Vellani's mother-in-law was present near Gandhi, just a few feet away, at Birla House. It was she who had held the falling body of the Mahatma in her lap, and her saree with Gandhi's bloodstains is a sacred possession of the family. Naturally, Vellani was most excited to be offered the role in the film. For him, portrayal of the character was a homage to his leader. 'The new generation does not know Gandhi well. The political leaders pay only lip service to Gandhi while killing his principles in day-to-day life. Therefore, it was necessary to bring forth Gandhi's ideals in a dramatic manner,' he said.[15]

Vimal Ahuja played the character of the most decisive man of the team, who has resolved to carry out the assassination at any cost. Throughout the movie, his character is shown to be living on the edge, and all his actions are aggressive. At the same time, the enormity of the job leaves him nervous and jittery in the face of the stout defence of Gandhi during the trial. Ahuja, a stage actor born in Rawalpindi, portrayed these minute nuances vividly, and his character is also to watch out for in the film. Ahuja had made his screen debut as the main character in an iconic thriller film *Bambai Raat Ki Bahon Mein* in 1967, which was directed by the prolific K.A. Abbas.

Veteran actor David Abraham once again came on board to essay a character in a Gandhi-related film. Having played a police officer in *Nine Hours to Rama*, the character actor portrayed the role of one of the conspirators who also acts as the judge in the mock courtroom trial. Since the legal drama is just a charade and the verdict is a foregone conclusion, the character of the judge is shown busy eating all the time, caring two hoots for what Gandhi's character has to say. David was convinced that the film was a bold and earnest attempt to spread the Gandhian values of truth and non-violence among the masses.

Talking about the movie in an interview, David said:

> Even though there are four characters in the movie, the focus is essentially on the thoughts and turmoil going on in the mind of the main assassin. The film attempts to put forth the clash of ideologies in a coherent manner and in the process has turned the original play into a beautiful film ... some bold people in this film industry once in a while attempt to do something different and experimental. Irrespective of whether such an attempt receives support or not from masses, at least intelligentsia should support such efforts.[16]

Iftikhar, another fine character actor, plays the part of 'time and history', which does not have anything to say of its own but makes use of Gandhi's quotes to raise allegations. Iftikhar said of his role in the film, whose importance he appreciated:

> I was very happy to be part of such an experimental film. There was no star on the set and everyone was equal who worked as a team. We got the script with dialogues ready fifteen days before the actual shoot and each one of us knew what was to be done. It resulted in the film being made in flat 16 days ... This film is not made with profit in mind. It is essential that such efforts receive the support so that filmmakers are encouraged to experiment in future too.[17]

Shot in courtroom drama style, the film puts the focus on the values and principles of Gandhi while throwing away the falsehoods and lies spread in his name. 'The symbolic courtroom drama is a graphic representation of the age-long conflict in man, between his conscience and motives,' said Vasudev.[18] He was convinced about the topic he had taken on. 'It has happened so many times in human history. The crucifixion of Christ and the assassination of Lincoln and Gandhi are examples of this. But conscience has always endured and prevailed, as history has borne out.'[19] It is made plain to the audience how many lies and wrong facts have been spread in the name of Gandhi. The accusers are smart enough to pick up the commonly held rumours about Gandhi in the society. The rumours are dressed up to hoodwink the common man and appeal to the popular consciousness.

Gandhi's character, defended convincingly by Zul Vellani, is shown as the composed one who never loses his cool. Though he is assertive in putting the right facts in front of the court and thereby in front of the whole society, there is a certain agony in his voice. An agony of having to defend his moral acts that are deep-rooted in Indian culture. With his deep baritone and composed voice, Vellani pulls off the role in a most convincing manner. The character is sure that the conspiracy being planned is morally and ethically wrong. Therefore, he disagrees with the idea of killing someone just because one does not agree with that person's thoughts.

He is allowed to refer to Gandhi's books and speeches during the proceedings of the trial, and that turns him into a strong believer of Gandhi's ideas and principles. The transformation of his character in the movie is revealing and educative. A lot of wrong information and falsehoods have been spread about Gandhi over the years in systematic campaigns, their objective being to vilify him and relegate him to a corner, to be ignored and forgotten. The film succeeds in tearing into every such attempt and putting the record straight.

Released in the birth centenary year of Gandhi, *At Five Past Five* was a stark reminder of his tragic assassination. The film also put the focus back on Gandhi's persona as the keeper of human consciousness and reconfirmed his place in the annals of world history. At the International Film Festival of India in 1969, the film won its director P. Kumar Vasudev the International Gandhi Award. It was Lalit Sehgal, the writer of the Hindi play, who had first approached Vasudev for making it into a film.

While Vasudev was busy exploring production houses in Madras, Sehgal found someone else to make the film. But things did not work out and the search continued, till Vimal Ahuja came forward to produce it. 'The plan was to get some big stars initially, but since the film was in English it was dropped. Moreover, [a] few image-conscious stars declined to play the role of assassin. After three months, we identified and found the actors suitable for the roles,' said Vasudev.[20] His approach was 'expressionism' instead of 'realism' while directing the film. Accordingly, each and every element of the sets represented something.

Kamal Bose, the cinematographer, was initially not really enthusiastic about the film. When approached to shoot the film, he did not think much about it, as he thought experiments like these were good only on paper and were non-starters. But when he heard the screenplay and saw the determination of the producer and director, he took it on as a challenge. He decided to set aside all traditional norms of cinematography to capture the dilemma of the characters. He used dim lighting to make the 'black and white' effective enough to capture the emotions of the characters. He said:

> All four characters were given different shades of light. The design of the set was made in such a way to symbolise traits. Thus, two ventilators are placed on two sides of the chair of the judge while an arch is in the middle. The idea was to showcase two eyes in the form of ventilators and an arch depicted brain of the human being.[21]

Even though Gandhi is not featured in the film, his presence cannot be missed for a minute. It is his spirit that fills the vacuum. The film tries to analyse the mind of the murderers as to why they were attempting to stop an old little man from doing his good work. Intelligently woven dialogues, spoken with conviction by Zul Vellani, made sure that Gandhi's viewpoint is presented succinctly. It is a pity that the film did not have a widespread commercial release.

Possibly, an experimental film like this, which had no songs, fights and the other usual tricks of popular films, and with a duration of about one hour, did not fit into the normal commercial exhibition space. In the end, not many people watched this film. Zul Vellani's son Anmol was studying at the University of Pune while the film was being made and remembers having seen the film only once, and that too at the preview theatre of Strand Cinema in Bombay. 'It was a private screening and limited to few people only. I saw it in 1974 with my wife,' he recalled.[22]

Veteran filmmaker Vikas Desai, nephew of composer Vasant Desai, recalls having attended the background music recording session for the film at Bombay Lab. He said, 'My uncle was very methodical in his approach and had done all the preparations before the actual recording. That was his practice and he was a man of homework.'[23] Vikas Desai, the co-director of renowned films like *Shaque* (1976) and *Gehrayee* (1980) with Aruna Raje, was studying at FTII when the film was being made in 1969. The editor of the film, Amit Bose, was also present at the recording session, and Vikas Desai recalls Bose's astounding reaction of 'Oh, my God!' upon hearing the innovative sound designed by his uncle.

The film's publicity material underlined the fact that even though it is a suspenseful courtroom drama at the surface level, it succinctly conveys the essence of Gandhi's philosophy. The conspirators, through an ironical mock trial staged by them, paying only lip sympathy to democracy and rule of law, have already made up their minds to kill the man. It also claimed that a film of this kind, an expressionist experiment, a fusion of drama and intellectual dialogue, had seldom been attempted. Instead of going down to the level of what is known as the 'box office', an attempt had been made to invite the audience to think of and participate in a conflict which is of concern all over the world. It was an honest attempt to bring a sense of conscience in the midst of the madness all around and to showcase compassion in the midst of brutality.

The film was cleared for unrestricted exhibition by the Central Board of Film Certification (CBFC) with only two minor cuts. It asked for deletion of an incorrect reference to the National Flag and to Independence Day in reel 6. It also asked for deletion of the underlined words ascribed to Gandhiji about his differences with Shri Subhash Chandra Bose in the sentence 'Unfortunately, Mr Bose was a devotee of violence.'[24]

The young producer Vimal Ahuja was confident about the success of such an unusual film. It was made in English especially for world-wide release to coincide with the International Gandhi Centenary Celebrations everywhere. 'We hope to sell this film to Television centres, not only in India but in the United States and United Kingdom. 20th Century Fox is already interested—not only for TV but for cinemas across the U.S. This will give us exposure both at home and abroad,' he had said in an interview.[25] Ahuja was inspired by veteran filmmakers K.A. Abbas and Inder Raj Anand and said, 'If people like them are proud of such a project and have faith in my doing it, surely it will not be long before the intelligent strata of cinemagoers in India would respond in like manner.'[26]

His faith was misplaced though. Such a brave attempt to present an alternative viewpoint raised hackles, of all the people, among Gandhian followers. Vithalbhai Jhaveri, who had made an epic five and a half hours documentary on Gandhi, and Usha Mehta, two prominent Gandhian thinkers, wrote an open letter of protest against the film, which was published in the *Times of India*. They said:

> The film and the play provide an opportunity to give visual form to Godse's banned statement and thus project a perverse image of the Mahatma on the minds of the people. The younger generation and foreigners not acquainted with India's freedom struggle are bound to feel that Gandhiji was the real culprit who deserved to die at the hands of 'patriots'.
>
> … Gandhiji is made to stand in the dock. Charges framed against him are mostly based on Godse's statement, sequence by sequence, a statement banned by the Government of India … The film has been given an award. Yet, the fact remains that both it and the play denigrate Gandhiji and damage the cause of national unity.[27]

In a strange turn of events, four years after the film received a universal exhibition certificate from the censors, a show-cause notice was served on producer Vimal Ahuja asking why the film should not be banned in the interest of public morality and decency. Ahuja was baffled by the timing of the notice because the film had already won the Gandhi award at the International Film Festival of India in 1969.[28]

It seems a protest letter by R.R. Diwakar, a former Union cabinet minister and a trustee of the Gandhi Smarak Nidhee, to the ministry of information and broadcasting had led the latter to issue the notice. According to Diwakar, 'the net effect of the film on his mind—made in the form of mock-trial of the Mahatma by the conspirators who had decided to kill him anyway—was that the assassins "perhaps had a case".'[29] The newspaper dubbed the entire sequence of developments as mysterious, as such a notice had been issued for a film that had won an award from the government itself!

Making a film on Gandhi's assassination in the centenary year of his birth was arguably an error of judgement on the part of the filmmaker. Possibly, the film in English was not intended for Indian audiences and was mainly aimed at overseas markets and film festivals. Being a small-budget film, it might have been difficult to release it commercially. Moreover, its running time of one hour didn't fit in the regular exhibition schedule. In effect, very few people managed to watch the film, and that too at private screenings, which were sporadic.

It was reported that a special screening of the film was arranged for the royal family of England. The producer Vimal Ahuja took a print of the film to London for the special screening, which was supposedly attended by Queen Elizabeth, her husband Philip and the newly declared Prince Charles, along with Lord Mountbatten. It is a pity that the film did not have a wide commercial distribution and exhibition in India.

Fortunately, a good copy of *At Five Past Five* exists in the vaults at the National Film Archive of India. A kind soul from Mumbai had personally deposited the print of the film, a rare one, at the NFAI in 2010. Watching it on a big screen in 16 mm celluloid format in the 150th year of Gandhi's birth was an unforgettable experience for me. Even after fifty years of its making, the film is a stark reminder of the importance of Gandhi's values in today's times. It only reinforces the greatness of the man and his timeless thoughts!

14

These Gandhis Didn't See the Light

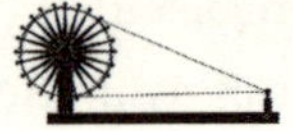

IT WAS TOUTED AS the best possible star cast in Hollywood for a Gandhi biopic in the late 1950s. Alec Guinness to play Gandhi, Lawrence Olivier as Lord Mountbatten, William Holden as an American doctor, Cary Grant as a British officer and Yul Brynner as Pandit Nehru. To top it all, David Lean was to helm the direction. One would imagine that with such a stellar line-up of artistes with a bouquet of Academy Awards between them, the film could turn out to be a masterful tribute to Gandhi on screen!

Alas, the proposed film, with *An Experiment* as the tentative title, remained an experiment only. The cinema industry has its own politics and economics at play when it comes to making a film. The idea of a biopic on Gandhi has fascinated many filmmakers across the world over the years. But, as fate would have it, almost all these projects merely remained on paper and never saw the light of the screen.

Gandhi was truly an exceptional and unique man such that a biographic documentary was made on his life when he was alive. A biopic in the form of a feature film on Gandhi was a very compelling idea for many a creative filmmaker. Surprisingly, it was the Western motion picture studios that had taken the lead in conceptualizing films depicting Gandhi's life journey for the screen before anybody else. And it was not that the topic was high on the minds of only the studio executives. The audience too wanted Gandhi's story depicted in film.

In fact, as early as in 1934, there was a curious American film viewer who had expressed a wish to see the life story of Gandhi on screen. While mentioning the other biopics being made on Queen Elizabeth and Napoleon in Hollywood, the writer says, 'Let's have more stories on the screen from true life and less from the make-believe world. How about bringing to the screen the little brown man of India-Mahatma Gandhi!'[1]

Indian film companies and filmmakers were, predictably, cautious and conservative about making a biopic on Gandhi as it was fraught with risk. Showing his life story in an impartial and unbiased manner to an audience that worshipped Gandhi as a Mahatma was always thought of as a big gamble. It was like playing with the emotions of millions of hearts. No one was ready to take on the mantle of doing cinematic justice to a life born once in a millennium; it was too big a challenge.

If this was the state of private film companies and studios, then the attitude of the Indian government was no different. Mounting a film on a father figure like Gandhi was a daunting task for the government too, and it was not ready to take up the job. Prime Minister Nehru was fully aware of this, and in December 1963 he made it clear in the Rajya Sabha that production of a film on the life of Gandhi was too difficult a proposition for the government department to take up. The government was not fit to do this, and it had no competent people to take up such a project … that was his matter-of-fact reasoning.

Many stories and legends have grown around Gandhi, both during his lifetime and after. Which ones to choose and focus on, and which ones to leave out and disregard would be a challenging and tricky exercise. Success for such a film was uncertain, but criticism assured! Gandhi had become a holy deity, only to be worshipped and not to be touched. And this applied even to telling his story on screen.

But efforts to make a biopic on Gandhi had started even while he was alive. It was a US-based production house that had conceived such a film as early as in 1947. A report in a Hollywood round-up in the *Film Daily* said that Gandhi himself had rejected a request from Jesse Goldberg of United Screen Associates to make a film on his life.[2] It is possible that the production house might have approached Gandhi to secure permission or seek his consent for the project and he declined.

The idea of making a biopic on him was revived after his assassination. In April 1948, it was reported that United Screen Associates was planning to make *A Great Soul*, a film based on the life of Gandhi.[3] The production house would have definitely wanted to chart a completely different path from the usual, if we take into consideration their past filmography. They had mostly produced pure action flicks, such as *The Lion Man* (1936), *The Gorilla Woman* (1937) and *Monsters of the Sea*. A biopic on Gandhi could have been 180-degree turn for the production house.

Since Western film studios had taken a lead in thinking of a Gandhi biopic, they needed active support of the government of India. Without the government's solid backing in terms of approval of the script and assurance of help in making available the infrastructure required for shooting and grant of the necessary permissions for shooting locations, these projects would not be possible. Having Pandit Nehru as the prime minister of the country, a keen supporter of the idea of a Gandhi biopic, made things easy for filmmakers who dreamt of such a challenging project. Nehru knew the importance of cinema as a medium and had favoured the idea of a Gandhi biopic all along. It is just that he wanted a foreign production to helm such a project, not an Indian studio.

Thus, a typical pattern emerged; an idea would be tossed by a Western studio or a prominent filmmaker. It would be followed by their visit to Delhi and a meeting with Prime Minister Nehru and other officials. After getting his in-principle approval, the script development and the scouting for locations would start. At the same time, Gandhi's close associates would be contacted, and efforts would be made to bring them on board to provide the much needed authenticity to the project. It also had another objective to ensure minimum opposition in India to the idea of a Gandhi film being made by a Western filmmaker.

But the Indian film industry, though itself reluctant to portray Gandhi's life on screen, had not taken kindly to the idea of Western filmmakers making a film on the Father of the Nation. There were protests and murmurs about such efforts from various quarters in the domestic industry. They couldn't digest the fact that foreign filmmakers were trying to attempt such a task when, in their view, there were several Indian film directors capable of helming such a project.

It was Baburao Patel, the maverick editor of *Film India,* India's biggest film magazine, who punctured these claims. He wrote a scathing piece just after Gandhi was martyred, criticizing the so-called desire of several Indian film companies to make a biographical film on him. The headline of his April 1948 editorial, 'Don't Murder the Mahatma Again', was a 'Warning to the Godse's of the Film Industry.'[4]

Known for his bold and forthright style, Patel wrote, 'The honest truth is—and every decent and sincere person in the industry will admit it—that there is not a single producing concern in India today capable of picturizing Gandhiji's life.' He wrote that there was not a single actor capable of portraying Gandhi on screen and not a single producer who could do justice to the subject. Patel said:

> We can never forgive a producer portraying Gandhiji in the shoddy manner for we have lived with Gandhiji, have heard him and seen him and we know that a man has yet to be born who can represent him on the screen or the stage. At present there is no one who can pose for a motion picture with even the remotest semblance with the world's greatest man of Malay the millennium.
>
> ... knowing as we do our current producers, it would be impossible for any one of them to infuse the picture with the spirit of Gandhiji, the greatness of his head and heart, and the divinity of his soul.[5]

According to Patel, the time was not ripe then for such a film, and such an effort was to be made only after a considerable time has passed, and then it was the government of the day which had to take a lead in appointing a committee of the best of brains to prepare the script for the film. Understandably, it would not be a very easy task to capture the life of the Mahatma in a single film, he wrote.

A month later, two-times Academy Award-nominated American actor Carrol Naish claimed that he was approached to play the role of Gandhi. He said in Los Angeles that the deal was still in the talking stage and the film was supposedly being produced by a wealthy British oil man, whose name he would not disclose. Apparently, the offer came after a conversation at a film party, when a British gentleman remarked that Naish talked like Gandhi. Naish said he was deeply interested in Gandhi's philosophy of life and he would closely resemble Gandhi if he could lose about 40 lbs (approximately 18 kg).[6]

The mysterious British man had promised to investigate who held the rights to Gandhi's biographies, including the picture rights. Naish claimed the man was not J. Arthur Rank, founder of Rank Organization and British National Film Company, nor anyone prominently identified with English films. But he was apprehensive about the whole thing, as it had its roots in a Hollywood party. He said, 'It would be tremendous break to portray the life of such a man as Gandhi and I hope this thing goes through. Of course, it might just be one of those things that develop at Hollywood parties.'[7] Evidently, a casual conversation was going to lead to nothing.

But plans for biopics on Gandhi continued to be floated. Somehow, the mystique around him had been steadily growing in the Western world ever since he appeared on the political scene in India. We have already seen how the charm offensive of Gandhi had invaded American society even though he had not set foot on their soil. Being leading producers of motion picture cinemas in the world, Hollywood studios were, therefore, keen to adapt Gandhi's story for the screen.

Hardly two months had passed after Naish's claim than came news about the making of a biopic called *Gandhi*. *Film India* reported that the life story of Gandhi was to be made in film by a new company, East-West Film Production, which had just been registered.[8] The names of Lord Sinha, John Sutre and F.W. Biber were mentioned as co-directors of the production house. It was also reported that England-based producer Vishnu Sen was contemplating a documentary on the life and teachings of Mahatma Gandhi and that he was in touch with Devdas Gandhi for it. Reports claimed that Sen had signed a contract with one of the biggest American film distribution companies to supply four Indian films. Again, nothing that these media reports said actually happened.

In August 1951, Ken McEldowney, head of Oriental International Films, began to toy with the idea of a biopic on Gandhi with the title *The Life of Gandhi*.[9] Flower seller-turned-film producer McEldowney was a self-made man in Hollywood. He had already produced a remarkable film, *The River,* in 1951, which was set in India. Directed by the well-known French filmmaker Jean Renoir, the first Technicolor film shot in India portrayed the story of an English family living in British India on the banks of the sacred Ganga. It was based on a short novel by Rumer Godden about her colonial childhood in Bengal. Satyajit Ray, then a budding filmmaker, was closely associated with this project, and Renoir was like a mentor for him during the filming.

It was reported that McEldowney was set to return to India to produce another film after completion of *The River*. Meanwhile, McEldowney met Devdas Gandhi for securing material on Gandhi for possible use in his full-length feature film. It was discussed in their meeting in London that the proposed film would be made for the Gandhi Memorial Film Library in New York. McEldowney was there to supervise the final Technicolour prints of *The River* and negotiated a deal whereby footages showing Mahatma would be turned over to him for use. The idea must have been in the pipeline for a very long time, as more than one year before this news there had been media reports about the proposed project.[10]

Variety magazine reported that Oriental International Film had planned production of a Gandhi film based on *Lead Kindly Light*, a book written by the American journalist Vincent Sheean.[11] The book is considered as one of the most remarkable books on Gandhi, and it was a week-long association of Sheean with Gandhi that had led to the memoirs. Sheean had a premonition of Gandhi's impending death, and he travelled from America to India just in time to meet him in January 1948.

Even though McEldowney had announced the film, it was not going to be a smooth affair as far as shooting in India was concerned. While shooting *The River*, the producer had faced a tough time in India. He felt there were too many challenges, including religion- and caste-related problems that his production house had encountered. The Indian laws also made it difficult for film equipment to be shipped into the country, and no budget could be set for shooting because production had never been undertaken by a foreign house in India before. Holy places and sacred animals were major sources of difficulty for a project in which many foreign technicians worked. To top it all, the production house had to make arrangements for preparing seven different types of meals for the Indians who were part of the project, according to their caste![12] Unfortunately, such dining ghettos are still prevalent in the film industry with different sets of artists eating separately as per their occupation even today.

Veteran Indian documentary filmmaker Ezra Mir aka Edwin Myers had also contemplated a film on Gandhi. Mir, who was visiting New York in 1948, had claimed that several Indian and British film producers were interested in making a film on Gandhi and that he himself might attempt a biopic on him on his return to India.[13] Mir later became a key figure in the documentary field in India and made many noteworthy short films and documentaries for the state-owned Films Division. But his Gandhi film remained only on paper.

During the same time, renowned filmmaker Gabriel Pascal toyed with the idea of making a film on Gandhi. Pascal, a Hungarian producer, was greatly influenced by Meher Baba, a well-known spiritual leader from India. He travelled with Meher Baba, spending substantial time gaining insights about the Indian way of life. It was then that he got drawn towards filming the extraordinary life of Gandhi. He held discussions with the Maharaja of Jaipur for the project, and the Birla family, a prominent business house, showed keen interest in financing the film. Pascal held several meetings with Devdas Gandhi and also succeeded in securing the consent of Prime Minister Nehru for the film. Nehru in his letter to Pascal said, 'I feel that you are the man who can produce something worthwhile. I was greatly interested in what you told me about this subject [the Gandhi film] and your whole approach to it.'

Initially, the plot of the film was to be based on Vincent Sheean's book *Lead Kindly Light*, for which the screen rights were bought. But Pascal found that the book was not very popular in India. He also secured permission from Navajivan Trust to use Gandhi's autobiography *My Experiments with Truth*, and engaged Gandhi's secretary Pyarelal to gather material for him. Hungarian-American writer Geza Herczeg travelled to India to work with Pyarelal on the script. Apparently, they managed to prepare a first draft film treatment titled *Mahatma Gandhi, Life of An Immortal* in October 1951.

This project attracted huge interest worldwide and found supporters in both India and the USA. But the script Herczeg developed wasn't a workable one, and Aldous Huxley, the noted British writer, was approached for the job. Pascal was not happy with Huxley's approach either. He said,

> He approaches spirituality like a scientist, with his mind and not with his heart. Just as his mysticism is more of a mental curiosity; it's a laboratory mysticism. He is cold and embarrassed by emotion. I don't think he understands that the dynamic force which moved Gandhi was his all-prevailing love.[14]

Realizing the importance of Gandhi's message being told in a feature film, noted international charity organization Ford Foundation came forward to finance the project.[15] Paul Hoffman, the head of the Foundation, was very upbeat about the project and asked Pascal to submit a budget. Pascal met the board of directors of the Foundation and submitted a budget of about $2 million.

Pascal and Gandhi shared one common connection, and that was George Bernard Shaw, the great author. Gandhi had read works of Shaw while in Yerawada prison and Shaw went to meet Gandhi during latter's visit to London in 1931. There was mutual admiration between these two great men. Pascal was the official cinematic interpreter of the great laureate and helmed many magnificent productions of Shaw's plays for the screen, including *Pygmalion, Caesar and Cleopatra* and *Major Barbara.* He was the only man who persuaded Shaw to permit him to produce his plays for the screen.

As things progressed, the Gandhi film project had ceased to be a mere film for Pascal and he thought, 'Gandhi was maybe the last grace sent to us by God. We are at crossroads; either we follow the Gandhian "non-violence" or we perish by the atomic war.'[16] Gandhi had influenced Pascal so much that the filmmaker turned vegetarian, to the extent possible for him, and also thought of giving up the bodily desires. Unfortunately, Pascal could not get the project moving for various reasons, including ill health and his other on-going productions. He passed away in 1954 at the age of fifty-six without making a film on Gandhi.

As more and more foreign filmmakers evinced interest in filming Gandhi's life, a concerted campaign started in India to discredit all such efforts. Writer Herczeg, who was working on the script for the Gandhi film to be directed by Gabriel Pascal, was particularly targeted. He was vilified as a publicity hound. And his interest in Gandhi's life was mercenary, people behind the campaign against him said. Some film critics in India strongly doubted that a Western writer or producer could do justice in depicting the life of Gandhi on screen. The campaign resorted to personal vilification, with Herczeg's ability, honesty and motives being wildly assailed.

The campaign against Herczeg was simply bewildering because he had not committed a single word to paper. Nor had he submitted a story outline for approval or consideration to the government. It was based, many believe, on the surging wave of nationalism and the chauvinistic attitude that had overtaken India since the country had gained Independence. The local film trade publications also joined the vilification campaign. One of the leading producers, Kishore Sahu, vented his anger in the presence of Herczeg:

> A stupid Indian killed Gandhiji once and this is a second attempt to murder him again. For I am sure that Messrs Herczeg and Pascal of Hollywood will kill even Gandhiji's memory. How can these American egotists with their arrogant airs and mercenary instincts ever make an honest and humble approach to a subject of such great spiritual stature from their long-distance acquaintance, when we, the sons of the soil, who have lived in his shadow, seen him walk and work, loved his smile and braved his frown, sighed and fasted with him through half-a-century, cannot even think of framing his life in celluloid for fear of distorting his hallowed memory?[17]

Greza Herczeg was in India meeting people and carrying out research for the script in 1951. During his visit, the Hollywood writer delivered a speech on 'Mahatma Gandhi and George Bernard Shaw' at Poddar College in Bombay on 14 September 1951. Before a packed audience of students and professors, Sahu, whom the students had invited to preside over, declared that he did not believe that any Western writer or producer could ever do proper justice to such a great subject like Gandhi, and least of all Herczeg and Pascal. 'It is presumptuous on the part of such persons to produce the life story of Gandhiji,' he said.

Sahu further said it was a pity that our leaders who are the trustees of Gandhiji's sacred memory have sold the Mahatma and his hallowed heritage to a foreign producer for a few dollars. 'Had they had the slightest respect for the memory of the Father of our nation, they would have harnessed the entire resources of our industry and our nation and themselves given to the world the greatest picture of all times,' the veteran producer lamented.

Having announced their plans to make a film on Gandhi, it was a race between Pascal and McEldowney to be the first to finish their projects. A representative of Pascal met Devdas Gandhi in New York to discuss the project. They made a preliminary agreement for use by Pascal of material the youngest son of Gandhi had. Pascal's plan was to start the film when he finished *Androcles and the Lion,* which he was working on at RKO studio. McEldowney, however, had a head start over his esteemed competitor. He already had his foot well into the Indian system of operating, having made *The River* here for United Artists Release.[18] (*Variety*, 1951)

Both Pascal and McEldowney made every effort to forge close connections with the Indian film industry. Both attended the special dinner hosted by the Motion Pictures Association of America at the Beverly Hills in Hollywood for the visiting Indian film delegation in October 1952. They were prominently photographed hobnobbing with leading lights of the Indian film industry, including actress Nargis, producer B.N. Sarkar of New Theatres Studio and actor David Abraham, at the special event.

Even as neither project was making much headway, there was yet another announcement of a Gandhi movie. *Motion Picture Daily* reported that a forthcoming movie on the life of Gandhi was to be titled *Amritsar*,[19] to be produced by Lloyd Young. The cast had not yet been finalized, but the shooting would happen in India while some indoor scenes would be shot in London, the report claimed. The screenplay was written by H. Kenn Carmichael, based on the original screen-story by Lloyd Young. *The New York Times* also reported this development saying, 'Movie is planned on the life of Gandhi; Receipts of Rights reported by Lloyd Young.'[20] It also said, 'Plans are underway for a feature film drama called "The Life of Mahatma Gandhi", based on the activities of the late Indian leader.'

Al Daff, a former Universal International executive vice-president, was closely involved in the production of this film. It was reported that the film was to showcase factual episodes from Gandhi's life, and rights to use material on Gandhi and his voice recordings were obtained through Navajivan Trust in India. Negotiations were underway with a major company for release of the film.[21] Daff visited India and met with government officials to discuss his plan. The shooting was to start in early winter in 1961. But this project too turned out to be a non-starter.

Llyod Young, a producer who had directed *The Stranger* (1954), sponsored by India's Film Division, was involved in yet another Gandhi biopic that was planned but didn't take off. In July 1959, it was announced that Film Productions International of Burbank would make two films on Gandhi. One would be a full-length feature and the other a short documentary. Both were to be made by Llyod Young Ltd., a company related to FPI, and to be shot on location in India. Executive Vice President of FPI Burton Martin declared that his production house has secured the concerned rights after discussions with senior Indian government officials and Navajivan Trust. It was reported that while the documentary would be made in cooperation with the Gandhi Memorial Trust, the feature would have a fictional plot. 'In accordance with the desires of the leaders of the Indian government, the actual person of Gandhi will not be a major role nor will he be impersonated by an American or European star.'[22]

All these efforts were aimed at making a feature-length biopic on Gandhi. But the short format of documentary was also explored. In 1961, New York-based Official Films Inc. announced that they were going to produce a series of biography films. It claimed the series would be 'an exciting new look at the inside stories of great lives'. It's appeal would be based on 'its dramatic use of historical and new film footage about great men (living and dead) of the past fifty years'.[23] Gandhi was the only Asian to feature prominently on the list containing the who's who of the world, including the likes of Sigmund Freud, Thomas Edison, Albert Einstein, Adolf Hitler and Winston Churchill.

Broadcasting magazine reported that the Gandhi segment of the series was okayed. It said, 'Having obtained official sanction from Government of India, producer Jack Harley Jr, has finalised plans to produce a telefilm documenting the life and times of Mahatma Gandhi as a segment for the Biography series, which Wolper Productions is producing for Official

Films.'[24] Ram Bagai was the technical consultant for the film, and he was to make available the footage on Gandhi from his private library.

Bagai, a trained cinematographer from the University of Southern California, was one of the first distributors of Indian films in the USA and had also served as the president of the Hollywood Foreign Press Association. Bagai's distribution firm Films of India, based in Los Angeles, brought Indian films to the USA for exhibition. Bagai was also a close Gandhi follower and later supported the US Civil Rights Movement led by Martin Luther King Jr. by donating the proceeds from the New York premier of V. Shantaram's *Do Ankhe Barah Haath* in 1965 to the Movement.

While Gandhi was alive, one gossip column in the film trade magazine *Motion Picture* reported a rumour floating in film circles that J. Krishnamurthy, the young Indian whose millions of followers called him 'Second Christ', may be prevailed upon to make a motion picture called *Untouchable* for Mahatma Gandhi. But Gandhi should wear more clothes, the column insisted![25]

While several projects were being announced, yet another major filmmaker from Hollywood put his hat in the ring. This time the project had the backing of Columbia Pictures. *Motion Picture Daily,* on 23 December 1954, reported that Columbia Pictures had entered into a deal with Otto Preminger winner of two special LAUREL Awards for 'new and daring types of motion picture entertainment', to make a film on Gandhi. Harry Cohn, the president and head of production at Columbia Pictures announced that the arrangements had been completed to produce a film, *The Wheel,* on the life of Mahatma Gandhi and Preminger would direct it.

The plan was to shoot only one version of the film to serve both the Western world and the huge Indian market. Therefore, all of the characters, both British and Indian, who would normally speak English would do so in the film, while those who would normally be expected to speak Hindustani would speak that language in the film. The report said that the Indian government had indicated its cooperation for the project.[26]

Reports also came in from Hollywood that two leading film studios were contemplating making two films on religious/political leaders from India.[27] MGM was planning to make one on the Buddha while Columbia was making a deal with Otto Preminger, twice-nominated director for the Academy Awards, to produce and direct one on Gandhi, tentatively called *The Wheel*. Both studios claimed that these two productions would be among the most important films ever done by them.

Preminger, known for his classic thriller *Laura* (1944), visited India in 1954 to do research for the Gandhi film and met Prime Minister Nehru along with members of Gandhi's family. After the discussions, Preminger revealed that his idea had been received with enthusiasm by Indian officials and that Nehru had promised to read the script and possibly make suggestions to give it historical realism. The film was supposed to be about Gandhian values than about the Mahatma's personality. Preminger's intention was to show the influence of Gandhi's principles on other men. Alec Coppel, who later co-wrote the screenplay for the Hitchcock classic *Vertigo,* was drafted in to write the script for this Gandhi film.

After returning from India in December 1954, Preminger revealed that the writer would shortly be sent to India to prepare a script so that he could begin the filming in 1955. He was pleasantly surprised to find a friendly feeling and hope for the future. 'Wherever I went and with all the people to whom I have spoken, a film about Gandhi would be warmly welcomed,'[28] the filmmaker said.

Most importantly, an Indian actor would be cast to play the role of Gandhi and the film was to be made using one of the widescreen processes, most likely Cinemascope. The theme would necessarily revolve around the life of Gandhi, but the focus would be on the outcome of his teachings and the course of the 'bloodless revolution' in India. In April 1955, news came in that Preminger would again travel to India in that summer and submit the screenplay for the approval of Prime Minister Nehru. The film was to be shot in colour under his Carlyle Productions banner for a Columbia release.

There was a constant buzz about Preminger's project, particularly in Hollywood and the US media. Each and every new development was reported with keen interest. The New York-based weekly *Variety* reported that the Gandhi biopic was to be made with Nehru's advice and added that Otto Preminger had set no financing or release deal as yet.[29] The shooting was to begin at the end of 1955, when weather conditions would be favourable in India. All the outdoor shooting would be done in India, but the base of operations was to be London. Once again, these efforts turned out to be in vain and the project was shelved. Preminger later directed one of the best courtroom dramas, *Anatomy of a Murder,* in 1959.

Austria-born maverick filmmaker Fred Zinnemann also came in the picture for depicting the life of Gandhi in film in the mid-1960s. The curious entry of Zinnemann in a Gandhi film project had the blessings of noted screenwriter Robert Bolt. The two had created magic on the screen with *A Man for All Seasons* in 1966, winning six Academy Awards, including the best picture and best director awards. Zinnemann had also won an Academy Award for his earlier film *From Here to Eternity* in 1953.

While Zinnemann had approached Bolt for *A Man for All Seasons*, this time it was Bolt who went to the filmmaker with Gandhi film project. Richard Attenborough, who eventually made *Gandhi*, also admired the work of Zinnemann and had said, 'I don't think I have ever been disappointed with a Fred Zinnemann picture.' Motilal Kothari, a London based Indian, about whom we will read more in the next chapter, also approved his name to take forward his dream of making a Gandhi biopic after his project with Attenborough was stalled.

While Zinnemann felt honoured 'to have been asked by Robert Bolt and Mr Kothari to direct a film of such importance', [30] he put forth three essential conditions to take the responsibility. He wanted all existing obligations to be dissolved to have a proper production machinery. That meant his production house Highland Films Ltd. would be the makers of the film, not Kothari's Indo British Films. Secondly, all executive authority concerning production to be in the hands of a professional executive film producer. And, creative control: script, casting and final editing would rest in his hands, subject to consultation with Robert Bolt. In short, Zinnemann wanted a set up like his film *A Man for All Seasons*.

By now, Robert Bolt himself had been drawn irresistibly towards Gandhi film project. In a long and personal letter to Zinnemaan, Bolt expressed his thoughts, 'I have to confess that my interest (in Gandhi film project) initially was moral. But it very quickly transmuted into an interest primarily artistic, as I realized both the fascinating difficulties and the electrifying opportunitics afforded by the project.' Bolt was personally dejected by Gandhi's assassination. 'This seemed to indicate that the appeal of his spirituality, goodness, selflessness or whatever it was, had been felt by me and masses of others in the West,'[31] he felt.

While elaborating on the moral theme of the film, Bolt wrote from his Surrey home,

> The difference between Gandhi and most of us lies in his inordinate strength of character. And this does make him a daunting, even mysterious, but not an incomprehensible figure. In writing this film therefore I should think I had failed if the film did not show both these things: The simplicity of his decision, and the forbidding strength required to implement it.

According to Bolt,

> The audience should go out comforted by the possibility of such a way of life, perhaps even with some idea of doing a bit better themselves, but they should not go out thinking either: "What a dear little man" nor "I see, it's really quite simple—I think I'll be a Saint too."[32]

As far as the artistic opportunities in the film, Bolt imagined the dramatic conflict offered on three fronts. First was the obvious conflict of Gandhi with the Powers-That-Be; the veteran writer was very right while describing the second one; the conflict with Gandhi's own people (who delightedly hail his moral purity so long as it is expedient to the political cause but are angered or puzzled by it when it is not, so that he is one moment a national hero and the next a bloody nuisance or even a traitor to the cause). And thirdly, the conflict with his kith and kin who willy-nilly share the dire consequences of his purity. 'The audience will be made to share the exasperation of his varying opponents,' Bolt wrote so because, 'our central figure is fascinating in himself, and is enmeshed in a drama of epic dimensions, set against an epic background. And he was blessedly full of surprises, the antithesis of a bore.'[33]

Bolt had given serious thoughts to casting in the film including the casting of Gandhi himself. While admitting the dilemma, he wrote, 'If we cast a European we face the problem of mere credibility. If we cast an Indian we face the problem of mere competence.' Even as he knew the final decision rested with Zinnemann, the director, he opined,

> I think a European actor masquerading as the Indian Gandhi is a lesser danger than an Indian actor of hopelessly inadequate ability … I do not think we want a Star of the magnitude of Lancaster or Cary Grant. But we do want an actor of proven ability and appeal, capable of sinking himself into a prodigiously difficult and rewarding character performance.[34]

The three collaborators, Bolt, Zinnemann and Kothari met over lunch on 21 October 1966 in London and chalked out a detailed plan to go ahead. As per the memorandum of the meeting prepared by Zinnemann, the actor to portray Gandhi would be an Indian. The script was to be finished by 1 January 1968, preparation of production until 1 June 1968, principal photography during June 1968 until March 1969, editing during March 1969 to September 1969 and first public screening was planned for late September 1969. These dates were highly desirable, it was mentioned, in view of the fact that the United Nations had designated a "Gandhi Year" ending in October 1969.[35]

A draft agreement was drawn up in December 1966 involving all parties including Richard Attenborough who was to quit Indo British

Films and transfer rights to Zinnemann. Despite everything falling in place as per his wishes, Zinnemann was still not ready to commit himself. Even as Kothari was insisting on signing of the agreement without wasting time, Zinnemann made it clear in a letter to his agent Christopher Mann that 'I am interested in the project for only one reason; the enthusiasm which Robert Bolt has for the material. It was my understanding with Robert Bolt that I would have no connection of any kind with the project until I am in a position to read the treatment which he hopes to have finished by September 1967.' He also stated that 'I have agreed to keep myself available to begin work on the film in 1968, if I should decide to proceed with the project.'[36] Finally, he said if these arrangements are insufficient to meet the requirements of Kothari, he would prefer to withdraw from the project immediately. Alarmed by this, Kothari conveyed that he was not trying to impose any requirements or condition upon Zinnemann.

Meanwhile, British author Geoffrey Ashe, who had written an excellent biography on Gandhi, came in the picture wanting to assist Bolt in writing the script. Ashe wrote to Bolt's agent in March 1967 saying, 'Believe me, my concern with the Gandhi film is just what I said—that this should be got right. It is a thing I care very much about.' Ashe said, 'The point really is that there are some very elusive things about Gandhi. I have already come across people who say they have read "hundreds of books," or profess to know all there essentially to know, and yet had missed important facts which I found for myself.'

Having travelled to India to do research on his book, Ashe had gained a certain perspective and he was curious to know, 'Apart from bibliography, I wonder if, in all his to-ing and fro-ing, the producer has ever bothered to walk without notice into an ordinary Indian village and ask ordinary villagers what Gandhi means to them? I did, and it shed a light which no book known to me would have given.'[37]

Two months later, American writer and producer Sidney Kaufman wrote to Robert Bolt and submitted a treatment note on the proposed Gandhi film. He was also trying to interest Kothari in his script. 'In submitting this treatment to you, I wish to state that I waive any claim of any kind whatever that may arise with or without grounds from your study or use of any material contained therein,'[38] he said. They also met in London and though Bolt was impressed by Kaufman, he didn't commit anything.

During this entire writing process, Bolt also seemed to have imbibed some of Gandhian ideas and therefore, instead of pocketing the monies due to him from MGM Studio, he wished that it be paid directly to Gandhi Famine Relief Fund in Bihar under Jayaprakash Narayan. In a letter to Kothari's lawyer, Bolt wrote, 'Incidentally, I have concluded that I don't want to make money for myself out of this particular project.'[39]

But somehow, differences arose between Zinnemann and Bolt on this crucial question of who was to play Gandhi. Bolt felt no Indian actors of remotely the required calibre were known, and instead suggested Tom Courteney or 'even Marlon Brando, though my word, he'd have to diet' for the title role. One would think them very strange choices for Gandhi, even though their acting prowess could not be doubted. On the other hand, Zinnemann was of the firm opinion that an Indian actor had to play the role of Gandhi. In a letter to Bolt, Zinnemann wrote that he could not direct a non-Indian actor as Gandhi. But before he could secure an agreement for an Indian actor, Zinnemann was drawn towards another film, *Man's Fate,* about the Chinese Revolution.[40]

All these were the failed attempts at making a biopic about Gandhi. But there were a few foreign films with stories directly focused on Gandhian ideas and values. In 1952, a Hollywood film *Thunder in the East* explored the theme of non-violence in conflict resolution. Based on the novel *Rage of the Vulture* by Alan Moorhead, the story of the film is set in India just after Independence. In the mythical Himalayan state of Kandahar, peace is disturbed, and in flows a plane full of ammunition. The local king is fighting with the guerrilla forces and the flying adventurer offers him the weapons.

The Gandhian Prime Minister, Ramji, was played by the four-time Academy-nominated actor Charles Boyer. He wears the white Gandhi cap, opposes the use of weapons, and believes in dialogue to resolve the issue. The film was produced by Paramount and directed by Charles Vidor. Even though the film has non-violence as its theme, ultimately the weapons are used to repel the attack.

Gandhi's philosophy was again the focus in a Canadian film, *Ordinary Magic,* released in 1993. Directed by Giles Walker, the plot revolved around Gandhi's satyagraha, a tool that could be used effectively in fighting injustice at local levels in modern Canada. The film was based on a novel *Ganesh (Young Adult)* written by Malcolm Bosse, who also wrote the script for the film with Jefferson Lewis. It is a story of a boy Jeffrey/Ganesha, who has been raised in India by his Canadian father who strongly believes in Gandhi's philosophy.

Ganesha moves to Canada to live with his aunt Charlotte after his father's death but retains his Indian way of life. When the ancestral home they are staying in is faced with a demolition notice by the local municipality, Ganesha adopts the strategy of 'satyagraha'. He and his aunt sit on their porch and decide they will fast until the notice is withdrawn. Slowly, friends and neighbours join in the protest, which leads to a debate on the development plan of the city.

The peaceful agitation turns into a public movement when violence is leashed on the protesters. In the end, the ancestral house is saved and the mayor reconsiders the city development plan. 'It is a charming film and the performances by Ryan Reynolds as Jeffrey/Ganesha and Glenne Headly as Charlotte are excellent. Both are completely credible.'[41] The 104-minute film has a sub-line that says, 'In all of us is a spark that can change the world,' echoing Gandhi's philosophy.

African leader Nelson Mandela, who famously fought against apartheid, was inspired by the values and principles of Gandhi. A documentary, *Together We lit up the Sky; Gandhi and Mandela in South Africa*, written and directed by Bettina Corke, portrays the initial journey of Gandhi in South Africa and then shows the parallels between the paths chosen by him and Nelson Mandela.

David Lean, the legendary filmmaker of *The Bridge on the River Kwai, Lawrence of Arabia* and *Doctor Zhivago* fame, had also thought of making a film on Gandhi after completing *The Bridge* film. He did extensive research on the subject and the proposed plot. He teamed up with writer Emeric Pressburger for developing the script. Both Lean and Pressburger travelled to India in 1958 and met Prime Minister Nehru. They also toured the Indian sub-continent for two months in Lean's Rolls-Royce for scouting possible shooting locations.

The story of the film was to be told from the point of view of a family of untouchables, an American doctor and an English policeman who marries a Muslim woman in India. Pressburger's approach to the subject was from a humanist perspective. Lean liked the initial idea and they discussed the casting, including Alec Guinness as Gandhi and Academy Award-winning actors William Holden and Yul Brynner for other parts. Pressburger wrote a long treatment note titled *Written in the Stars* and subtitled it with 'An Experiment'.

The screenwriter scribbled, 'Gandhi has often said that his life was an experiment in Truth. I think it was richer than that. I would call it an experiment in human values. Our film should be the same.' Though Lean had pinned high hopes on the script, the final treatment note by Pressburger was not liked by him. 'I don't know what happened in the meantime, because the script was just awful,' Lean remarked, and moved on to start another project, *Lawrence of Arabia*.

When compared with Attenborough's *Gandhi*, the treatment by Pressburger suggested a more humane approach and better understanding of Gandhi's persona. Had the Lean-Pressburger film come about, it could have portrayed Gandhi in lesser Halo while keeping the canvas at a smaller scale compared to Attenborough's film.[42]

Lean had always admired actor Alec Guinness and his work and thought he could portray the role of Gandhi effectively. In fact, while discussing his own Gandhi film project, Richard Attenborough was startled to hear that Prime Minister Nehru's personal choice for Gandhi's role was also Alec Guinness. 'The nationality is unimportant,' Nehru declared. 'All that matters is that he should be very good. Besides, the idea of being portrayed by an Englishman would have made Bapu laugh a great deal.' Guinness, though, was wise enough to decline this prestigious role gracefully and eventually played a Hindu Brahmin in Lean's *Passage to India* in 1984.

Cary Grant was proposed to play the role of a British police officer, William Holden an American Doctor and Yul Brynner Pandit Nehru in the film. The thespian actor Lawrence Olivier was to star as Lord Mountbatten, and John Gielgud as Lord Irwin. Lean who was pinning high hopes to make such a big project happen had confessed to his producer Spiegel:

> There had been many times when I have fought-in my own mind-to keep you away from my next project but the size of this film as it unfolds calls for the greatest producer of the industry and in my opinion, you are him. We have both reached our creative zenith together, and as you once said, we ought to have our brains tested if we don't join hands again.

The necessary meetings for the film took place in Delhi with Nehru and other government officials, but despite Lean's wish that 'this will work out wonderfully', it could not. Somehow, Sam Spiegel, Lean's frequent collaborator in producing his movies, was not at all convinced about this project. Also, for some reason, Spiegel, who had produced two of Lean's films, did not like India at all. According to Lean, 'He had a lot of charisma … but Sam and India did not work together. There are two types of people, those who come to India and want to leave on the next plane and those who fall in love with it. Spiegel left immediately.'[43] But for Spiegel, David Lean would have made his Gandhi film.

Lean's name was to once again crop up in the context of a Gandhi film when he showed interest in a biopic of the Mahatma based on Robert Bolt's script titled *Gandhiji*. After Zinnemann's exit, Bolt decided to join hands with Lean and there were hectic parleys with Robert O'Brien of MGM Studio in this regard, including the issues of sharing the profits. In one of the treatment notes, Lean wrote, 'I have tried to show the steady flowering of the rigidly correct moralist into the carefree and compassionate Saint.'

While sharing the news of rapid progress made with Lean on the project, Bolt wrote from Rome to his agent, 'David (Lean) is very excited by the Gandhi Treatment. Hates the idea of working in India again, but thinks I have achieved "the bones of what could be the best film ever made" and that he simply must do it. Before David had read it, I had a very nice call from Bob O'Brien in New York saying that they were similarly excited and wanted to go ahead.'[44] In fact, since Lean got involved in the project, it was decided that the film will not only be directed by David Lean, but will be produced by his company Faraway Productions.

As an interesting aside, even the secretary of Ian Fleming, best known for James Bond novels, liked Bolt's treatment note of *Gandhiji* very much. Margaret Ramsay, Bolt's literary agent sent the treatment note to B. Griffie Williams for her confidential reading saying, 'This is the version that Lean saw which persuaded him to make the film.'[45] Mrs Williams found it fascinating and wrote back saying, 'It seems that RB (Robert Bolt) has, like myself, a great sympathy with Gandhi—as far as I have read I feel that there is not enough accent on the politics. I hope it works out well because it is such an interesting subject.'[46]

As writer and director, the partnership between Bolt and Lean was one of the greatest in the film history and their bonhomie was crucial for the Gandhi project. This sentiment was echoed by Bolt's agent Margaret Ramsay when she wrote that, 'The really good thing about Lean, is that when he and Bob get together on a project, Lean puts so much of himself in it, that it is unthinkable, apart from death, that he should abandon it.'[47] But by December 1969, the things were still in limbo with no contracts signed by MGM in part due to repeated change of leadership at the studio. This had clearly upset Bolt who had toiled hard on the script, but the film had not gone on the floor.

Moreover, Richard Attenborough was still in the picture trying to get the financial backing from other sources. But Bolt's heart was with Lean. He thought of Gandhi film as ideally David Lean's type of film and not Attenborough's. It was because of Lean's greatly superior experience and his proven capacity to drive a big project to a successful conclusion in the teeth of extended difficulties, according to Bolt. Also, Lean had time and again made repeated assurances that Gandhi would be his next film.

While staring at the bleak scenario of the film not getting ahead, Bolt shared his doubts with Kothari. He wrote:

> This is perhaps a mean-minded suspicion for me to harbour in the face of his (Lean) warm declarations to me of his intention to do the film at all costs but it is possible that he does not entirely know his own mind. He has a highly personal reason for wishing not to spend a long period of time in India.[48]

Incidentally, Lean was married to Leila Matkar, an Indian from Hyderabad.

Due to his own health complications, Bolt couldn't work more and gave his script to Attenborough for a princely sum of 1 British Pound. Attenborough liked the script very much and wrote, 'Bob's achievement in containing the story within this length, of making one perpetually anxious to know what happens next and to give the feeling by the time you have reached the end, that one has really come to know this extraordinary man, is a feat which I am sure few writers in the world could have accomplished.'[49] In the end though, the final script of *Gandhi* written by Jack Briley had no resemblance to Bolt's.

The subject of Gandhi had fascinated David Lean his entire life, but in the end he could not make a film on him. While reminiscing about the subject Lean recalled, 'I worked on Gandhi with Robert (Bolt) and then gave up because I thought we weren't getting a good enough script. If we were doing a film about Gandhi, it had to be more or less the bible. Simply wonderful.'[50] It was also true that his film Ryan's Daughter (1970) was ruthlessly panned by American critics calling it a 'piece of bullshit'. It affected Lean's confidence so much that 'David lost his nerve and feared that his script for Gandhi was not good enough.'[51]

In fact, he went into a shell for nearly fourteen years before making *A Passage to India* in 1984.

Apparently, Lean did not see Richard Attenborough's *Gandhi*. When asked specifically whether he had seen the film, Lean told, 'I have and I haven't. In India I saw a pirated tape which was a good half-hour short, and it was an appalling quality. So I can't really say that I've seen *Gandhi*.'[52] One can only imagine what Lean's film could have been, with such a prominent cast in the hands of a filmmaker whose three films had won a staggering nineteen Academy Awards. Lean's last wife Sandra also thought 'what a great film David could have made' on Gandhi and 'it was sad that he never got round to directing it.' But when she asked Lean's colleague Don Ashton, production designer on *The Bridge on the River Kwai*, he said, 'It's good he didn't, he'd probably still be doing it!'[53]

Ironically, when all these efforts were happening to make a biopic on Gandhi without any fruition, there came out two films focusing instead on his assassin: Mark Robson's 1963 *Nine Hours to Rama,* and Kumar Vasudev's 1969 *At Five Past Five*. They have already been described in detail in earlier chapter. While the first film was banned in India, the second went into oblivion.

15

Kothari and Attenborough: The Men Behind *Gandhi*

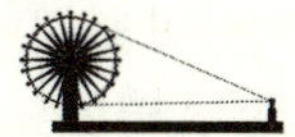

TO BRING GANDHI'S EXTRAORDINARY life story on screen, there had to be a man possessed with faith, passion and fierce inspiration. Motilal Kothari was one such man. Like A.K. Chettiar, who crisscrossed the world in search of footage of Gandhi and then put together the first-ever biographic documentary film on him, Kothari was equally motivated to pursue his dream of telling the life story of Gandhi through a feature film in a grand manner. He was neither a film man nor a man with big money. He had not even visited a film studio in his life at the time of embarking on the film project he did. Yet he saw the dream.

For years together, Kothari moved heaven and earth in pursuit of his obsession, which bordered on madness, with a commitment and devotion that only Gandhi could inspire. What else would have prompted Kothari to go and seek Richard Attenborough, an actor and producer who had not directed a single film till then, to propose a film on Gandhi! The two men encountered many problems and challenges in the process, but didn't give up on their noble mission. Kothari's idea became Attenborough's purpose, but it took almost twenty years for their dream to come true and for the world to see the grand vision of both on screen.

Born in Tasgaon in the Satara district of Bombay province, Motilal Kothari was deeply influenced by Gandhi. As a student, he had actively participated in the freedom struggle and had met Gandhi thrice. The first time he met Gandhi was when the Mahatma had come to Phaltan in the Satara district on a fund collection tour in 1925. The function was held in a decorated pandal built by the local Jain community to receive him, and Gandhi was not pleased by all the pomp and show. He remarked, 'Why have you used so much foreign cloth to honour a saint of yours who himself prefers to go naked?'

Kothari met him again in 1932 when Gandhi was in prison during the Civil Disobedience Movement. His third meeting with Gandhi was when Kothari had come from England to meet and deliver certain personal messages from some Englishmen to Gandhi in 1946 at Birla House in Bombay. It was a Monday, Gandhi's Day of Silence, but they talked for more than half an hour using written notes. These three meetings over a period of twenty years had deeply influenced Motilal Kothari.[1]

A short and stout man, Kothari moved to London after the assassination of Gandhi, and took a job at the Indian High Commission. It was not an easy decision for him, though. He felt that he was running away. At the airport while leaving India, an inner voice told him, 'Aren't you running away—and why?' A few years later he suffered a heart attack and the same voice confronted him again, 'And where will you run now?'[2] That was the time Kothari decided that the life story of Gandhi needed to be told through a powerful medium, and what better medium it could be than cinema.

He then made it his life's mission to bring this unique story on screen in such a way as to make it immortal, like its hero. Gandhi had become a legend in his lifetime, and his reel version would continue the legend for many generations to come. Kothari was inspired to write. 'I decided

I had to try to do something, however small, which I believed to be a positive step for humanity.'[3] There were auspicious signals too in the beginning for the project. Getting the film and television rights of one of the best biographies on Gandhi, written by American author Louis Fischer, was nothing less than a blessing. Fischer offered it to Kothari without charging him any money.

In July 1962, Kothari met Richard Attenborough, who was thirty-nine at the time and had become a fairly successful actor and producer after serving in the Royal Air Force during the Second World War. When Kothari mooted the idea of making a film on Gandhi, it clearly startled Attenborough. 'Although I felt extremely tentative in terms of committing myself to mounting a movie on Mahatma Gandhi, the subject matter already exerted a strong attraction. I felt the chances were he would prove to be quite a character!' he recalled.[4]

Attenborough thought he was in no way fit enough to direct this film because he had 'no reputation' compared with other filmmakers who had attempted such projects earlier. Kothari was not disheartened and gave him the biography of Gandhi by Louis Fischer to read. Thus began the eventful journey of these two men, which was to take a roller-coaster ride for many years.

Attenborough was totally enthralled by the Fischer biography when he read it while on a vacation. His uncertainty about the project changed into something of positivity towards it by the time he finished reading the book. But even as his close colleagues and advisers were sceptical about the whole thing, it was his actress wife Sheila, with whom he was paired in many films, who backed him fully in going for the project. For a film like this about a national icon, it was necessary to have the consent of the Indian government, and Attenborough's friendship with Louis Mountbatten came in handy in working the wheels.

Mountbatten, the last Viceroy and first Governor-General of India, actively facilitated the process and got in-principle approval for the film from his close friend Prime Minister Nehru. This was in May 1963. The same month, Attenborough met Nehru, B. Gopala Reddi, the minister for information and broadcasting, and Indira Gandhi in Delhi to take things forward. Dublin-based Gerry Hanley was immediately engaged to write the first draft of the screenplay, with initial financial help from Rank Organization, a major production house in London. Things were falling into place at a fast pace.

Much before meeting Attenborough, Kothari was keen on engaging Robert Bolt to write the film. In October 1961, Kothari wrote to Bolt through his lawyer Laurence Harbottle expressing his desire to get the writer on board. Bolt's agent Margaret Ramsay immediately replied saying, 'I think if you were to wait until early next year for Bob (Bolt) to know about this film, you might possibly get him to do it for you ... I think he would make a remarkable film-script of this subject.'[5]

Bolt was then working on the script of *Lawrence of Arabia* while his play *A Man for All Seasons* was also being premiered. Kothari wrote another letter to Ms Ramsay expressing happiness over this development and said, 'As you may have gathered the subject in question has practically become an obsession with me, and I shall always remain grateful for any assistance you may be able to give me.'[6] But as it happened, Bolt conveyed his unwillingness through a letter saying, 'it is absolutely out of the question for him to consider doing another film script in the foreseeable future'.[7]

Kothari was not willing to take a no and dashed off another letter, this time by hand, to avoid postal delays. He was convinced that Bolt would do full justice to the project and wrote,

> I could hardly overemphasize either my own devotional interest in wanting to make this film or my genuine conviction that Mr Bolt should do the script. All those who are associated with me share my view and will not only agree to wait for any reasonable period of time to make it possible for Mr Bolt to undertake this work, also go to almost any length of trouble to create conditions that would be conducive to his completing the script in the shortest possible time.[8]

Meanwhile, Kothari and Attenborough were clear about the basic outline of the film. They knew it was impossible to cover all of

Gandhi's life in a three-hour movie. The film was not going to be about the Indian National Congress, and it was also not intended to be about India's freedom struggle. Gandhi's relations with his sons and his controversial experiments with sexuality in his old age were also not to be part of the film. In a note for the script writer, Motilal Kothari had singled out three aspects of Gandhi's work: his identification with the poor, his struggles against injustice, and, finally, 'his determination to practice continually everything himself first, before he asked others to do it'.[9]

Eventually, when the film was finally released, the opening title-card summed up the vision of its makers:

> No man's life can be encompassed in one telling. There is no way to give each year its allotted weight, to include each event, each person who helped to shape a lifetime. What can be done is to be faithful in spirit to the record and try to find one's way to the heart of the man.

A production company named Indo-British Films was specially established for making the film, with Kothari and Attenborough as its directors. The company entered into an agreement on 19 June 1964 whereby Louis Fischer assigned the film rights of his two books, 'The Life of Mahatma Gandhi' and 'The Essential Gandhi' for nominal consideration.

But the first draft Harold Hanley, noted American writer who was roped in to write screenplay, attempted was for a film of more than five hours! The condensation of a life as extraordinary as Gandhi's was always going to be a big challenge. That didn't deter the makers. In May 1963, Attenborough travelled alone to Delhi while Kothari couldn't because of his heart trouble. Attenborough met with Prime Minister Nehru to present the draft script and seek his opinion.

Nehru was keen that Academy Award-winning actor Alec Guinness should play the role of Gandhi. But Guinness was certain that an Indian actor should portray the character of Gandhi, not a foreigner like him. Nehru also felt that in skill and technique, Indian artistes in the 1960s were not of sufficient calibre to take up such a challenging role. And, most importantly, he told Attenborough, 'Whatever you do, do not deify him—that is what we have done in India—and he was too great a *man* to be deified.'[10] Nehru also announced in the Rajya Sabha: 'I have had a number of talks with Mr Richard Attenborough and, in my judgement, the British producer is mentally equipped to undertake the production and strikes me as a good man for the work.' Nehru's blessings were a very good omen for the project.

Not immediately, though. Nehru, the most supportive of the project, died shortly afterwards in 1964. Then there were problems with the finances. The Maharaja of Baroda, the initial Indian backer of the film, was very difficult in negotiations, and Rank Organization, the British financier, backed out of the project. Quite unexpectedly, a major film organization, Embassy Pictures of Joseph Levine, stepped forward to support the film, along with a major Hollywood studio, Paramount. An agreement was made between Indo British Films and Embassy Pictures in July 1964 for the financing of the film. To get totally involved in the production, Kothari resigned from his position at the Indian High Commission in London while Attenborough declined a major acting role in an MGM production, *Operation Crossbow*.

With everything now in place, the announcement of the film with a budget of five million dollars was made at a gala function at the Hotel Savoy in London on 15 December 1964. At the function, Kothari, with Attenborough standing beside him, said:

> [Gandhi is] the only man, at least in our century, who has shown by his own practice, a way of life that suggests a hope of solution of the outstanding world problems of today … If we succeed, even approximately, in portraying in our story, the rare and exquisite courtesy and compassion, humour and humility, courage and wisdom of this unique man, I believe that people, all over the world, coming out of the cinemas, will say to themselves … How good it is to be a man, and how wonderful it could be to try to be a good human being.

Despite the excitement of a possible grand project of this size in the air, one thing was of major concern for the novice producer-director pair. No casting was decided then, including for the main role of Gandhi, and it was quite a daunting task for the first-time director Attenborough to select one for it. Even though he very much did not want a non-Indian actor to be playing Gandhi, he tried to get well-known British actors like Dirk Bogarde, Peter Finch, Albert Finney and Tom Courtenay for the role, but failed. The film had now hit a roadblock, because no eminent actor was part of the cast and the draft script was too scratchy to move ahead with.

Nonetheless, the launch of the film was also announced with much fanfare in India. Kothari addressed a well-attended press conference at Hotel Taj Mahal in Bombay in February 1965 and said the film would be a faithful reproduction of Louis Fischer's biography. He held another press conference on 7 February 1965 at Hotel Poonam in Poona, the city where the bulk of the shooting was planned to be done. Kothari said the film, besides emphasizing Gandhi's major achievements in eradicating untouchability and his belief in non-violence, for which he had struggled all his life in South Africa and India, would also depict Gandhi as a human being right from age eighteen. At the press conference, Kothari also emphasized that the film would not be a mere documentation of Gandhi's political achievements and preachings. It would be much more than that, he said.

Filmfare magazine reported the announcement of the film, noting that it was to be made in a spirit of reverence:

> The producers have five names, none Indian, for the role of the Mahatma but no casting has actually been done yet for the film. Shooting is to begin in India in October. According to Motilal Kothari, the Indian concerned in the project as executive producer, the only criterion for the casting will be the best person for each role.[11]

It was also reported that the Gandhi Bhavan in Pune would be one of the locations for shooting some of the key sequences of the proposed film.[12] It said that sets consisting of replicas of Gandhi's Ashrams in South Africa, as well as that of Wardha and Sevagram, would be built for the shooting, which would start on 25 January. An American financier had agreed to invest Rs 2.5 crore, and the rest of the amount required for the Rs 3 crore project would be invested by the Maharaja of Baroda. The report also said the story for the film had been approved by Nehru and his successor Lal Bahadur Shastri, as also by Morarji Desai and Indira Gandhi, the latter in her capacity as the minister of information and broadcasting.[13] Moreover, approximately 1500 feet of film in Technicolour was shot in India in 1965.

To move forward on the script, Kothari got the eminent writer Robert Bolt, even though the latter had reservations about the capability of Attenborough as a director. It was a bizarre situation for the film to proceed. As a writer, Bolt had established his credentials in the industry with critically acclaimed films, including *Lawrence of Arabia* and *Doctor Zhivago,* for which he had won an Academy Award. Compared with him, Attenborough had no major success to claim as director. Therefore, in a strange turn of circumstances, Kothari toyed with the idea of dropping Attenborough as the director of the Gandhi film. To make matters worse, the inability of the makers to get a prominent actor to play Gandhi prompted Embassy Pictures to drop out of backing the film.

In the face of all these challenges, Kothari made a short visit to India in 1966, and the media got hold of him in Bombay to quiz him about the progress of the film. He was asked the question that was on everyone's mind—who was to play the all-important role of Gandhi? 'It's strictly off the record,' Kothari said. But he divulged that production of the film would commence in October 1966.[14]

It was reported in the Indian media that despite all these roadblocks, Motilal Kothari was certain that his Gandhi film would be completed by early 1969. The scriptwriter Bolt was in India along with Kothari, and he remarked that the film would essentially be for entertainment and 'hopefully they will get something more than that'.[15] The involvement of Bolt created widespread interest in the film and there were many enquiries in the industry about it. David Lean was also reported to have remarked, 'It could well be the motion picture of the decade.'

Meanwhile, Kothari also made efforts to engage new screenplay writers, but failed. Then, war broke out between India and Pakistan, which meant shooting could not be started, at least for a few months. Attempts were also made by Kothari and Attenborough to engage 20th Century Fox for financing the film, but they were wary of involvement in another Gandhi film after producing *Nine Hours to Rama*, which was a big failure.

Kothari was relentless in his pursuit and got American writer Donald Ogden Stewart, who had won an Academy Award for *The Philadelphia Story* in 1940, to take forward the screenplay. Steward prepared a screenplay, called *The Day Gandhi Died*, which was not what Kothari and Attenborough had envisaged. Their predicament worsened when Nehru's successor Lal Bahadur Shastri also died in January 1966, stalling progress on many major fronts—the script, the casting and the finances. At that point, Kothari wanted a full commitment from Attenborough, failing which it was decided that both would proceed separately to take forward the project and only come together to conclude a deal, if possible.

Kothari renegotiated with Robert Bolt, and in came the well-known director Fred Zinnemann. Bolt and Zinnemann had successfully worked together on *A Man for All Seasons* (1966) for which Zinnemann received the Academy Award for Best Director. Attenborough then opted out saying, 'Zinnemann is a truly great director, one of the best in the world, and if I have to relinquish my dream, well, I could hardly hope to imagine a better person to whom I could pass it on.'[16] Kothari wrote to Christopher Mann, the agent of Zinnemann in October 1966 specifying the details for production of the film. He was keen that Indo British Films should be the makers of the film and he be credited as the Executive Producer.

On both these points, Zinnemann had different ideas. He wanted to produce the film under his own banner Highland Films and in a letter to his agent Christopher Mann specified:

> Mr Kothari should have any title he desires, so long as the words "Producer" and "Director" don't appear in it; otherwise, we would be in for endless and serious misunderstandings. I am sure that the proper and fair way can be found to express the importance and magnitude of his contribution to the picture, but since he has had no professional experience, he should not ask for executive authority—even by implication—on an enormously difficult production of this size.[17]

But Robert Bolt knew the importance of Kothari in a project of this magnitude. He was also aware of the fact that even though Zinnemann and Bolt were respected names, that alone was not sufficient for Indian government, whose help and cooperation was crucial. He wrote to Zinnemann, 'What the Indian government wants, and has said it wants, is some degree of Indian participation, at a respectable level. They do not trust their own filmmakers who enjoy no higher a reputation for probity than do our own. But they do trust Moti Kothari.'[18] Therefore, Bolt wanted to find an amicable solution on this crucial issue about Kothari's involvement as well as credit in the film.

To bolster his case for active and honourable position for Kothari, Bolt further wrote, 'Moti Kothari has the confidence of the Indian Government because he is a known follower of Gandhi, meaning that in some measure at least he is a practicer of what Gandhi preached … He was personally known to Nehru and is to the present premier, Mrs Gandhi. Nehru gave his personal blessing to the project so long as it was guaranteed by Moti's active participation. The same is true of Mrs Gandhi. He has also interested Mountbatten … The point lies in the degree of goodwill towards Moti which is implied by such a gesture.'[19]

Since 1961, Kothari was consumed by the thought of making a Gandhi biopic and Bolt was one of his first collaborators on this project. Even though Bolt was reluctant initially to work on the film, Kothari pursued him relentlessly and, in the process, the noted writer was charmed by the Gandhi magic. He felt that notwithstanding Kothari's lack of professional experience in the film industry,

> Moti Kothari's knowledge of the subject, the locations and personalities involved, the ways and means, the correct channels and the useful channels, is vast. To me his greatest asset (apart from the intensity of his belief in the project) is his friendship with such people as Fischer, Miss Lester, Horace Alexander, Jayaprakash Narayan and other key figures in Gandhi's life, with some of whom I have already had invaluable recorded conversations.

Moreover, Bolt told Zinnemann, 'If it is desired, there are rich well-wishers in India who would be willing to invest rupees in the venture upon Moti Kothari's guarantee.'[20]

During the meeting on 21 October 1966 between these three collaborators, it was decided that 'in order to satisfy Indian expectations and to forestall Indian suspicions (unhappily inflamed by *Nine Hours to Rama*), Mr Kothari ought to be appointed a Director of the operating company' and his credit on main title would be "Film Initiated by Motilal Kothari" and a further credit in final roll-up to reflect his factual contribution in the making of the film. A draft agreement was then drawn up to finalize the details in November-December 1966.

Nothing much came out of this arrangement either. David Lean then re-entered the scene to pursue his old ambition of making a film on Gandhi. MGM studio was considered a possible financier. But the film was delayed because Lean and Bolt got busy with *Ryan's Daughter*, which took three years. During all this impasse, Bolt remained steadfast in the ability and doggedness of Kothari. At every juncture, whether in terms of rights or contracts, he tried to protect the interests of Kothari because he knew that the latter had no steady income and his only pre-occupation was to see a film made on Gandhi.

Bolt's feelings found expression in a letter written by his agent Margaret Ramsay in March 1968 addressed to Lee Steiner, agent of David Lean. She wrote, 'I still think that the initial reason for his writing the film was something over and above biz considerations. There is something about the story of Gandhi which in fact ought to make people behave with just one grain of Gandhi purity, and Bob's support of Kothari has shown very great integrity and responsibility towards the rather unprotected inceptor of the whole thing.'[21]

Kothari was a patient man and he decided to wait. But he was not sitting idle. His original dream of releasing the Gandhi biopic in the birth centenary year had not materialized, but he made every possible effort to successfully organize a few cultural events to commemorate the seminal occasion in England. Meanwhile, Attenborough went on to direct *Oh! What a Lovely War*, *Young Winston* and *A Bridge Too Far*, apart from acting in a few films.

The relentless zeal with which Kothari still pursued his dream, trying to draw the best possible minds to come on board is simply amazing. Thus, he got in touch with D.G. Tendulkar, the man who had written the widely acclaimed *Mahatma,* an eight-volume biography of Gandhi. Kothari wanted to explore the possibility of getting inputs from Tendulkar for the script that was being prepared. On the letterhead of Indo-British Films Limited, Kothari presented himself as executive producer of 'In Production *Mahatma Gandhi*'. In the letter to Tendulkar, dated 6 January 1967, he wrote:

> As early as 1963 Panditji had written to you about the film on the life of Mahatma Gandhi that I am trying to make. Although I have been to India three or four times I did not trouble you because things had not taken any final shape or form. At long last I have now interested Mr Robert Bolt to undertake the writing of the final script. I think it would be very useful if you two met. I wonder, therefore, if you will be kind enough to spare some time during our stay in Bombay from the 15th to the 18th of this month ... In any case it would be a genuine pleasure to meet you in person as I am a great admirer of your wonderful work 'Mahatma'.[22]

Curiously, much before Kothari had approached Richard Attenborough with his Gandhi film idea, he had thought of an Indian filmmaker to helm the prestigious project. That Indian filmmaker was the renowned director V. Shantaram. In 1961, Kothari met him and made him a proposal to direct the Gandhi film. The meeting took place on the sets where Shantaram was shooting his film *Stree*.

When Kothari broached his idea, Shantaram was thrilled. Right from his Prabhat Film Studio days, Shantaram had always espoused the cause of the country's freedom struggle and had tried to portray nationalist sentiments through his films. While agreeing to direct the film, he said the Gandhi project had to be presented as a national one and the film had to be made accessible to the common people. While agreeing to direct it, Shantaram also said he would not charge a single penny for it.[23]

According to Shantaram, it was better to have the government of India on board to support the film so that Gandhi's thoughts and ideas would not only reach out to the Indian masses but also internationally. Kothari agreed and promised to take things up with Prime Minister Nehru. But even after three months, things were not progressing on any front, and finally Shantaram himself wrote letters to Nehru asking for an appointment to discuss the project, but nothing came of it. With no response from either Kothari or Nehru, Shantaram was left disappointed. He had strongly believed he could successfully bring out the spirit of Gandhi's character on screen. Years later, when Attenborough's *Gandhi* was released, he strongly criticized the movie for its lopsided depiction of Gandhi and its dominant Western viewpoint.

While the impasse with Bolt and Lean continued and the project was in a limbo, Kothari suffered a heart attack in September 1969 and finally succumbed on 15 January 1970. Even while carrying a major heart ailment, he didn't leave any stone unturned to take forward his dream project. For the short and stout man that he was, the constant travel and other responsibilities must have taken a heavy toll on his body. But Kothari had a premonition that he might not live for very long.

During one of his many meetings for the film, Kothari shared his inner thoughts with veteran Marathi filmmaker Ram Gabale in Pune. Gabale was closely involved with the making of the Gandhi film at almost every stage and had developed an intimate friendship with Kothari. 'We are taking so much of trouble to complete this film. But

I don't know why, I always feel that I might not be able to live to see the completed film,' Kothari told him.[24]

A man with an endearing smile, who chased the dream of making a feature film on Gandhi for so long, was not to see the fruit of his relentless efforts. For years together, Kothari was a possessed man, going after every possible person and institution to see that the life of Gandhi was brought on screen. It was only his relentless efforts that had brought together some of the best creative minds in the British, American and Indian film industries to picturize the story of an extraordinary Indian leader. His legacy was to continue in the actual making of the film with Kothari's son Raj, an editor at BBC, joining the crew in the editing department.

Attenborough was gracious in acknowledging the real inspiration behind the monumental effort in mounting a film like *Gandhi*. He wrote:

> In 1963 Moti and I had together determined to make the film. The inspiration emanated from Moti, and I resolved that if ever again the opportunity arose for me to assume the task of bringing Gandhi's words and love to the world, nothing would give me a greater sense of fulfilment or indeed a better opportunity of perpetuating the name of Motilal Kothari.[25]

It was only fitting then that when *Gandhi* was finally released in 1982, the film was dedicated to Motilal Kothari, as well as to Pandit Nehru and Louis Mountbatten. What could have been a better tribute to the man when Attenborough also dedicated the Academy Award the Gandhi film won to Motilal Kothari.

Kothari's determination and devotion to Gandhi brought miracles. Despite the many hurdles he faced, and even though Motilal Kothari was not alive to see it, Gandhi's life story was finally portrayed on the silver screen in 1982. Motilal Kothari's story is best described in his own words. 'If my film is made, it is a triumph of perseverance, of faith—and I want young people everywhere to know this and be heartened by this.'

Why the Hell Do You Want to Make a Film About Gandhi?

During their first meeting on 7 July 1964, the maverick American producer Joseph E Levine asked a question to Richard Attenborough and his exact words were, 'Why the hell do you want to make a film about Gandhi?'[26] Obviously, this was not the first time Attenborough faced such a question and also not the last time. Even though, it has been a dream for several filmmakers, both Indian and foreign, to bring Gandhi's life story to the screen, the prospects of mounting such a film had its own challenges. Braving several obstacles and uncertainties, Attenborough was the one who finally managed to make his film *Gandhi* and termed it as 'a human biography'.

Right from the day when he met Motilal Kothari in London on a cold morning in 1962, Attenborough kept at it, struggling to find actors, manage finances and find a suitable script. In the process, the dream of Kothari became his too. Despite being asked so many times by so many people and studios as to 'why the hell' he wanted to make a film on Gandhi, Attenborough persisted with his mad dream. Finally, in November 1982, after about twenty years of struggle, the film was released worldwide to both critical acclaim and commercial success.

I first saw the film as a nine-year-old in a tiny tent-cinema theatre in a small village in Maharashtra. Apart from watching the odd Films Division documentary that popped up now and then, nothing much was available in terms of moving images on Gandhi in the 1980s. So, seeing Gandhi's life story unfold on a big screen made one relive those historical moments that one had only read of in textbooks. The film was released in the dubbed Hindi version too for better connect with Indian audiences.

After the arrival of television in India, watching the film became a yearly ritual for many. Every 2 October, Gandhi's birthday, the film was shown on national television and watched and rewatched by many. Without going into the strengths and weaknesses of the film, one has to admit that here was a full-length feature film that first dared to bring alive the Father of the Nation on screen. People will debate the fact that it was made by a foreign filmmaker and not an Indian, but it was a feat no other filmmaker could manage before.

Gandhi's life, from the time he set foot in India in 1915, mirrors that of the freedom struggle of India. His story is so complex and yet so engaging that one has to carefully sieve out the facts from the chaff of myths, and actual events from the fictional tales that had built around him. And be vigilant about not getting caught up by the controversies about his life.

Attenborough was very clear in his mind that his film was not going to analyse and probe Gandhi's life and actions. Cinema is first and foremost a medium of telling stories. Filmmakers can adopt different approaches to tell their stories. Attenborough had decided his approach and he explained it thus: 'I work as an actor works to involve an audience by engaging their emotions, to interest them in the story you are putting before them ... I have no interest in being remembered as a great creative filmmaker. I want to be remembered as a storyteller.'[27]

Having made more than forty trips to India before the actual production started, Attenborough, in the end, succeeded in telling the story in a simple narrative format. It is not an easy task to put a life story on screen in a three-hour capsule. It becomes more difficult and challenging if that story is about an extraordinary person like Gandhi. Attenborough therefore decided to keep only the important events from Gandhi's life in the plot and not bring in every person or leader of the freedom movement. The guiding mantra was to bring the spirit of Gandhi alive, and he and his team succeeded to a major extent in achieving that feat.

It was the selection of Ben Kingsley to play the role of Gandhi that clinched the matter for Attenborough. Kingsley almost lived the character, and in the process succeeded in making people believe his portrayal of Gandhi. It surely helped that Kingsley, born as Krishna Pandit Bhanji, was of Indian origin, but the astonishing fact was that he had not set foot in India before this assignment! A white actor with brown paint on his face would have looked incredulous and unconvincing in this role. But it was not only about looks. For the 'spirit' to come alive, the mannerisms and body movements, the gait and diction, had to be correct.

For Kingsley, 'The most difficult challenge was to convey Gandhi's titanic energy with his great stillness. This polarity exists throughout his character and this was the problem in playing him.' The more difficult part was to portray Gandhi's charm, together with his toothless grin. Gandhi walked a lot. That long stride of his made people almost run to keep up with him. Also, an actor in his role had to project his inner strength and the affection in his kind eyes. An actor trying to portray the challenging role of Gandhi had to keep all this in mind.

A Shakespearean stage actor, Kingsley, with no previous film experience, got it right miraculously—to such an extent that while the shooting was going on, people came up and bowed before him on the sets. Apart from shaving his head and learning to do Yoga, he lost about 10 kg by turning vegetarian. The extraordinary performance won him an Academy Award for best actor in 1983, despite that year seeing one of the toughest competitions in that category, including Paul Newman for *The Verdict,* Dustin Hoffman for *Tootsie,* Peter O'Toole for *My Favourite Year* and Jack Lemmon for *Missing.*

Naseeruddin Shah, considered to be one of India's finest actors, was one of the strong contenders for this coveted role, and he so badly wanted to be cast as Gandhi that he thought, 'If it were to be an Indian actor, it had to be me.'[28] While there was a buzz about who was to play Gandhi, Shah was also looking at the bigger picture. 'I was dying to get the role not because I was so keen to play him but because international stardom was beckoning, and I thought I had a very good chance of bagging the part. When I was rejected I wasn't devastated because the "screen test" in London had convinced me that the whole thing was rigged,' Shah recalled.[29] But despite being overlooked, when he saw the film he was gracious enough to admit, 'Ben was quite wonderful, he got everything right except Gandhiji's ear-to-ear smile. I was not at that time skilled enough to have pulled it off the way he did, though.'[30]

That, though, didn't prevent Shah from further analysing Kingsley's portrayal of Gandhi, and, true to his forthright style, he is blunt in his opinion:

> My acknowledgement of Ben Kingsley's performance does not mean I was bowled over by it—in fact, I think he fell short on many scores—the smile for one, the voice for another, the muscular body, the assumed sitting/walking postures in which he looked far from comfortable, but he got the essence of the character, I have to admit, and he served the purposes of the film, which frankly conformed closely to the Hollywood formula (without the gratuitous violence of course) of the 'good guy versus the bad'.[31]

Years later, Shah got to play Gandhi's role in a play Mahatma v/s Gandhi directed by Firoz Abbas Khan in 1998. He put his all energy into the role and remembers:

> I finally got to play Gandhi ji in a play by Ajit Dalvi and I think I gained more insight into his psyche in that than I would have by acting in the Hollywood movie. This play showed Gandhi ji as a fallible human being, as an almost tyrannical father and a completely unbending person in many aspects of his life. I was able to empathize with Gandhi's son Harilal as well as with Gandhi himself.[32]

Despite Gandhi's worldwide popularity, it was very surprising that Gandhi as a subject of a feature length film had very few backers in terms of financiers. Perhaps, it was a sign of the changing times, where the matters of money were far more important than any ideology. This resulted in a very long struggle, of almost twenty years, for the Attenborough film to find financial backers for the film. Most of the studios including MGM, Warner Brothers, Paramount etc. thought it an unviable venture with no commercial prospects. Ironically, when the film got completed it was a completely different scenario, and all the major studios in America vied with each other to release and distribute the film worldwide.

In a way, the magic of the Gandhi phenomenon was on display here. From the newsreel era, when he was certainly a major star, Gandhi as a talkie hero seemed to have again appealed to everyone. The wishes of Motilal Kothari also got fulfilled, in the sense that the world got to know and appreciate once again the teachings of Gandhi in an era of atom bombs and the Cold War indicating the decline of humanity. Certainly, the will of the makers got reflected in the end product. The renowned film critic Roger Ebert was effusive in his praise of the film and said, 'This is the sort of rare epic film that spans the decades, that uses the proverbial cast of thousands, and yet follows a human thread from beginning to end.'[33]

The film starts with the assassination and funeral ceremony, thus establishing how popular he was among the people in the first few frames itself. The first forty minutes of the film are devoted to depicting his successful experiments in non-violence and satyagraha in South Africa. The narrative then shifts to India. Gandhi's India tour, undertaken to familiarize himself with the country, is one of the highlights of the film. The four-minute sequence is a visual delight, showcasing India through its diverse social and geographical contours, to the melodious background score by Pandit Ravi Shankar.

Another four-minute scene tries to capture the Dandi March for its sheer dramatic value. Gandhi's epic march had been widely covered by newsreel companies and one gets to see the motion picture cameras placed along his route. This was, in a way, an acknowledgement of the arrival of Gandhi on screen through newsreels. Of course, Gandhi's visit to London to attend the Second Round Table Conference is shown in the film in the newsreel format. It helps in establishing the film as an authentic record and takes viewers back to the black-and-white era of newsreels.

Gandhi was a man of the masses. His life was an open book. But the film also manages to depict a few tender moments between the Gandhi couple. Kasturba had been a solid rock in Gandhi's life, giving him the strength to carry out his public activities. The scenes in the film showing their time together in South Africa beautifully portray it. In India, the scene in which the couple enact their marriage rituals at the banks of a river is a very poignant one. It succeeds in conveying the strong bond between them. During the final moments of Kasturba, no words are spoken, which shows how inseparable the man and his wife were. The sad face of Gandhi conveys his love for and oneness with his partner of sixty-one years.

Much has been written and said about Kingsley's performance. But Rohini Hattangadi was equally brilliant in her portrayal of Kasturba. An alumnus of the National School of Drama, Hattangadi was only twenty-seven when she played the role of Kasturba, which won her numerous accolades. The memorable performance depicting the transition of her character from youth to old age in a graceful manner, got Hattangadi the BAFTA award for best supporting actress, the only Asian to win the honour. Selected for the role over acclaimed actresses Smita Patil and Bhakti Barve, Hattangadi delivered her emotions in a subtle but forceful manner, managing to carve out an individuality even while in the shadow of her great husband.

Cinema is a medium of possibilities. Attenborough's *Gandhi* could be viewed through different prisms, and one can say many things about it. But ultimately it is the tale of a man who led his people for their liberation from a mighty power. The dramatic moments in his life are captured vividly on screen. Attenborough took cinematic liberties to include and exclude many events and personalities from Gandhi's life story. That was inevitable. The focus of the film was to narrate Gandhi's story and capture the spirit of his personality. To a large extent, it is an authentic film. And if anyone wants to know the man's story, this three-hour viewing is a beginning of that journey. The film, justifiably, went on to garner as many as nine Academy Awards, including for best film, best director and best actor.

Attenborough certainly did not heed the advice Nehru gave him before the production was to start. 'Look, he had all the frailties, all the shortcomings. Give us that. That's the measure, the greatness of the man. Whatever you do, do not deify him …' Nehru had told Attenborough. The director used his artistic freedom and chose to tell the story in a simple manner without going into an analysis of Gandhi's actions. Perhaps the nature and format of the biopic itself compel a filmmaker to avoid analysis. The film is not a documentation of a time period. The focus of the biopic as a genre has traditionally been on the actions of an individual, and Attenborough's *Gandhi* sticks to that. Film historian Ashish Rajadhyaksha sums it up succinctly, 'The film generates an interest in the individual—or rather, the Individual—and the events are little more than dramatic props with which to highlight their greatness.'[34]

Eventually, critical analysis apart, Richard Attenborough's *Gandhi* became the first biopic feature film on the Father of the Nation. It told a simple story about a complex man.

After the release of Attenborough's *Gandhi*, it was not necessary now for filmmakers to tell the entire story of Gandhi once again, thus paving the way for them to focus on various aspects of Gandhi. One could choose a particular event, a relationship or an ideology from his life and explore the multiple layers in a cinematic manner. Attenborough's *Gandhi* also encouraged Indian filmmakers to venture into portraying these nuances boldly. Then there were other stalwart freedom fighters, some of them close colleagues of Gandhi, whose lives found their way into biopics. Gandhi appeared in them, not as a focus, but through the prism of the different points of view of these people.

16

Gandhi in Many Avatars

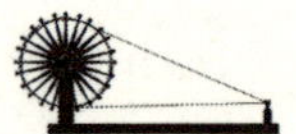

A FULL-FLEDGED BIOPIC FEATURE film on Gandhi took almost thirty-four years to be made after his demise. That is a long and considerable time. But the successful reception of Attenborough's *Gandhi,* released in 1982, gave the much-needed fillip to the aspirations of many Indian filmmakers to explore various facets of Gandhi's life. Many of them, including masters like Satyajit Ray, had earlier shied away from the challenging task of making a film on Gandhi for the big screen. The release of Attenborough's film and its good reception proved to be a turning point for them.

There was also a sufficient gap now, from Gandhi's times, for the Indian film industry to gather courage and take a relook at Gandhi's persona through different lenses. Perhaps this time gap gave the Indian filmmakers the necessary space and freedom to explore his life in a neutral manner. The burden of 'Mahatmaship' could now be thrown away, to see the man behind it and throw light on some of his controversial actions and relationships.

But trust the Indian filmmakers to come up with something absurd just to garner cheap publicity. Just a few months after Attenborough's *Gandhi* was released, a well-known Indian producer and director I.S. Johar announced his version of a Gandhi film in May 1983. From all records, it was a mere publicity stunt. The maverick filmmaker, always known for publicity gimmicks, announced that the film was to be financed by American Cable TV Company. And that was it; he did not give any more details. Obviously, he was just indulging in hype and drama to be in the news, cashing in on Gandhi's name than anything else.

Despite the successful reception of Attenborough's *Gandhi*, both critically and commercially, nothing much happened in the Indian film industry for more than ten years by way of any Gandhi film. Finally, it was veteran filmmaker Shyam Benegal who decided to take the plunge and focus on the early years of Gandhi in South Africa. His film was a cinematic exploration of what made Gandhi prepare for his larger role in India. The film, *The Making of Mahatma/Gandhi Se Mahatma Tak,* in English/Hindi, respectively, was released in 1996, featuring the events that made Gandhi a political saint.

Based on *Apprenticeship of a Mahatma* written by Fatima Meer, who also wrote the screenplay for Benegal, the film focused on Gandhi's twenty-one years in South Africa, where he conceived and experimented with the idea of satyagraha with enormous success. The biopic, produced jointly by National Film Development Corporation (NFDC) of India and South African Broadcasting Corporation (SABC), explored the leader's two-decade struggle in South Africa.

Gandhi's early life with family in Africa, the efforts he took in organizing the Natal Congress, and his efforts to support the British in the Boer War were the focus areas in the film. Benegal portrayed this important portion of his life as a preparatory phase, on which Gandhi would expand after his return to India, to don the mantle of the leader of India's freedom movement. According to Benegal, 'This is a more intimate story. It is concerned with so much that had to change in Gandhi before he became the Mahatma.'[1] Attenborough's *Gandhi* had touched upon the African segment of Gandhi's life, but Benegal focused fully on it, making a detailed study of Gandhi's early experiments.

Writer Prof. Fatima Mir, an author and historian based in South Africa, had described in her book the transformation of a very young and shy man into a leader of the masses. Benegal recalled:

> When I read the book, I found it had a great deal of relevance for the world today ... My story is actually of a personal transformation. He went to South Africa as a young lawyer, not very sure of himself but when he came from South Africa, he was already the Mahatma.[2]

Most people know and are aware about Gandhi's life after he came back to India from South Africa in great detail. He had become famous as a Mahatma and the hero of the Indian population in South Africa. But the details of his early days in South Africa are not very well known. The film focused precisely on this period in Gandhi's life. The spotlight was on the early struggles of a man who was trying to stand on his feet and at the same time becoming aware of bigger issues, such as racism and injustice. It was also the time of his personal struggles and choices, which saw him adopting sexual abstinence and turning vegetarian. The process was not simple, as it involved a confrontation with his wife and family, and the forming of his own opinions and ideologies. He was young and raw and trying to form and realize his ideals.

Rajit Kapur, who played this young Gandhi, portrayed the character remarkably well. Since no moving images are available of Gandhi's time in South Africa, Kapur was on his own as far as any reference point for an actor was concerned. While Kingsley played a gentle Gandhi, Kapur's Gandhi was a youthful but maturing Advocate Mohandas. He was aggressive and straightforward in his approach in dealing with issues faced by outside men in a foreign land. For Kapur, Gandhi's autobiography *My Experiments with Truth* was like a bible for preparing for the role.[3] This book dwells a lot on Gandhi's African years and gave Kapur a broad framework on which to base his acting. Kapur brought out the emotional intensity and empathy of the man, with a compelling performance in the film.

As an actor, Kapur's fondest memories are of the last scene in the film, where his hair was cut live on camera to transform him into the image of Gandhi which we know. 'I thought I found the soul of Gandhi at that moment when I walked out to give that shot with *Raghupati Raghav Rajaram* playing in the background,' he recalled.[4] More than 100 people on the set stood transfixed seeing the physical and mental transformation that happened in the actor in front of their eyes. Pallavi Joshi played Kasturba convincingly and credibly. The silent yet powerful personality of Kasturba and her companionship with Gandhi were brought out by her brilliantly.

The highlight of the film was the long march Gandhi led to protest against the tax on Indian settlers in South Africa. Arguably, it was the first political march undertaken in history in a totally non-violent manner. The film succeeded in throwing light on the transformation that had happened in Gandhi's life and how the seeds were sown in South Africa for the tree that bore fruit later in India. Benegal beautifully traced the graph of the slow and steady growth of an unsure man into a leader with tremendous self-belief. There were several moments of Mohandas finding his course of action in the film. The film showcased the evolution of a simple and common man into a mass leader by his adoption of new means of political struggle and, in the process, becoming a Mahatma.

Sardar Patel was one of the closest colleagues of Gandhi in the freedom movement, apart from Pandit Nehru. A leading advocate from Gujarat, who left a flourishing legal practice to follow Gandhi, Patel was a staunch supporter of his leader. Despite having differences of opinion with Gandhi, Patel stood by him till his last breath. Gandhi treated Patel like a brother and said, 'He has earned the nickname of being my yes-man. He does not mind it. He even flaunts it as a compliment … Ever since he decided to cast his lot with me, my word has been law to him.'[5]

A man instrumental in the unification of the country after Independence and a leader who knew the value of cinema surely deserved his story to be told on screen. Renowned filmmaker Ketan Mehta took up such a project and directed the Hindi film *Sardar,* which was released in 1994. The film, scripted by the eminent playwright Vijay Tendulkar, highlighted the last few years of Patel's life in the run-up to India's freedom. Well-known actor Paresh Rawal played the main lead of Patel, while Annu Kapoor enacted the role of Gandhi.

The film opens with young Patel criticizing Gandhi but then getting drawn to the freedom movement after listening to him. Patel was just six years younger than Gandhi and they enjoyed a great bonhomie on account of their common Gujarati background. While speaking at the Haripura Congress session in 1938, which had been very well organized by Patel, Gandhi said, 'Sardar and I are close to each other, we are as one, we work alike and we think alike.' The love and affection between them was, however, not reflected in the film, except in the scene of their last meeting before Gandhi is killed. Moreover, Gandhi is portrayed in the film as a weak and helpless leader who is almost resigned to the events that unfolded in the days before India's Independence, a far cry from the actual facts.

Next to come was a significant story of a staunch Gandhi follower in *Kuhkhal* (The Price of the Freedom), an Assamese film in 1998. Directed by the renowned filmmaker Jahnu Barua, the film focused on the situation in Assam in 1942. The Congress unit in a remote village, Sarupathar, misinterpreted Gandhi's call for non-violent political action and decided to sabotage a train. Kuhkhal Konwar (Kushal Konwar), the president of the unit, understood the real essence of Gandhi's message and tried to convince his committee against such a sabotage plan, but failed to change their mind. Kuhkhal accepted complete moral responsibility for the crime. C.A. Humphrey, then the British head of the district, wanted a scapegoat, and Kuhkhal was the perfect candidate, as he was not only honest but also a member of a powerful royal clan of Assam.

Based on a true incident, the main focus of the plot was on how the lead character, despite being not very well educated, but who believes in ethical values, chooses to face exemplary punishment. A very strong follower of Gandhi, Kuhkhal became a victim of his own principles. Barua recalled, 'I have always liked the two ideas of Gandhi; non-violence and Swaraj, and I was moved by the character of Kuhkhal.'[6]

According to Barua, Gandhi in independent India has never been properly introduced to students and young Indians. 'In fact, he was wrongly introduced. Gandhi means only bhajans and a holy person. Because of this wrong perception, generation after generation never came to know how to respect Gandhi and his values. Half of our problems could be solved if we follow his values in their true spirit,' Barua lamented.[7] Though Gandhi is not shown physically in the film, his presence can be felt through this staunch follower.

Seven years later, Barua was to make another interesting film on Gandhi, which garnered critical acclaim. *Maine Gandhi Ko Nahi Maara* (I didn't kill Gandhi), released in 2005 in Hindi, was an intriguing narrative revolving around the life of a retired professor, Uttam Chaudhary, who falls victim to dementia. In his unstable mental condition, he starts believing that it is he who killed Gandhi at Birla House while playing with a toy gun. The long sessions of arguments eventually bring up many social and political aspects of that hateful incident of Gandhi's assassination in the contemporary context. Once again, Barua was fired up in his passion to present Gandhi before the new generation. He said, 'I was very much conscious of the fact that today's generation does not respect Gandhi.'

Gandhi's assassination, though a tragic event, is the most memorable incident from his life for many people. Therefore, the protagonist in the film is obsessed with that incident. The approach of the plot is indirect, and the last speech of the protagonist says it all. The film is also about how young people are suffering a lot because they do not know of Gandhi's values and have not adopted them. Barua also tried to emphasize Gandhi's idea of Swaraj.

> Assam is very rich in terms of natural resources from tea, oil, forest products, etc., one of the richest in Asia. But in independent India, no textbooks explain it properly. Students do not know how tea

> is made and oil is extracted. What Gandhi said about Swaraj, that know your country, know your resources, use of indigenous things. He used Charkha, a symbol of our identity. If he was alive, Charkha would have been replaced by indigenous computers![8]

Barua wove into the plot a Gandhian family with a great deal of love. Barua said, rather sadly:

> I had to bring him in very tactfully. It would not have worked otherwise. As a filmmaker I had to use this cinematic element to bring focus. No one can negate that Gandhi was [is] irrelevant [today]. He is everywhere but forgotten. All are using him, but his values are forgotten. I have taken a negative stand to provoke the things, positively. So that people can appreciate. Lot of young people told me that it opened their eyes. True value of Gandhi has never been truly conveyed. We have been killing Gandhi every moment. More than half of the problems could have been easily solved if we had followed his principles and values.[9]

The positive response to these films on Gandhi encouraged other filmmakers to portray the lives of other important political and social leaders who were contemporaries of Gandhi. These biopics threw light on these leaders and their work, which paralleled Gandhi's. Sometimes, few of them had also crossed paths with Gandhi. Obviously, a very different approach is followed to project Gandhi from these leaders' point of view. These movies tried to analyse Gandhi's many actions in a critical way. But then, Gandhi was never against introspection.

One such tall leader was Dr B.R. Ambedkar. The man who led the struggle of untouchable sections of the Indian society had confronted Gandhi many times. A film by the same name as the leader was released in 2000 in multiple languages. Renowned filmmaker Dr Jabbar Patel focused his lens on this important social revolutionary in India. Dr Ambedkar's tryst with the Indian nationalist movement during the heyday of Gandhian politics occupies an important part of the narrative.

In the film, Gandhi is depicted vis-à-vis Ambedkar at their first meeting in Bombay at Mani Bhavan, then at the Round Table Conference meeting in London, and finally at the Aga Khan Palace, during the deliberations on the Poona Pact.

Gandhi was seen through the eyes of Dr Ambedkar as a Sanatani, a religious Hindu leader whose only aim was to protect Hinduism and not to emancipate the depressed classes. Ambedkar claimed to be the sole voice and representative of the depressed classes in India. During the Round Table Conference, there were bitter clashes between them. Even so, Gandhi was all empathy for Ambedkar. Gandhi wrote:

> I have the highest regard for Dr. Ambedkar. He has every right to be bitter. That he does not break our heads is an act of self-restraint on his part … The same thing happened to me in my early days in South Africa where I was hounded out by the Europeans wherever I went. It is quite natural for him to vent his wrath.[10]

Months later, after the Poona Pact was signed in 1932, Ambedkar had to say to Gandhi, 'I have been surprised, immensely surprised to find so much in common between Gandhi and myself. If you devoted yourself entirely to the welfare of the Depressed Classes, you would become our hero.'[11]

The versatile actor Mammootty played the role of Dr Ambedkar in a most convincing manner, with forceful body language and powerful speech delivery. The strong performance brought him the National Film Award for best actor. Even though there are only a few scenes when Gandhi comes on screen, his role was essayed by Mohan Gokhale in a subtle and gentle manner. The contrast in their acting styles was too stark to be ignored. The strong physicality of Mammootty, with his booming voice, overpowers and completely dominates the meek and listless Gokhale. 'Gandhi comes across as a politician while meeting Dr Ambedkar. The clashes were bound to happen due to the difference in their ideologies even though their goal was common,' said Dr Patel.[12] But this difference in their ideologies didn't prevent Dr Ambedkar from rushing immediately to Birla House when he heard the news of Gandhi's assassination. Next day, despite his poor health, Dr Ambedkar walked some distance in the funeral procession.

Another political adversary of Gandhi was V.D. Savarkar. A film was released depicting his life story in 2001. Ved Rahi's bilingual film *Veer Savarkar*, made in Marathi and Hindi, vividly portrayed the personal hardships that Savarkar underwent at the Andaman jail. Savarkar's faith in violent struggle to overthrow colonial rule was at complete variance with Gandhi's ideology of non-violence. Gandhi's meeting with Savarkar was an important moment in the film. The film tried to recreate the second, and the last, meeting between Gandhi and Savarkar in Ratnagiri in March 1927 at the latter's house. They had first met in London's India House in 1906. The 1927 meeting revolved around the issue of caste reforms, untouchability and the Shuddhi Movement.

While Gandhi opposed Savarkar's Shuddhi Movement, or reconversion of people to Hinduism, Savarkar differed with Gandhi on his insistence on maintaining the 'varna' system. They never met again after 1927. Later, Savarkar became one of the accused in the murder of Gandhi and was subsequently acquitted due to lack of evidence. Like Motilal Kothari, who initiated the idea of a Gandhi biopic, the cause of a film on Savarkar was championed by the renowned music composer Sudhir Phadke. Like the film on Gandhi, it took several years for Phadke to finally realize his dream of a biopic on Savarkar.

The revolutionary nationalist Bhagat Singh believed in armed revolution to gain freedom for India. He differed with Gandhi's ideology of non-violence, and this was depicted in Rajkumar Santoshi's patriotic offering *The Legend of Bhagat Singh*. The biopic, released in 2002, portrayed conflicts and conciliations between the different ideologies of Bhagat Singh and Gandhi. In fact, as many as five films were released that year focusing on the revolutionary freedom fighter. Bhagat Singh's tryst with Gandhian politics in his early life had an interesting parallel with his image of a socialist revolutionary. But there is a twist in the tale—the film showcased Bhagat Singh's growing popularity, almost threatening the leadership of Gandhi. Surendra Rajan, who played

Gandhi in the film, made a caricature of the character by gesticulating angrily while reacting to Bhagat Singh's act of throwing a bomb in the National Assembly.

Also, Gandhi's character was denounced for not making enough efforts to stop Bhagat Singh's hanging, which is historically far from the truth. Gandhi had sent a Congress delegation to Viceroy Irwin to plead for commutation of the death penalty for Bhagat Singh and also wrote letters asking the government to reconsider their decision. In fact, his last letter was sent on the very day on which the British government hurriedly carried out the hanging of Bhagat Singh for fear of pressure building up to stop the shameful act.

In cleverly placed situations in the film, Gandhi's ideas and his sentences were countered strongly by Bhagat Singh, his replies almost amounting to retorts that both suited the plot as well as gaining applause from the audience. Well known filmmaker and then Chairman of Central Board of Film Censors (CBFC) Vijay Anand considered Gandhi's portrayal in the film to be weak and unfair. He said, 'He (Gandhi's character) doesn't even hold his head high. I told the filmmaker he was the Father of the Nation. Don't let him look like a cow.'

Shyam Benegal was once again behind the camera to focus on the story of Gandhi's colleague-turned-political adversary Subhash Chandra Bose. A revolutionary and charismatic leader, still revered by people, Bose had tried to wage an armed struggle against the British government by raising an army of staunch followers. *Netaji: The Forgotten Hero*, released in 2004 and directed by Benegal, threw light on Bose's struggle to raise the Indian National Army to fight the British colonizers. It also touched on Bose's ambivalent relationship with Gandhi.

Despite being an advocate of armed revolution, Bose remained a great admirer of Gandhi and his respect for the Father of the Nation was intact till his tragic end. Gandhi reciprocated the feelings of the young leader. He refused initially to believe the news of Bose's death and was convinced only after many months. Sachin Khedekar, with his close physical resemblance to Bose, brought out the various nuances of the character very well.

The film opens with a scene from the Tripuri Congress session in 1939, where Bose, who has been elected president, confronts Gandhi when asked to step down on the insistence of the latter. Bose is not convinced about the effectiveness of the strategy of non-violence when the Second World War is at India's doorstep. Both Gandhi and Bose decide to go their separate ways to pursue their common goal of freedom for India. The meeting between them shown in the film ends on a cordial note when Gandhi calls Bose his 'strayed son'. This sets the tone for the film to showcase Bose's armed struggle, a story that is now part of folklore.

The majority of these biopics focusing on important national leaders tried to short-change Gandhi as far as his portrayal on screen was concerned. While admittedly the inter-personal relationships between Gandhi and these leaders were vexed, it has to be kept in mind that all of them were engaged in pursuing a common objective. Gandhi, on his part, never brought his differences with other leaders to a personal level; for him, it was ideas that were always important. Therefore, one is amused to see some of these 'biopic' films trying to make their chosen leader bigger in stature than Gandhi by showing the latter in a poor light. Almost all the portrayals of Gandhi in these films tried to trivialize his role and importance in the freedom movement. One might defend it by calling it as cinematic liberty, but it cannot be at the cost of historical accuracy.

Gandhi was arguably one of the most photographed men in the world since the invention of the camera. Many well-known photographers had clicked and captured his many moods in several memorable photographs over the years. One of them was the celebrated *Life* magazine photographer Margaret Bourke-White. British Broadcasting Corporation (BBC) made a twenty-nine-minute documentary in 2004, *The Worlds Most Photographed: Mahatma Gandhi*, which was directed by Louise Hooper. It also told the story of another renowned French photographer, Henri Cartier-Bresson. He had managed to take photographs of the mortal remains of Gandhi, which became among the most publicized images of the event worldwide. He had reached Birla House moments after Gandhi fell to bullets and could click photographs of the pistol used, the bloodstained clothes and the bullet-ridden body of the Mahatma. He remained at the venue, clicking photographs of people mourning by the side of Gandhi's dead body. These were poignant moments of grief marking the final moments of the great man at Birla House. The next day, Cartier-Bresson also managed to click some of the most iconic images of the funeral ceremony showing the nation in mourning.

Among the many images associated with Gandhi's associations in the public memory, one popular image is that of his three favourite monkeys. A sculpture of three monkeys sitting in a row, one with its eyes closed, one its ears closed and one with its mouth closed, is believed to have been presented to him by some Japanese visitors. The monkeys symbolize the popular saying, 'See no evil, hear no evil, speak no evil', and have become part of Gandhi memorabilia. In Kamal Haasan's *Hey Ram*, released in 2000, the protagonist Saket Ram reinterprets these monkeys as one that has ears only for him (Gandhi), won't open its mouth against him, and is blind to the current state of affairs. And all of them live in a world of Gandhi-esque fantasy. It is this interpretation in the film, written and directed by Haasan, that set the tone for the bilingual period drama in Hindi and Tamil, presenting an alternative ideological viewpoint of India's Partition and Gandhi's assassination.

It is a tale of an archaeologist, Saket Ram, played by Kamal Haasan, who turns into a militant ideologue after a series of personal tragedies, including the murder of his wife during a communal riot in Calcutta just before India's Independence. His hatred towards Gandhi, whom he blames for appeasement of Muslims, grows, even as his next would-be wife sings Gandhi's favourite bhajan '*Vaishnav Jan To*' at a family function.

Viewers get the first glimpse of Gandhi, played by a well-built Naseeruddin Shah, during his peace efforts in riot-affected Calcutta. Ram questions Suhrawardy, the premier of Bengal, for his complicity in the atrocities to which Gandhi was a mute and helpless spectator. Shah, after failing to get the coveted role in Attenborough's *Gandhi* in 1982, realized his dream to essay the character after eighteen years. But he does not have fond memories of the film. He recalls, 'The film required me to wear prosthetic makeup all over my face and I must say I hated the experience.'[13]

Shah also wrote about getting to play that elusive role:

> My curiosity to know if I could (pull off Gandhi's role), however, was finally stilled many years later when I played Gandhi on the stage in a hugely successful production; and merely repeated that performance in a film (*Hey Ram*) with so much prosthetic on my face it could have made a Mongolian actor resemble Gandhi if his head were shaved and he wore granny glasses.[14]

It is Shreeram Abhyankar, a Tamil-Maharashtrian man from Thanjavur, who influences Saket Ram, and the latter slowly gets drawn towards extreme ideologies, politically opposed to Gandhi. Gandhi is referred to as a 'treacherous person' and his role as a 'Mahatma' is questioned. Atul Kulkarni portrayed the character of Abhyankar brilliantly with his intense delivery of dialogues and probing eyes. It won him the best supporting actor award at the National Film Awards. Saket Ram then resolves to kill Gandhi for his policy of Muslim appeasement. He finds himself at the same hotel in Delhi where Nathuram Godse is staying, nursing a similar motive. Eventually, after many twists and turns, including the death of his close Muslim friend Amjad Khan, played by Shahrukh Khan, Ram realizes the value of peace and non-violence, but it is too late.

During a scene at Birla House, Gandhi is shown carried in by men in a chair, and he is sitting like a resigned man in a pensive mood. Later, when the protagonist comes face to face with his target, he is a changed man. He is introduced to Gandhi as the man who saved many Muslims during the riots. Gandhi approvingly refers to him as 'My Ram from the south!' The only time Gandhi's character feels real in the film is when he cracks a joke on himself while haltingly attempting to speak Tamil. Ram makes his way in front of Gandhi to seek forgiveness, but Gandhi asks him to join in his proposed visit to Pakistan. The very next moment, Gandhi is killed by Godse.

The killing scene is shot in the most stereotypical Indian 'filmy' style, where Gandhi was thrown into the air after being hit by bullets and then falling on the ground with a thud! Considering the fact that an actor of such fine calibre as Naseeruddin Shah was involved, this particular scene was most galling to watch. When asked about it, Shah confessed, 'It was Kamal Haasan's idea. In fact, he demonstrated how it should be done. He was trying to make a film that would please every kind of viewer, I think.'[15]

Thankfully, such a distasteful scene was rendered poignant by a soulful rendition of Gandhi's favourite bhajan '*Vaishnav Jan To*' in the background by D.K. Pattammal. One of the finest exponents of Carnatic music, Pattammal had sung many patriotic songs during the heydays of India's freedom movement invoking Gandhi's name. So, it was thoughtful of both Kamal Haasan and composer Illayaraja to get her to sing the bhajan, she already being eighty years old. The recording equipment was taken to her house, and when 'told that the song was to be played at Gandhi's death in the film, the redoubtable lady resorted to emotional recall to add sigh and sob at appropriate intervals!'[16]

After all the Gandhi bashing in the three-and-a-half-hour film, Haasan's ambitious project tries to salvage itself in the end when the protagonist Ram collects the spectacles and sandals of Gandhi as precious memories for keepsake. In a memorable last scene of the film, these memorabilia are handed over to Tushar Gandhi, real-life grandson of Gandhi. Saket Ram's room, full of images of Gandhi, is shown filled with bright sunlight filtering in from the open windows.

Commenting on his motive in making such a controversial film, Kamal Haasan said, 'I come from a family of Gandhi bhakts. But I am nobody's bhakt. I had a controversial opinion on Gandhi when I was a teenager. This film is my apology to him. I never call him Mahatma because I wanted to see his face behind such a big halo.'[17]

It is anybody's guess whether he succeeded in seeing the face, leave alone the soul of the man, through this film.

17

Imagining Gandhi in the Present Times

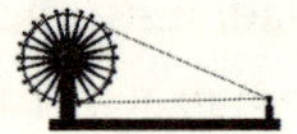

IT IS A FAVOURITE national pastime for many Indians to talk about how Gandhi has become irrelevant. Almost everyone has an imaginary axe to grind about one thing or other related to Gandhi. The man and his ideology are of no use for the new generations, we are told every now and then. Moreover, Gandhi bashing and ridiculing him have been successfully made into a career by many, particularly on social media. The anonymity these platforms afford has made people make shameful utterances on Gandhi without verifying the truth. It is also believed that the rapid advances in science and technology have made Gandhi's concept of development regressive and old-world. Funnily enough, Gandhi and his values have blissfully survived all such attacks, and in fact every such criticism has given him a new lease of life.

Therefore, against all these odds, Gandhi made a strong comeback on screen in the new century. The man who was considered a thing of past, slowly being forgotten, got a fresh lease of life on screen in the new millennium. Filmmakers explored new meanings in his principles and scrutinized his life in greater detail. In the process, Gandhi was no longer kept on a high pedestal. He was humanized. Cinema tried to tell stories of him that are ordinary, yet showing him as an extraordinary man. In fact, the new millennium has seen many more films focusing on Gandhi's life than the period before. It is a rediscovery of sorts, to imagine him to be present in the current times. It is also an exploration to find answers to the problems of our times by using his methods and ideals.

If you don't succeed by attacking a man's ideology, then try to find something controversial or juicy in his private life: this has happened with many in the past who have been torch bearers for successive generations. Gandhi is no exception and has faced relentless scrutiny from all quarters. Because he dared to do and experiment—something few can even dream of. Moreover, he wrote about these experiments time and again, caring too hoots about what people had to say. Therefore, Gandhi's private life has always been a matter of curiosity for many. His peculiar way of living—at least, that is how society saw it—based on the principles he himself derived from his life, has been debated and analysed endlessly. It started during his lifetime and continues even now in great detail.

Among the many curiosities and complexities of his personal life, his relationship with his sons has invited a lot of criticism from many quarters. A great leader who led the nation was a failure, many think, when it came to bringing up his sons. His relationship with his elder son Harilal, particularly, was a matter of anguish for both him and Kasturba. Despite efforts from both sides, the chasm between father and son could never be bridged. Filmmaker Feroz Abbas Khan looked at this difficult relationship in his film *Gandhi, My Father*. Released in 2007, the film, written and directed by Khan, highlighted Gandhi's love for the nation and his commitment towards social reformation at the cost of his family.

To generations born after India became an independent nation, Gandhi has been presented in two very extreme ways. One put him on a pedestal, eulogizing his 'sainthood' and making him a demi-god, while the other hated him and believed him to be the cause of all evils in India. These were very convenient and easy positions to take, because it suited the people and organizations that propagated those views for years. But not everyone was ready to take such extreme positions. Feroz Abbas Khan wanted to explore the middle path. 'I felt that humanizing Gandhi was, perhaps, the way that I could relate to him,' Khan said.[1] 'The idea of Gandhi is much bigger than the personality of Gandhi.' The Mahatma is going to be there forever, but there is also a Bapu, a father and a family man.

Gandhi, My Father is a moving tale of the misunderstandings between father and the son, that leads to bitterness and anguish in their lives. Akshaye Khanna as Harilal, Gandhi's eldest son, tried to bring the turmoil and the bitterness of lack of love from his father on screen. Harilal was constantly under the stress of being the Mahatma's son, whereas what he wanted was to lead a normal life, away from the constant glare of society. But being Gandhi's son meant that was not possible. It led to both father and son growing apart. In the midst of Gandhi's public life, the letters exchanged by them are testimony to the anger and hurt that had crept in between them.

Darshan Jariwala, who played Gandhi, depicted the anguish and helplessness of a father in a convincing manner. Having been offered the role accidentally, Jariwala went through a course of Vipassana meditation to prepare for this important assignment. 'It was necessary to empty out the weight of ordinariness from my being and to subsume my sense of self completely in order to even begin to attempt this character,' Jariwala confessed.[2] Coming from a Gujarati background, just like Gandhi, certainly helped both Jariwala and Shefali Shah, who played Kasturba, in getting the right mannerisms, body language and dictions of Bapu and his wife. It is a story told from the point of view of Harilal, Gandhi's eldest son, and of course the Gandhi that emerges is obviously very different from Gandhi's public image.

It was a vexed relationship from the beginning. Gandhi, true to his nature, held himself responsible for all the misdeeds of Harilal. It was his lust that had led to the birth of this son when his own father was lying on his deathbed, he believed. Thus, the relationship could never be repaired. The film portrays seven to eight meetings between them, but they are all marked more by silence than any exchange of words. All along, Gandhi, the father, tries to call back his estranged son, but the latter is stubborn in his refusal to return. Was Gandhi a prisoner of his circumstances or did Harilal fail to see his father in a true and broader perspective? The film raises these questions and tries to explore the inner turmoil of both. Steadfast in his beliefs, Gandhi is finally a broken father, anguished by his son's erratic behaviour. And then, perhaps, also by the way, India became independent with a huge blood-stained partition.

As was the case with several filmmakers, Khan was certainly a changed man after making his own interpretation of Gandhi for the screen. 'I am more inspired by Gandhi after having made a film on him. It is his ideology that is the answer for the troubled times we are in and it would be so for all the times to come,'[3] he said. Khan succeeded in presenting a very compassionate view of the irony of the relationship between a famous father who believed in the service of mankind and a son who wanted to chart his own path.

As per the Hindu tradition, the soul is immortal and the body perishable.[4] After the cremation, one's ashes are immersed in the holy waters as part of the last rites. Immersion of Gandhi's ashes, therefore, was a very poignant event. The ashes were immersed in various rivers and seas in different parts of the country in 1948. The vast amount of footage available of these ceremonies is a true testimony of the devotion and faith people had towards their leader. A 2010 film, *Road to Sangam,* released in Hindi and directed by Amit Rai, tried to capture those very emotions. The film presented a fictional account about an old Ford V8 engine that carried the ashes of Mahatma Gandhi to Triveni Sangam in Allahabad and its mechanic Hasmat Ullah.

A Muslim mechanic is given the job of repairing an old engine. He is blissfully unaware of the fact that it had transported the ashes of Gandhi. He is caught in a complex situation after a powerful bomb explosion rocks his town leading to the arrest of innocent Muslim youths of his locality. A strike to work is called by the prominent leaders of his community to protest against the unjust treatment meted out to the arrested youths by the police. Will he support the protest and abandon the repair of the engine, or go against the wishes of his community? The film focuses on the contemporary political scene and conflicts of identity. In the process, it manages to hold a mirror to the society, suffering from the resurgence of communalism after six decades of Gandhi's martyrdom.

Next year came a short English film, *Crumpled Paper Titled Gandhi,* showcasing the story of a ten-year-old boy's tryst with truth through a page on Mahatma Gandhi in a textbook. The nine-minute film, released in 2011, was written by Shahzeb Kothari, along with Mirat Trivedi. Kothari directed the film portraying the journey of the boy learning and unlearning Gandhi through events in the course of a single day.

An Unlikely Combination: Gandhi and Hitler

No two men could be so different—Gandhi and Hitler. The men who shaped world history in their own ways during the two decades of the 1930s and 1940s were starkly contrasting in personality and ideology. One believed in non-violent methods while the other tried to finish off an entire ethnic group of people. This clash in their ideologies was what the makers tried to focus on in the film *Gandhi to Hitler,* released in 2011. Initially titled *Dear Friend Hitler,* the film, directed by Rakesh Ranjan Kumar, is based on the two letters written by Gandhi to Hitler and was released at the sixty-first Berlin International Film Festival.

Obviously, in a nation where Hitler's autobiographical manifesto *Mein Kampf* is so popular that it sells almost in equal numbers as Gandhi's *The Story of My Experiments with Truth,* it was a very clever effort on the part of filmmaker to have the names of these two in the title to draw audiences. They certainly can't be blamed though. As early as in 1935, there was a funny incident involving the name of these two contrasting personalities. It so happened that when a drama named *Vicky* was being staged in Gaiety theatre in London, the German Ambassador took objection to naming a character of a small page-boy as Hezikiyah Hitler, on the ground that the name suggested Jewishness. The government ordered that the name be changed. The theatre people, in their own wisdom, changed it to George Bernard Gandhi![5]

The film starts with a disclaimer: 'Although the letters, which the film is based upon, are true and there is historical evidence to support the same, there is no proof that the letters ever reached the dictator during World War II, or that he ever read them.' Gandhi is then shown writing a letter to Hitler in 1939 from his Ashram in Wardha. The scene then shifts directly to April 1945, when Russian forces have surrounded the city of Berlin and the German army is in the process of surrendering before them. Funnily enough, Hitler is shown reading Shakespeare in his bunker in these trying final moments!

It is a tale of the last few days of the Führer of the Third Reich. The filmmakers tried to show how the Gandhian principles of love and peace are the way ahead for humanity, whereas adherence to Nazism invites nothing but destruction. Even though Gandhi's name is used in the title, there is very little of Gandhi in the film. He is infrequently brought on screen to mouth his usual philosophy while marching through the countryside. It feels as if Gandhi was out on a walk freely distributing his sermons!

A parallel story is shown, in which a Gandhian housewife is longing for her husband who is in the midst of action in the Second World War. There is yet another story of Netaji Subhash Chandra Bose and the Indian National Army. Raghuvir Yadav, an otherwise competent actor, missed the plot completely and ended up doing a caricature of Hitler. Though this seemed to be unintentional, it helped in showing what the filmmakers probably did not have on their minds as far as portrayal of the dictator was concerned!

The premise of the film was enticing—the clash of two very different ideologies emanating from the East and West. But its lacklustre production values and very weak screenplay ensured that the film fell completely flat. The entire Indian cast playing the foreign characters reminds one of the similar mistake made by Mark Robson in *Nine*

Hours to Rama. The result is the same; the film looks entirely unreal and inauthentic as these foreign characters converse in Hindi.

Gandhi Is Back

Generation after generation has imagined and romanticized about what it would be like if Gandhi lived in their midst. People want him to come back and show the light once again to humankind. They look up to him to provide solutions. Some filmmakers have toyed with this popular theme and have explored the idea of a Gandhi living in their own current times. Curiosity as to how Gandhi might have acted and reacted to current issues of their own times has inspired filmmakers to take a relook at Gandhi. A short Hindi film *Reincarnation*, released in 2012, imagined such a theme, focused on a return of Gandhi to earth. Reincarnation is possible for a noble soul like Mahatma on screen!

The plot of *Reincarnation* revolves around Siddhartha, a middle-class youth who gets a recurring dream that he is Gandhi and is getting shot by an assailant. He wakes up screaming every time he sees this dream and finally decides to seek help from a psychologist. The dream, however, continues to appear. Eventually, his mother and relatives begin to believe that there must be something to his dream. As word spreads about his dreams, he starts getting attention as well as respect from people around. They bow before him, touch his feet and seek his blessings, thinking him to be the reincarnation of the Mahatma.

Slowly, Siddhartha gets lured by all this attention into behaving like Gandhi by changing his mannerisms and dressing style. People call him for prayer meetings, and he addresses them Gandhi style. The media takes notice of this strange phenomenon and the news reaches the prime minister. He invites Siddhartha to accompany him on a tour to Pakistan to resolve the issues created by the bloody Partition.

This time, however, the dream returns, but with a twist. The man receives a big jolt when he realizes that he was not Gandhi, as he had been imagining himself to be, but the one who shot Gandhi! Sumeet Raghavan played the title role of Siddhartha in the film directed by

Gaurav Bakshi. There are some moments in this short film where he reveals the twin personality syndrome of the character effectively. The theme had interesting possibilities, but the film failed to explore them in any deep way.

The Gandhian model of political activism came into focus in a film, *Satyagraha,* in 2013. Renowned filmmaker Prakash Jha did a contemporary take on the Gandhian tool of satyagraha against political malpractice and corruption. It is a tale of an idealistic man, played by Amitabh Bachchan, who starts a peaceful agitation against the corrupt system in a new-age Gandhian style. Loosely based on the nationwide campaign launched by social activist Anna Hazare, the film portrayed the use of modern media as a tool in the fight. Earlier known for his realistic films, here Jha seems to have lost his cinematic touch. Sadly, he resorted to an item dance number to sell the story of *Satyagraha.*

The use of satyagraha as a weapon to fight against injustice and malpractices was once again dealt with in a Tamil film. The only novelty in the brilliantly done fictional narrative was the protagonist—Gandhi! A. Balakrishnan's Tamil film *Mudhalvar Mahatma* (Welcome Back, Gandhi) released in 2014 showed Gandhi's return to his country after sixty years of his death to resume his satyagraha movement. The film focused on the social, political and economic malpractices prevailing in India, and the contemporary relevance of the Gandhian ideology of satyagraha and non-violence. Once again, the theme of reincarnation was at play in this film.

Disgusted with the state of affairs in the country, Gandhi decides to return and start a new struggle against politicians and industrialists. Unlike *Lage Raho Munna Bhai*, in this film Gandhi is not present in the form of a spirit. He is real and wants to establish *Ram Rajya*, a dream close to his heart. S. Kanagraj plays the role of Gandhi, who returns to India after getting the blessings of Lord Shiva. His thoughts and principles find followers in the chief minister of a fictional state, played by the veteran actor Anupam Kher. Once again, it was the nationwide mass movement led by Gandhian activist Anna Hazare that provided the fillip and inspiration to explore such a story. Balakrishnan, who had earlier made a biopic on veteran Tamil leader K. Kamaraj, claimed to have been inspired by Gandhi's philosophy. He said,

> I had been reading up a lot and as I delved into books on Gandhi and by Gandhi, I realized there was so much about his philosophy that is relevant today. His approach to simplicity and his selflessness are inspiring. Here was a man born into riches and who ended up wearing just a dhoti. It's difficult to read about Gandhi and not do something about what it arouses in you.[6]

The regional cinema continued to explore various themes espoused by Gandhi. A Kannada movie, *Gandhiji Kanasu* (The Dream of Gandhiji), released on 15 August 2014, advocated the cause of village sanitation. Village development was one of the major programmes propagated by Gandhi, and the movie is based on real incidents from north Karnataka. Five of Gandhi's dreams are dealt with in the film, including showchalaya (sanitation), cleanliness, free movement of women and the need for universal education. The film was produced and directed by Ramesh Paravenaikar.

What if a someone resorts to satyagraha, Gandhi's favourite tool, to fight for his rights in modern times? Anant Mahadevan tried to explore the answer in the context of the current realities in his Hindi film *Gour Hari Dastaan: The Freedom File,* which was released in 2014. The protagonist of the film becomes the butt of jokes when he resorts to satyagraha in Bombay to get what is his right: a Tamra Patra honouring his participation in the freedom struggle.

But one of the most progressive cinema industries in the country seems to have given little attention to Gandhi or his values and principles. The Malayalam cinema has traversed innovative themes right from its inception and several eminent filmmakers have portrayed humanist stories on screen. Somehow, Gandhian themes have found little or no representation in such stories. A stray portrayal of a Gandhian, here and there, is all one can find. The strong influence of communist ideology since the start of Malayalam cinema, could be one reason behind this.

A major exception to this trend can be seen in the cinema of Adoor Gopalakrishnan, a master filmmaker. His films exhibit a rare blend of Gandhian values, history and politics that is deeply rooted in the soil of Kerala. His film Mathilukal (Walls) (1990) is an unusual love story between a prisoner and a lady inmate, whom he has not seen. Based on autobiographical novella of renowned Malayalam writer Vaikom Muhammad Basheer, the film is a slice of life account set in 1942-43 when the nationwide Gandhian struggle for freedom was at its peak.

Jailed on the charges of sedition, Basheer, played brilliantly by Mammootty, engages with fellow political prisoners one day. In a delightful sequence, when he asks who has seen Gandhi everyone raises their hands. Who has touched Gandhi, he asks next and no one answers. It is Basheer who raises his hand in triumph. Seeing Gandhi and touching him is a matter of pride to him.

The Master storyteller was at work again in his 2002 film Nizhalkkuthu (Shadow Kill) that portrays a powerful indictment of capital punishment while emphasizing on the importance of Gandhian values. It is a story of a hangman, set in the pre-Independence era. The twist comes when his freedom fighter son, a follower of Gandhi and who spins Charkha, is asked to carry out an execution when his father takes ill. In a subtle and understated portrayal, the film throws lights on the outright negation of values of non-violence and dignity of labour.

A Boy's Tryst with Gandhi

Gandhi is gone long back but he is very much part of our daily lives and a 2015 Bengali film *Babar Naam Gandhiji* showcases how a street kid appropriates him in his struggle to live and to study. Filmmaker Pavel's debut offering was an interesting take on life in a metropolis while also providing a perspective on the values and principles of Gandhi in today's times. Kenchodas Mohandas Karamchand Gandhi is the name of a boy who is raised in the streets of Kolkata and thinks his father is Gandhiji.

Kencho, a street-smart kid, ekes out a living by begging. But he also uses his intelligence to earn some extra money. Due to his friendly attitude, he is also the darling of all the neighbourhood. He decides to join a well-known school, where he is insulted for his surname of Gandhi. His struggles begin, but there is a helping hand in the form of Pavel, a young man who runs an NGO for street children. The NGO manages to get Kencho a birth certificate and other documents required for school admission, and the goons chip in with money for the admission fee. There is a beautiful scene showing Kencho asking questions of a Gandhi statue while the rain lashes on.

Next year, a Kannada filmmaker, Sushil, explored Gandhi's story in animation, in a film titled *Yamalokadalli Gandhi*. This six-and-a-half-minute animation movie was a good attempt to convey the ideals of Gandhi using the earlier-mentioned motif of the three monkeys.

Gandhigiri

'Gandhigiri' has become a term used by youth in India to describe any action based on Gandhi's principles. This term came to be used after Rajkumar Hirani's tremendously successful film *Lage Raho Munna Bhai*. Trying to cash in on the popular term, a film of the same name was produced in 2016. It was yet another NRI-return narrative, telling the story of a veteran freedom fighter who transforms four outlaws using Gandhi's principles. The broad theme of the film, directed by S. Mishra, bears close resemblance to that of V. Shantaram's *Do Ankhen Barah Haath*.

The film starts with a quote; 'A small body of determined spirits fired by an unquenchable faith in their mission can alter the course of history - Mahatma Gandhi.' Newsreel visuals of the Quit India Movement are then shown. The narrator informs the viewers that many princely states had tacitly encouraged the freedom struggle in their respective jurisdictions, and one of the royals, Maheshwar Singh, was a staunch supporter. As a result, the British government exiles him as bonded labour to Mauritius. He doesn't sit idle there either. Gandhi's teachings prompt him to take up the cause of labourers in Mauritius.

Renowned actor Om Puri plays the protagonist who is felicitated on Pravasi Bhartiya Diwas for his contribution in fighting for the rights of fellow labourers. He declares his intention to go back to his native region and spread the values of Gandhi, à la Gandhi returning to India from South Africa! He then meets four people from different backgrounds who have strayed from the straight path and decides to reform them. An honest attempt to tell the story, however, becomes a farce as a result of inept acting and poor production values. An otherwise great actor, Om Puri is lacklustre in his portrayal of the Gandhian man and could not salvage the film.

Pitting Gandhi against the nationalists who were proponents of armed revolution has also been a favourite pastime for many armchair writers and researchers. *Gandhi vs Aazaad* in 2016 was a similar attempt to show the 'other side' of Gandhi, which the world has not seen yet, claimed the director Abhay Kumar. According to him, Gandhi got promoted as a hero, but true heroes like Chandrashekhar Azad and Subhash Chandra Bose went unheard, and that was the premise of his plot. Time and again, this accusation has been hurled at Gandhi. This alternative narrative has gained some ground in recent times but with very little or no historical evidence. Kumar himself played the title role of Chandrashekhar Azaad in the film, in addition to writing and directing it.

The real life of a Gandhi follower turned into a reel story in a 2016 film titled *Anna*, directed by Shashank Udapurkar. Drawing parallels between Mahatma Gandhi and Kisan Baburao Hazare, the 'Anna' in the film, it was a reflection on the life of a contemporary Gandhian activist. A retired man from the Indian army achieves a turnaround in his own village by leveraging the collective energy of fellow citizens for the overall development of the village. It was a living example of Gandhi's Gram Swaraj. He then ventures to go beyond the boundaries of the village and works for the cause of fighting corruption, which is now nationwide.

Utilizing fasting as a weapon to cleanse the system and making clever use of mass movement, Anna Hazare had once again brought the focus on Gandhi in the early 2000s. Many questions were raised about the high moral position assumed by Hazare that had resulted in the popular mass movement he brought about. These aspects apart, the film did try to cash in on the newly acquired 'Gandhi' status of Hazare because of the perceived similarity of his role (in working against corruption) with Gandhi's leadership of the freedom movement.

Gandhi always believed in personal and social cleanliness. Village sanitation was on the Eighteen-point Constructive Programme envisaged by him. The newly elected Indian government led by Prime Minister Narendra Modi in 2014 put the focus back on Gandhi's favourite programme by launching the Swachh Bharat Abhiyan/Clean India Mission to develop a clean India. A film, *Toilet Ek Prem Katha*, released in Hindi in 2017, developed a fictional tale on this theme. It was about a newly married couple's efforts to construct toilets in their village. Directed by Shree Narayan Singh, the film portrayed the bride's determination to secure personal dignity. She takes the matter to court and receives wide media attention. The efforts yield results at the policy level, and the government finally decides to build toilets in the village.

The similar theme of cleanliness was the focus in a Hindi short film *Silver Gandhi* released in 2020. Based on a true story of a person who is inspired by Gandhi's emphasis on cleanliness decides to dress like Mahatma but with a change; he puts silver paint on his body! The director Avinash Nanda believes that the film would encourage hundreds of Indians to choose a life of cleanliness and hygiene.

#Gandhi

Social media has now become a new-age sensation, with interactive online platforms enabling people to communicate on real-time basis. News travels fast across continents and time zones. It would have been amusing to see how Gandhi would have coped with the constant onslaught of social media. It has also become a very effective tool for organizing mass protests, and the world has seen the power of its reach in recent times. In such a situation, when a common man decides to take on the establishment, he becomes a social media hero.

When a retired widower inadvertently takes on the establishment, he (here the nondescript Ram Nath Gadhvi) becomes a social media sensation—*#Gadhvi*. This was the name of a film released in 2018, which took into account the prevalent social media trends. Written and directed by Gaurav Bakshi, the film, whose alternative title is *He thought he was Gandhi*, presented the clash between a Gandhian Gadhvi and a hired goon, Omkar.

It is also a tale of a retired government employee taking on the government to expose the corruption in the system. But Ram Nath Gadhvi is no ordinary Gandhian. He has started believing himself to be the reincarnation of Mahatma Gandhi! Sanjay Mishra, who played a local goon in *Gandhigiri*, returns to play the protagonist, Gadhvi, in this film. Only by shattering this apparent delusion can Omkar succeed in his mission of suppressing the swelling anger against his masters, the establishment.

The film takes a serious turn when Gadhvi becomes a social media hero—and the only way to bring Gadhvi down seems to be to bring down his core beliefs. The satire works like a thriller, where one is kept guessing who exactly Gadhvi is. Is he really a reincarnation of Gandhi? Will Omkar succeed in bringing him down? Will the truth set him free? Are we what we are destined to be? Or can we create our own destiny?

The assassination of Gandhi has always fascinated filmmakers. Like a haunted story, it has filmmakers lingering around it, trying to examine it from different angles by mixing truth and fiction to tell their own version of the incident. Questions have been raised about the killing many times and much has been written about the lack of preventive measures taken by the police department despite the frequent death threats that came his way. The questions were not without reason, though.

The Special judge in the Gandhi assassination case, Atmacharan Agrawal, had remarked: 'Had the police acted on the intelligence available, the tragedy would probably have never happened.' Taking a cue from these observations, *The Gandhi Murder*, directed by Karim Traïdia and Pankaj Sehgal, tried to explore a theory of political conspiracy.

It is a story of three policemen who learn about Gandhi's impending murder. The trailer says that behind every assassination there is an untold truth and implores the viewer to witness the biggest truth in Indian history. It also adds that the balance between war and peace rested in the life of one man. The film, claiming to be based on verified facts, takes the view that the assassination of Gandhi was made possible due to inept handling by India's police and security services, which could easily be exploited.

Initially, the name of the film was *Solar Eclipse: The Depth of Darkness*, which was changed to *The Gandhi Murder.* Stephen Lang, known for his role as Colonel Miles Quaritch in *Avatar,* played the role of the DIG of police while Jesus Sands starred as Gandhi. The Indian actors Om Puri and Naseer were also cast in the film. It was the last acting role of Puri, one of the best of Indian actors, who passed away after this movie was completed. The Spanish actor Sands was also the co-producer of the movie. Veteran Algerian director Karim Traïdia, who was nominated for the Golden Globe for *The Polish Bride* in 1998, directed the film, along with Pankaj Sehgal.

The promotional publicity for the film, made in 2019 during the 150th birth anniversary of Gandhi, claimed, 'It is widely argued that Gandhiji was murdered because he betrayed Netaji Subhash Chandra Bose.' The film had its usual flaws; non-Indian actors playing Indian characters and falling flat. The film was shot in Sri Lanka, not India, and it clearly affected the authenticity of the plot. It was also a poor attempt to link Gandhi's assassination with the murder of Abraham Lincoln, trying to prove a theory that these deaths help bring countries together.

Co-director of the film Sehgal said as much in one of his interviews: 'Our intent is to show Gandhi's immense contribution to India post-Independence, which is something that very few people understand. They don't understand that his assassination was bigger than any of his other contributions … India was on the verge of a civil war.' In another interview Sehgal said, 'The film demonstrates that the assassination was not an act of a single assassin, but a collective plan hatched within the corridors of power of the newly independent India.'[7] Even though the Central Board of Film Certification (CBFC) had cleared it, the film was not released in India on account of the threats received by the producer and director.

Kasturba was a constant companion of Gandhi's since they were thirteen years of age and till her death in 1944. Her story has been as fascinating as that of Gandhi. Hers was an extraordinary life—of an uneducated woman who became the wife of a barrister but did not lose her individuality. As Gandhi's wife and then as the mother of his sons, Kasturba had been a pillar of support for Gandhi in his private and public life. Though she was in the constant shadow of the larger-than-life figure of her husband, Kasturba was also an independent-thinking woman and asserted her rights with quiet dignity. She lived in India raising their sons while Gandhi was in England pursuing his law studies.

During his early days in South Africa, she joined him and stood with him constantly in his public activities. Gandhi, in his autobiography, wrote about her early days as a satyagrahi, 'According to my earlier experience, she was very obstinate. In spite of all my pressure she would do as she wished. This led to short or long periods of estrangement between us. But as my public life expanded, my wife bloomed forth and deliberately lost herself in my work.'

When she passed away at Aga Khan Palace in Poona, Gandhi was with her in the final moments. He described his companion of sixty-two years in moving words:

> If anything she stood above me. But for her unfailing cooperation I might have been in the abyss ... She helped me to keep wide awake and true to my vows. She stood by me in all my political fights and never hesitated to take the plunge. In the current sense of the word, she was uneducated; but to my mind she was a model of true education. She was a devoted Vaishnav. But she had obliterated all feeling of caste from her mind and regarded a Harijan girl with no less affection than her own children. She personified the Kasturba Gandhi ideal of which Narsimha Mehta has sung in '*Vaishnava Jana*' hymn. There were occasions when I was engaged in a grim wrestle with death. During my Aga Khan Palace fast, I literally came out of

> the death's jaws. But she shed not a tear, never lost hope or courage but prayed to God with all her soul.[8]

Though so much of writing is available on Gandhi, Kasturba receives only passing references. Therefore, it is a welcome sign that filmmakers are now coming forward to tell her story on screen and *Gandhi Ki Prerna Kasturba* was one such film released in Hindi in 2019. Directed by Manish Thakur, the film was based on Dr R.K. Paliwal's play *Kasturba*. Amid all the celebrations in Gandhi's 150th birth anniversary year, only a few people remembered that Kasturba also shared the anniversary. Thakur's film is an effort to celebrate the occasion and put the focus on a strong woman who lived in the shadow of her illustrious husband.

Gandhi As a Young Boy

Gandhi's life had been an extraordinary one, to say the least. Filmmakers over the years have tried to explore different aspects of this multifaceted personality. So, right from putting his entire life journey into film to dissecting his relationships and his formative years in South Africa, filmmakers have tried to unravel the intrigue that Gandhi was. Somehow, no one had looked at his childhood in a detailed manner. Multiple National Award-winning filmmaker P. Sheshadri decided to focus his lens on the young school-going Gandhi and the various influences from his parents and friends.

Based on renowned Kannada writer Bolwar Mohamad Kunhi's novel *Paapu Gandhi Bapu Aada Kathe* (From Monu to Mahatma), *Mohandas*, made in three languages—Kannada, English and Hindi—is an earnest attempt to look at Gandhi's early years, from age six to fourteen. Major portions of the movie were filmed at Rajkot and Porbandar where Gandhi spent his childhood from 1875 to 1883.[9] Gandhi got married when he was just thirteen. The film also portrays the influence of his father Karamchand and mother Putlibai, and of the mythological stories from Indian epics, on Gandhi.

Gandhi himself has written about his growing-up years in his autobiography, but not in much detail. The vast amount of literature on Gandhi delves into his values, philosophy, and of course his leadership of the freedom movement in India, but says little about his childhood. Sheshadri explained the motive behind making the movie he did:

> Gandhi's childhood was very important to understand him as a person. We all know very little about Gandhi as a child. I felt this story is relevant for all the children across the world and perhaps to the parents too. If we recall our own childhood, we find many similar incidents. Each one of us have had our share of mischief and misadventures. What was different about Gandhi? How we grow with those experiences is crucial and that determines what you become.[10]

To portray an illustrious man like Gandhi, whose visual memory is so alive and fresh among not only one but several generations, surely poses a multitude of challenges for actors. They do not have the liberty to go too far from the actual image of the man lest it should be frowned upon. One can only attempt to take a certain amount of liberty in imagining and exploring the character of Gandhi on screen. His physicality, looks and mannerisms are too strongly etched in the public consciousness to be ignored. At one end, an actor has not much to do except to try to look like Gandhi. If one gets the physicality correct, it is easy. But the real test then is to bring the spirit of the man alive, going beyond his physicality. Therefore, for an actor to essay Gandhi's character on the silver screen is always a huge challenge.

Naseeruddin Shah, who had wanted to badly play Gandhi in Richard Attenborough's film in 1982 and after eighteen years played Gandhi in *Hey Ram*, says he explored various layers of the man in the popular play *Mahatma vs Gandhi*. As an actor, the role gave him a certain satisfaction. He said:

> The difficulties with playing a character like Gandhi or Einstein whose practically every move and every word on record are

> enormous, the way he walked, the texture of his voice, his body language—all that has to be replicated closely and unless the results match the original you are deemed to have failed.[11]

To prepare for Gandhi's character, Shah watched Vithalbhai Jhaveri's epic five-and-a-half-hour documentary *Mahatma*. He also listened to many audio tapes of Gandhi's speeches to get the tone and diction right.[12] While comparing Gandhi with other historical characters in terms of enacting them, Shah said, 'It's different playing Ghalib, whom no one alive has seen and who is not on record, so the actor can use his imagination. Therefore, the responsibility of playing a part like Gandhi is enormous; the audience must not only get the picture of him that they know and love but must also be told something new about him.' In his typical wry humour, Shah sums up his experience of portraying Gandhi, 'The biggest challenge I faced while playing him was to lose weight and learn how to spin the charkha!'[13]

Gandhigiri: Mahatma Meets a Don

Of all the films that took a relook at Gandhi and interpreted his actions for the present times, there was one in the new millennium that made Gandhi cool again—Rajkumar Hirani's *Lage Raho Munna Bhai*. It was a brilliant yet hilarious idea of bringing Gandhi together with a Don. The potent combination of this unlikely pair resulted in one of the most remarkable portrayals of Gandhi on screen. Hirani has carved a niche for himself by making films that deliver simple yet powerful messages, and he deployed the right mix of art and entertainment in this new-generation 'cool' movie. A laugh-riot that depicted the relevance and triumph of Gandhian philosophy in today's times, the film was a huge hit and brought back the focus on Gandhi.

The spotlight on Gandhi this time was every bit positive as the Gandhi presented here is not an eccentric or a faddist old person but a loving and caring figure, like a grandfather. He is the same old Gandhi, wearing a white khadi dhoti with bamboo staff in hand. He smiles profusely through his toothless mouth and has gentle manners. And here he is, trying to teach a few life lessons to a local don, of all people, in Mumbai. The odd combination of a Mahatma and a don provided for a delightful and funny comedy. It worked brilliantly to present one of the most popular and contemporary cinematic interpretations of Gandhi.

Piqued and disturbed by the fashion of Gandhi-bashing in vogue, Rajkumar Hirani, an FTII alumnus, decided to make a film about Gandhi. Hirani confessed that it was Attenborough's *Gandhi* that opened his eyes and said,

> Gandhi bashing was a fashion until I watched Attenborough's *Gandhi*. He was just a chapter in my history lesson and a face on our currency until then. Attenborough's Gandhi shook me as a filmmaker. I got glued to his life through books written by various authors to know more about him. I always thought that someday I will make a film on him and Attenborough was responsible for Lage Raho Munnabhai.[14]

Wishing to make a satire on the present state of India, Hirani wrote a story about a young boy who had met Gandhi in 1945. The boy is hit by a British soldier and goes into a coma, only to wake up fifty years later in a hospital in independent India. But somehow, the script was not going as per Hirani's plan to make it entertaining and engaging. He had already made a hugely successful film *Munna Bhai MBBS,* about a goon with a golden heart. The pair of Munna and Circuit, played so adorably by Sanjay Dutt and Arshad Warsi, respectively, was already in place. It had captured the popular imagination. Suddenly Hirani hit upon an idea—that the plot could become interesting if Gandhi, the symbol of non-violence, met up with Munna Bhai, the don! His collaborator and co-writer in many films, Abhijat Joshi, a Gujarati who was brought up in Ahmedabad, joined him to develop the idea into a script, and the rest is history!

Hirani was very clear in making the film relevant to the present generation. 'We had to present Gandhi to the younger generation in an entertaining way. We, therefore, decided to ignore some aspect of Gandhiji's teachings, like khadi or prohibition of alcohol, and stuck to the core of his philosophy—truth and non-violence.'[15] His co-writer Joshi had done a lot of research by reading the diaries of Mahadev Desai, Gandhi's trusted secretary, for years, much before the film happened.

Joshi was also deeply influenced by the writings of the Marathi writer Sane Guruji, on whose seminal book an iconic movie, *Shyamchi Aai,* was based. Though it was Hirani's idea of combining Gandhi with Munna Bhai, Joshi was on the same page. He said, 'It was important for us to dispel the myth about Gandhi being a sedate, ascetic person. We wanted to show his other side—witty, humorous, light-hearted and creative.'[16]

The movie tells the tale of a local don, Munna Bhai, who falls in love with Janhavi, a radio jockey. In order to meet her, he takes part in a quiz on Gandhi. Kidnapped professors help him win the contest, and he presents himself before her as a Gandhi expert! When invited to give a lecture on Gandhi to inmates of an old-age home, he had to spend days and nights studying in a library. When Gandhi was alive, people used to wait to catch a glimpse of him, sometimes by stopping the train he was travelling in in the dead of night. But Munna Bhai's study is so intense that Gandhi himself appears before him and gives 'darshan'!

There starts a quirky journey together, of an unusual combination of Gandhi and a don. Gandhi is there to advise Munna Bhai and also to bail him out of tricky situations, but using his age-old tools of truth and non-violence. Hirani is a proven master in combining humour with deeper sentiments. Here too, he uses his skill beautifully to transfix the audience with this unlikely duo on their delightful journey.

The film popularized the word 'Gandhigiri', and it came to symbolize protest with love! It was a clever packaging for Gandhi's mode of agitation. Noted screenwriter Abbas Tyrewala coined the word 'Gandhigiri'; it simply meant you can win over the enemy with love and goodness instead of feeling anger and hatred for him. Director Hirani has this knack for connecting with the masses using words and symbols that stay in their minds. More importantly, the connect is with their hearts, and that too without use of too much technique. The challenge was to encapsulate Gandhi's principles and apply them in the daily lives of common people.

The word 'Gandhigiri' rhymes with 'dadagiri', a typical Mumbai slang word that does not have positive connotations and stands for the behaviour of throwing one's weight about. So, the coining of a word using Gandhi's name was a play on 'dadagiri' but meant exactly the opposite! But it turned out to be a real game-changer, not only for the film but for defining Gandhi's philosophy in the current context. It had its desired effect, in the sense that the young generation adopted it into their lingo!

Gandhi's character in the film uses the current vocabulary and responds to the banter of Circuit and Munna in the same style. He is not in preaching mode here. He uses humour to convey the same philosophy of the Mahatma but using contemporary slang, and not by giving staid sermons. That really connected with the young generation. Gandhi now was one among them. He came out as a human character, not...as 'one'...who prescribes ideals and principles from a high pedestal.

Hirani made Gandhi one among us, like an elderly person in the family who is approachable and helpful. The character of Gandhi in the film is mischievous and talks with a naughty smile most of the time. For him, the medium of Radio was the familiar one, but this time it was two-way communication. Gandhi went live on FM Radio, spoke to people and gave life lessons through Munna, the goon. The special show on radio was called 'Mahatma's Magic' in the film. The solutions and advice given by Gandhi are on topics as diverse as truth, tolerance, corruption, marriage, and one's civic duties. Hirani's magic was in creating scenes that showed the audience how Gandhi would have reacted to the problems in their daily lives. That became a benchmark. And that made Gandhi relevant.

Acclaimed actor Dilip Prabhavalkar, who has essayed many memorable roles in Marathi cinema and theatre, brought to the screen a loveable Bapu. In fact, initially he had not been assigned Gandhi's role. He had given an audition for one of the characters in an old-age home in the film. But it was his infectious smile, much like Gandhi's, that did the trick. When Hirani and Vidhu Vinod Chopra, the producer of the film, noticed it, they felt that Prabhavalkar could do Gandhi. Prabhavalkar did not very much resemble Gandhi physically. But that did not come across as a handicap. His soft voice tinged with humour and his lyrical dialogue delivery contrasted very effectively with the aggressive and brash Mumbai slang of Munna and Circuit.

Prabhavalkar initially was not very sure of this eclectic combination of Gandhi pairing up with two goons. He was anxious about how people would react to Gandhi being mingled up with bad characters like a mafia don.[17] But he pulled off his role very convincingly. Again, the Gandhi conceived here by Hirani is dark brown in complexion, bordering on black, because it was Munna Bhai's, a don's, imagination of Gandhi. So he cannot be a regular Gandhi!

The spirit of Gandhi came alive on screen through Prabhavalkar's innate strength and gentleness. What also helped was his wide smile. Gandhi's ear-to-ear grin is famous, and Prabhavalkar enacted it with full empathy. He considered the character of Gandhi as 'the most important role in my career and one of the toughest ones!'[18] In the process, Prabhavalkar was instrumental in making Gandhi 'cool' again for the millennial generation. He too prepared for the role by watching newsreel footage of Gandhi and listening to his speeches for getting the diction right. The personality of the actor is a very important factor in portraying a unique character like Gandhi, Prabhavalkar said.

Even in the new millennium, filmmakers have been sceptical about making movies on Gandhi. Producer and director of *Lage Raho*, Vidhu Vinod Chopra, had confessed his anxiety. 'We feared a ban on the movie, considering the sensitivities of people towards Mahatma Gandhi. Our main concern was that it shouldn't get banned. It was difficult and scary; we didn't know whether we will be banned or we will get applauded.'[19]

The film turned out to be hugely successful, not only commercially but also in spreading the relevance of Gandhi's thoughts and teachings in the modern world. It got the rare distinction of becoming the first Hindi film to be shown at the United Nations when it was screened on

10 November 2006. The film was also shown as part of the Tous Les Cinema du Monde (World Cinema) section at the prestigious Cannes Film festival in 2007.

Curiously, the film also generated tremendous interest in Gandhian ideals, which were then translated into action on the ground. Several innovative protests were launched, taking a cue from the film, both in India and abroad. This was a modern way of non-violence and satyagraha—two of Gandhi's best teachings—at its best.

While there has been spurt in portraying Gandhi for the screen in recent years, the efforts to film his assassin's life has also gained traction in the industry. As per reports, veteran director Rajkumar Santoshi is in the process of making a film *Gandhi Vs Godse* based on Asgar Wajahat's play *Godse@Gandhi.com.*[20] The plot is to be focused on last years of Gandhi while the play explores the dialogue between both as they try to understand each other's viewpoint.

As the world celebrated Gandhi's birthday in 2021, another movie *Godse* was launched by director Mahesh Manjrekar. Calling it to be 'The Deadliest Birthday Wish ever', the filmmaker told the viewers 'to get ready to witness a story no one dared to tell before!'.[21] Manjrekar, who is already working on a biopic of V.D. Savarkar, claimed, 'People do not know much about Godse other than he's the man who fired at Gandhi. While telling his story, we neither want to patronize nor want to speak against anyone. We'll leave it to the audience on who is right or wrong.'[22]

It is all very well to tell the stories claiming to be of different ideologies but the manner of the film's announcement was certainly not in good taste. But then Gandhi would have certainly laughed at all such attempts. His life and principles have faced severest of scrutiny all these years and have still survived to give hope to the mankind!

18

Kurmavatara: The Gandhian Ideas for Salvation

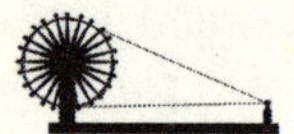

IN APRIL 2011, ALL of India had been stirred up by the anti-corruption movement led by a social activist, Anna Hazare. A self-styled follower of Gandhi, Hazare had adopted a similar set of tools as used by the Mahatma. And that got people calling him the 'new-generation Gandhi'. It was not only that Hazare, a former army man, was a vegetarian and wore a khadi dhoti with Gandhi cap, but also that he fasted in protest against many ills in the political system—all of which had captured the popular imagination.

A multiple National Award-winning filmmaker, Girish Kasaravalli, was perturbed by the development. It compelled him to explore the notions of ethics and morality, that had a major role in Gandhian philosophy, and to examine them in the current context. That led him to make *Kurmavatara,* a Kannada film released in 2013, which looked critically at these issues. It succinctly brought forth the universal importance of Gandhi's views and advocated Gandhi's ideas for the salvation for the universe, like Lord Vishnu's incarnations. It was a seminal film that broke new ground in presenting the thought that Gandhi and his concepts are far more important than the actual man.

The story of the film is about a retired government employee who dons the role of Gandhi for a television serial, and how he slowly falls for the charms of the Mahatma. Selected for the role simply for his close physical resemblance to Gandhi, the man, while enacting the role, imbibes the values and principles of Gandhi, and the reel story takes a different turn in real life for him. It is a film within a film, and Kasaravalli used this technique brilliantly to delve into the many layers of Gandhi's persona as well as the prevalent socio-political dynamics in India.

Based on a Kannada short story written by Dr K. Veerabhadrappa, the script and screenplay were written by director Girish Kasaravalli, an FTII alumnus and one of the finest filmmakers in the country today. Even though Kasaravalli had read the story earlier when it was published, he felt an urge to reinterpret and adapt it to the socio-political situation that obtained in 2011. According to him,

> The movement led by Anna Hazare was a political activity whereas the movement orchestrated by Gandhi had a philosophy. Its aim and purpose went beyond the freedom movement. It encompassed our lives, our community; It was a dharma for him (Dharma not in a limited sense of religion but as *Dharayeti iti dharmaha* … One that leads our life).

For Gandhi, means was equally important as aim. For every activity he attached ethics. The old Gandhian in the film says that and hums a verse to that effect. Ethics and morality played a major role in Gandhian philosophy.[1] Therefore, the context was very important, and Gandhi's story had to be told linking it to the present environment, Kasaravalli felt. At the same time, he was intrigued by the question everyone faces, 'Could Gandhi's philosophy be implemented in today's world?'

That question becomes pertinent in today's times:

> Because the whole of post-globalization world is moving in the opposite direction. Today it is marketing and attracting larger clients to increase our profitability are the benchmarks. The publicity is the key factor. Gandhi was against advertisements and profit-driven marketing. Ethics do not play any role or if it plays it will be a negligent role. The consumer driven marketing strategy wants to change need into greed; in such a situation Gandhian approach looks ineffective.

Accordingly, Kasaravalli invested his own thoughts into developing the original story to make a strong script. 'To make Gandhian approach, which is relevant for all times, to work we need to question our notions of development, modernity and profit-driven strategies. To make it happen we need a political will, people need to adopt an austere lifestyle,' became the focus of his narrative.

Gandhi's assassination has lured many creative thinkers as well as filmmakers all these years. Louis Fischer's seminal biography of Gandhi starts with that dramatic scene, as does Richard Attenborough's film *Gandhi*. *Kurmavatara* takes the cue and begins with the same scene, but it is a shooting of Gandhi for the shooting of a television serial, *Mahatma*! While this is being filmed, there is a tongue-in-cheek comment from the other actors who are playing Gandhi's colleagues.

Though the director of the TV serial, played by Apurva Kasaravalli, is very happy with the shot taken and the assistants applaud the excellent take, one of them remarks, 'But the crowd was too thin. People will compare it with other films. This pales in comparison.' His colleague defends the film, saying the other films were international co-productions. 'This is just a small-budget TV serial. Despite severe constraints, we have made sincere efforts.' The comment is a pointer to the sad reality of the struggle independent filmmakers go through to make a film of their choice, as compared with the high-profile filmmakers who are backed by big production houses in their large-scale ventures.

The plot revolves around Anand Rai, a government employee who is on the verge of retirement. He has two things in common with Gandhi; he has not watched a single film or television serial in his life and he is a workaholic. When the director of the TV serial approaches him with an offer to play Gandhi, he immediately declines, saying he is not an actor and not interested in acting. His family members then prevail upon him to accept the role for their financial security and for a better future for his grandson. The man relents.

In the first scene, a reluctant Rao is to feature in an emotionally-charged scene, where the Partition of India is being discussed in a meeting. Gandhi's close colleagues Sardar Patel and Maulana Azad are some of the characters present. But the first-timer Rao, who is nervous and does not know how to act, that too in front of the camera, can't get the emotions right. He has been an emotionless man, his son reveals. Even when his wife died, he didn't cry. He didn't go to see his wife battling for life in the ICU. The director humiliates Rao in front of everyone on the sets. That is too much for the hapless Rao and he weeps silently. That is what the director wanted. The unit captures his emotions on camera successfully. Their purpose is served.

Rao, who did not care much for Gandhi initially, starts slowly getting into the skin of the character. While a discussion is going on about the low TRPs of the Gandhi serial, Rao's analysis is spot on when he remarks, 'These days when Gandhi himself is not popular, how can this serial be?' Still, his own acting leaves much to be desired. Rao's son, eager to make quick money through his father, tells him, 'You have no love or respect for Gandhi, therefore your performance as Gandhi is not good.' He gets him a few books on Gandhi to read. He also takes Rao to meet an old follower of Gandhi's who had taken part in the freedom struggle. The freedom fighter has a piece of advice for Rao. Though people believe that Gandhi's messages regarded non-violence, freedom and a casteless society, he also gave equal importance to ethics in public life, which is very rare in today's times.

Kasaravalli wanted to show the quiet transformation in Rao. 'Anand Rao, who didn't care much for either Gandhi or his philosophy, starts to become Gandhi for the role. But gradually, he develops a liking for Gandhi, initially in physical resemblance (trying to imbibe his traits and mannerisms) and later in his values,' said Kasaravalli. It reflected in the introspection Rao goes through, 'As I started playing Gandhi, I realized how much I had wronged my wife and my son,' said Rao in the film.

But Rao is not alone in this journey. The director of the TV serial, though young, has his own take on Gandhi. 'Everyone has their own understanding of Gandhi. Some are right and some wrong. Each one has his own version of Gandhi. This is my Gandhi,' he says, when confronted about his interpretation of Gandhi in the serial.

Making a film on Gandhi in India, and that too in the new millennium, has its own challenges. Even after seventy plus years have passed since his death, Gandhi is still a hot potato to handle for any creative filmmaker. Kasaravalli too had to face these hurdles. He said, 'The biggest challenge was the representation of Gandhi. I didn't want a film wherein Gandhi is totally idolized. It has to be a film about Gandhi, the Father of the Nation; Gandhi, the politician; Gandhi the idealist; Gandhi the husband; and a father.'

These facets of Gandhi have contradictions amongst themselves. While agreeing with his political philosophy, Kasaravalli confessed, 'I had problems with some of his attitudes. I also wanted that to be brought out. I could do that as my protagonist Ananda Rao isn't a hardcore Gandhi follower. That helped me to spell out some of my apprehensions.'

With his firm convictions, Kasaravalli also tried to depict many Gandhis in the film. For that to achieved cinematically, he used a film-within-film approach. He told, 'Another feature of the film that fascinated me was that there are many Gandhis in the film. One is multi-faceted Gandhi himself with all his idiosyncrasy. There is another Gandhi which Anand Rao imagined by reading books and literature on him. There is one more Gandhi which the TV Director had visualized by looking at 'Gandhi' the film made by Richard Attenborough, and last but not the least, Gandhi as I wanted to be presented.'

As a creative filmmaker, 'This kaleidoscopic presentation of Gandhi was what thrilled me the most,' he said. Kasaravalli was aware that it would raise hackles and said, 'I knew some of the Gandhi loyalists would object to my demystified portrayal of Gandhi, one in which he is presented as a man who has many human weaknesses like you and me. And they criticized the film for that.'

To all these approaches, we can safely add the viewpoint of the audience which is treated to this many-faceted depiction of the Father of the Nation. As in case of other films, each viewer would firm up his or her own opinion after seeing the film, and that is also the beauty of this masterpiece from Kasaravalli.

There is another character in the film, who is Rao's old boss. His son Iqbal has ambitions to act in a film, and he approaches Rao. Since Rao is the lead character in the serial, his recommendation gets Iqbal a role. But that role is of Nathuram Godse, Gandhi's assassin. Iqbal is so keen to fulfil his dream to act that he is even ready to wield a gun for it, but his Muslim father wants none of it. The father is fully aware and conscious of the communally surcharged atmosphere prevalent in the society. A Muslim playing the much-hated character of Godse would further vitiate it, he felt. 'Our people won't approve of Iqbal playing Godse's role. Ask the director to cancel it. At least superficially there is a semblance of peace. Let us not disturb it. Transforming the truth into a lie and a lie into the truth has become a game plan these days' is his telling comment.

The transformation of Rao and his attraction to the path of Gandhi is not an easy one. The price is too heavy, and Rao realizes it to his own peril towards the end of the film. He has to give a bribe to release his son from police custody, and that shameful act is the last straw for him. He is now resigned in his disgrace and says, 'I am a bad actor. I made a grave error in trying to play Gandhi. Now, I have even lost the moral right to do so. Let's finish the shoot somehow and be done with it.' Putting Gandhi's values into daily practice is not everybody's cup of tea. Even if one wants to tread that path, society will make every effort to put a spanner in the works. Rao realizes the burden of carrying the cross of a Mahatma in the end.

Shikaripura Krishnamurthy, who played Anand Rao, who in turn played Gandhi in the TV serial in the film, carried out his performance most convincingly. A Sanskrit professor with no real training in acting, Krishnamurthy showcased the slow transformation of the man, just by being himself before the camera. The moral dilemma he faced and the anguish of his past mistakes were emoted well by him. Krishnamurthy himself was fascinated by the Gandhian principle of truthfulness and simplicity in thought and action.[2] Initially hesitant to act before the camera, Krishnamurthy adapted well and raised his performance under the apt direction of Kasaravalli.

Towards the climax of the film, torn between the real and reel worlds, Anand Rao finally breaks down. He wishes for his tryst with cinema to end somehow and to finish the ordeal he had been undergoing since the shooting of the serial started. It had to happen, Kasaravalli said:

> But the world around him starts looking in his Gandhi incarnation a possibility of commodifying Gandhi. It is not just an irony but a sad state of affairs. So, when Ananda Rao tells the actor who plays Godse please kill me and be done with it, the irony turns into remorse (*vishaad*).

Like many filmmakers around the world, Kasaravalli too was captivated by Gandhi's persona while making a film on him. He shared:

> Many writers and artists of Karnataka whom I like, are Gandhians in their political philosophy. I am not an expert on Gandhi like them. Hence, I can't be called a Gandhian, but his philosophy has shown me light on many occasions. While writing the script I had to read a lot about Gandhi and his philosophy and it has enriched my understanding of life and human values.

According to Hindu mythology, Kurmavatara is the second avatara (incarnation) of Lord Vishnu. 'Kurma' is a Sanskrit word meaning tortoise. Lord Vishnu took the form of a tortoise to help the gods and demons to churn the ocean to obtain the nectar of immortality. Vishnu supported the holy mount Mandar, which was the axis on which the churning was done. During the process, the shell of the tortoise cracked from the weight of the mountain.

Gandhi with his world view and ideas was an avatara for our thinking universe, according to Kasaravalli, and his views would help support it. At one end, the entire world is busy embracing consumerism like there is no tomorrow, which will eventually take the world where there will be no tomorrow. 'Even the present COVID19 pandemic is a result of our too much of greed that has come after the abuse of ecology over the years,' he said.

At the same time, Gandhian views and principles, though very useful, are difficult to imbibe. Or at least we think they are difficult to implement in everyday life. *Kurmavatara* succinctly brings out this dichotomy. Kasaravalli's genius lay in showcasing this fine balance that is required to overcome this difficulty, something much required for humanity to survive. The narrative of the film is slow and languid and one feels that some brisk editing could have helped engage the viewers better.

It is a pity that such a brilliant exploration of Gandhi has not received a wider audience. The film won the National Award for Best Film in Kannada in 2011 and was screened in many prestigious festivals across the world. Still, not many people have seen the film, and it surely deserves the wider patronage of cinephiles. It is a cinematic gem from Kasaravalli and one of the best interpretations of Gandhi on screen.

The incarnations of Lord Vishnu do not happen frequently. As Lord Vishnu lifted the universe on his back to save the world, in the form of Kurma, so are the principles of Gandhi essential for our survival. Kasaravalli's *Kurmavatara* is a timely pointer to the importance of the Gandhian world view for sustainable development of the planet. Gandhi is so simple and yet so difficult at the same time. The *Kurmavatara* showcased Gandhi is very much relevant, for today and tomorrow!

Postscript

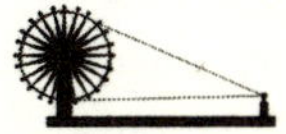

> The screen is an odd thing. Outside of beauty or talent there are unknown reasons which makes a man or a woman fit with the camera. I call them screen animals.
>
> —Jean Renoir

BY ANY STANDARD OR yardstick, the personality of Mohandas Karamchand Gandhi was not made for the movie camera. His looks were unimpressive. From no angle was he photogenic. His personality was also not overbearing. His first impression was not always the lasting impression. His bare body, in fact, repelled many people, mostly Westerners. In his later years he was bald, an old man with a voice one could hardly hear beyond a distance. All these qualities made for no great view for the screen.

But there was a charm and a personal magic about him. It grew over a period on anyone who met him or tracked him. It was enough to have only one conversation with Gandhi to get influenced by him.

Moreover, his life was an open and transparent book. He lived in the midst of people, in the constant gaze of crowds and cameras. There was sincerity, frankness and candidness in him towards everyone, and in his gestures. And as Renoir remarked, there were several unknown reasons at work making Gandhi a screen animal. That, perhaps, explains why he is one of the most photographed and filmed men in the world.

Ever since the medium of moving images was introduced in India, Gandhi has a very interesting and unmissable appearance in almost every Indian film and that is of a chronicler. Gandhi, in the form of photographs, sits on the walls of the government offices, police stations and courtrooms that feature in almost every other film in India. He has an important high seat from where he watches all the goings-on happening right under his long nose. The viewers cannot miss him—his all-familiar appearance with the bald head, round spectacles and white shawl wrapped around his thin body. On a lighter vein, it is a shame that he has not been credited for these appearances, and that too having appeared without charging a single penny!

Then there are the statues of Gandhi shown in films. Many a times, they assume an active role, and other characters in the film engage in conversation with them. They could be questioning him about his or their own past actions. It could also be a sharing of personal sorrow and anguish. Sometimes there are confessions too. It is as if a character is compelled to talk to the Gandhi statue, a God-like figure, to empty out his mind. Never mind a recent order of the Karnataka High Court, which ruled that a Gandhi statue is not a place of worship.[1] The court order obviously had a different context, but reel characters will likely continue to treat Gandhi statues in high esteem and indulge in frank conversations with them.

Another interesting and unique connection Gandhi has with cinema is to do with the viewers—the common man. For many years there used to be a Gandhi Class, a seating arrangement in cinema theatres meant only for the very poor. The front few rows in cinema halls, particularly in south India, were priced very low compared with the proper seats, as in the balcony. How this came to be called Gandhi Class is a mystery, but it was believed that these Gandhi Class viewers, mostly working-class men who could afford only cheap tickets, were the ones who would decide whether a film was a hit or not. If they liked the movie and hooted and whistled, then the film distributors understood that the film was headed for a long run. In a way, Gandhi Class was a tribute to the man who identified himself with Daridra Narayana and at the same time ironical, because once again his name got associated with the cinema industry.

It is indeed a miracle that a man who had neither the face nor the body suited for the screen has been filmed so much. When Gandhi arrived on the social and political scene in India, he 'dressed like a coolie and lived practically on air', as described by the Secretary of State Edwin Samuel Montagu in 1916. Even that little semblance of dressing was discarded in quick time and he dared to do what no political leader could think of doing. He had no qualms about appearing bare-chested and wearing only a short dhoti on screen. No political leader worth his crisp white khadi designer dress can even think to do so in the present times.

The Bhakti tradition in India has it that God can be realized in two ways: saguna and nirguna. Devotion to a deity which one believes in is saguna bhakti. For many people in India, the persona of Gandhi has been the manifestation of God in the modern times. His image, therefore, occupies the mind and consciousness of a large number of Indians. The world of cinema knew this very well and in one of the early newsreels filmed during his lifetime, a saguna image of Gandhi was shown superimposed on the entire map of pre-Independence India through a slow-animation graphic!

Yet another close and intimate connection of Gandhi with cinema comes in the form of Indian currency notes. Every time a viewer goes to a cinema hall to buy tickets, he has to pass on a currency note through the small and crampy ticket window. It happens every day in countless nondescript villages and mofussil towns across India. Gandhi has the distinction of being the only person whose picture has been printed on Indian currency notes without break till now. He is sitting pretty on these currency notes of various denominations, smiling his famous wide grin. He is probably smiling at the irony of his picture being used on currency notes for a pleasure he never enjoyed.

As a 'chronicler' on screen, Gandhi is only a mute spectator. He watches all the happenings around him with a benign smile on his face. In a way, he has witnessed, through those kind and compassionate eyes behind those famous round spectacles, almost everything that has made or unmade the idea of India all these years. And he will continue to watch, because Gandhi is almost indispensable to Indian cinema.

Notes

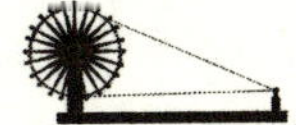

1: Raghupati Raghav Rajaram

1. D.G. Tendulkar, *Mahatma,* Publications Division, Government of India, New Delhi, 1951, p. 143.
2. Press Information Bureau, Government of India. *Press Release*, New Delhi, 27 September 2019.
3. John Turner, *Filming History: The Memoirs of John Turner*, British Universities Film and Video Council, London, 2001, p. 132.
4. John Turner, *Filming History: The Memoirs of John Turner*, British Universities Film and Video Council, London, 2001, p. 133.
5. John Turner, *Filming History: The Memoirs of John Turner*, British Universities Film and Video Council, London, 2001, p. 133
6. *American Cinematographer,* 1955.
7. British Board of Film Censors, Bombay and Bengal 1920 to 1950, NFAI, Pune.
8. *Motion Picture Daily*, 4 February 1948.

9. D.G. Tendulkar, *Mahatma*, Publications Division, Government of India, New Delhi. 1951, p. 143.
10. *Film India*, March 1948, p. 62.
11. *Film India*, March 1948, p. 62.
12. Press Information Bureau, Government of India, *Press Release*, New Delhi, 27 September 2019.
13. M.K. Gandhi, *An Autobiography or the Story of My Experiments with Truth.* Navajivan Publishing House, Ahmedabad, 1940, p. 312.
14. 'People and Ideas: Gandhi', *Vogue*; New York, Vol. 111, Iss. 4, (1 March 1948): 196, 197.
15. A.K. Chettiar, *In the Tracks of the Mahatma*, edited by A.R. Venkatachalapathy; translated from Tamil by S. Thillainayagam. Orient Blackswan Private Limited, Chennai, 2007, p. 24.
16. *The Collected Works of Mahatma Gandhi* (Electronic Book), Publications Division, Government of India, New Delhi. 1999. Vol 24, p. 35.
17. Gautam Kaul, *Cinema and Indian Freedom Struggle*, Sterling Publications, New Delhi, 1998, p. 15.
18. Gautam Kaul, *Cinema and Indian Freedom Struggle*, Sterling Publications, New Delhi, 1998, p. 16.
19. Louis Fischer, *The Life of Mahatma Gandhi*, HarperCollins, London, 1950, p. 157.
20. *Exhibitors Herald*, 14 January 1922.
21. *United Pictures Newsletter*, December 1922.
22. Dr Sadanand More, *Lokmanya Te Mahatma,* Vol. 2, Rajhans Publication, Pune, 2007, p. 731.
23. Navajivan, CWMG.
24. *The Collected Works of Mahatma Gandhi* (Electronic Book), Publications Division, Government of India, New Delhi, 1999, Volume 27, p. 47.

2: It's Not Vidur; It's Gandhiji!

1. *Report of the Indian Cinematograph Committee 1927-28*, Central Publications Branch, Government of India, Calcutta, 1928.
2. J.B.H. Wadia, *NFAI Oral History Project*, Pune, 1984.

3. *Report of the Indian Cinematograph Committee 1927-28*, Central Publications Branch, Government of India, Calcutta, 1928.
4. *Screen*, 28 November 1958.
5. *Bombay Chronicle*, 13 August 1921.
6. *Film India,* November 1940.
7. *Harijan*, 28 April 1946.
8. *Harijan*, 8 May 1937.
9. British Board of Film Censors, Bombay and Bengal 1920-1950, NFAI, Pune.
10. *The Film Daily*, 1930.
11. *Harijan*, 27 May 1930.

3: Hail, Deliverer!

1. Gandhi's Salt March, accessed 10 October 2021, https://www.mkgandhi.org/articles/Gandhis-salt-march-the-tax-protest-that-changed-Indian-history.html
2. D.G. Tendulkar, *Mahatma*, Publications Division, Government of India, New Delhi, 1951.
3. Sudhir Kakar, *Mira & the Mahatma*, 'Penguin' Viking, New Delhi, 2004.
4. *The Collected Works of Mahatma Gandhi* (Electronic Book), Vol 48, p. 419.
5. *The Collected Works of Mahatma Gandhi* (Electronic Book), Vol 49, p. 16-17.
6. Gandhi's Salt March, accessed 10 October 2021, https://www.mkgandhi.org/articles/Gandhis-salt-march-the-tax-protest-that-changed-Indian-history.html
7. A.K. Chettiar, *In the Tracks of the Mahatma: The Making of a Documentary*, Orient Longman Private Limited, Chennai, 2007.
8. British Board of Film Censor Records 1920-1950, NFAI, Pune.
9. B.R. Nanda, *Mahatma Gandhi: A Biography, Complete and Unabridged,* Oxford University Press, New York, 1958, p. 298.
10. *The Collected Works of Mahatma Gandhi* (Electronic Book), Vol 49, p. 17.

11. *Radio Mirror*, April 1938, p. 91.
12. E.S. Jones, *Mahatma Gandhi*, Hodder and Stoughton, London, 1948, pp. 21–22.

4: Gandhi's Talkie Debut

1. *Motion Picture Herald*, April–June 1931.
2. *The New York Times*, 1 May 1931.
3. *Motion Picture Herald*, 30 May 1931.
4. *Motion Picture Herald*, 23 May 1931.
5. *The Film Daily*, 31 May 1931.
6. Paul Addison, 'The Political Beliefs of Winston Churchill', *Transactions of the Royal Historical Society*, 5th Series, Vol. XXX, 1980, p. 26.
7. *Exhibitor Daily Review*, 6 October 1928.
8. James Mills, *Bell & Howell Filmo Topics Magazine*, January 1932.
9. *The Hindu*, 1 May 1931.
10. Leah Weinryb Grohsgal, *Newsreel or Not Real*, Humanities Magazine, Spring 2019.
11. Charles Peden, *Newsreel Man,* Doubleday Doran & Company, New York, 1931, p. 15.
12. *Associated Press*, 31 March 1942.
13. *Cinema*, June–July 1931.

5: The Mystery Man in London

1. *Movie Makers Magazine,* March 1932.
2. James A. Mills, *Filming Mahatma Gandhi,* Bell & Howell Filmo Topics Magazine, 1932.
3. James A. Mills, *Filming Mahatma Gandhi*, Bell & Howell Filmo Topics Magazine, 1932, p. 2.
4. *Movie Makers*, March 1932.
5. James A. Mills, *Filming Mahatma Gandhi*, Bell & Howell Filmo Topics Magazine, 1932.
6. Mira Behn, *The Spirit's Pilgrimage,* Longmans Green, London, 1960, p. 131.

7. Muriel Lester, *Entertaining Gandhi*, Ivor Nicholson and Watson, Essex, London, 1932, p. 32.
8. Muriel Lester, *Entertaining Gandhi*, Ivor Nicholson and Watson, Essex, London, 1932, p. 36.
9. *Movie Classic*, November 1932, p. 58.
10. *Movie Classic*, May 1932, p. 67.
11. *Time*, 5 October 1931.
12. *The Collected Works of Mahatma Gandhi* (Electronic Book), Vol 54, p. 282.
13. *Bombay Chronicle*, 17 December 1932.
14. *Free Press Journal*, 16 December 1932.
15. *Mauj Majah* (Gujarati newspaper), 29 August 1937.

6: Mahatma in the Popular Consciousness

1. www.vijaybhatt.in.
2. Gautam Kaul, *Cinema and the Indian Freedom Struggle*, Sterling Publishers, New Delhi, 1998, p. 251.
3. *Young India*, September 1925, p. 321.
4. S. Theodore Baskaran, *The Eye of the Serpent*, East West Books, Madras, 1996, p. 16.
5. S. Theodore Baskaran, *The Eye of the Serpent*, East West Books, Madras, 1996, p. 16.
6. Kumar Shahani, *The Saint-Poets of Prabhat*, Filmworld, Bombay, 1980.
7. M.K. Gandhi, *Young India*, 25 May 1921.
8. https://www.thehindu.com/features/cinema/Blast-from-the-past-Desa-Munnetram- 1938/article13430576.ece
9. *Film India*, January 1940.
10. https://www.mkgandhi.org/autobio/chap62.html
11. *Film India*, October 1938, p. 52.
12. Bapu Watve, V. Damle and S. Fattelal, a Monograph, NFAI, Pune, 1985, p. 28.
13. S. Theodore Baskaran, *The Eye of the Serpent*, East West Books, Madras, 1996, p. 103.
14. *Film India*, October 1948.

7: Gandhi Sees a Talking Picture

1. www.vijaybhatt.net.
2. Louis Fischer, *The Life of Mahatma Gandhi*, HarperCollins, London, 1950, p. 492.
3. Rajmohan Gandhi, *Mohandas: A True Story of a Man, His People and an Empire*, Penguin Viking, New Delhi, 2006, p. 520.
4. *Motion Picture Herald*, 27 May 1944.
5. *Picturpost*, 15 June 1944.
6. Shantikumar Morarjee, *Gandhijina Sansmarano Ane Biji Saambharano*, Balgovind Prakashan, Ahmedabad, 1963.
7. *The Collected Works of Mahatma Gandhi*, Vol 37, p. 65.
8. *Film India*, January 1943.
9. M.K. Gandhi, *Letters to Sardar Vallabhbhai Patel*, Navajivan Publishing House, Ahmedabad, 1957, p. 56-57.
10. *The Collected Works of Mahatma Gandhi* (Electronic Book), Vol. 88, p. 17.
11. Urwish Kothari, https://theprint.in/opinion/heres-how-indian-films-of-the-1930s-and-1940s-used-gandhi-in-their-ads/296271/
12. *Film India*, January 1940, p. 7.
13. *Film India*, January 1943, p. 39-41.
14. https://static.pib.gov.in/WriteReadData/specificdocs/documents/2021/nov/doc2021112011.pdf
15. Mridula Mukherjee, *The Selected Works of Jawaharlal Nehru*, Oxford University Press India, New Delhi, 2009, p. 311.
16. *Collected Works of Mahatma Gandhi* (Electronic Book), Vol. 88, p. 17.
17. *CWMG* (Electronic Book), Vol. 45, p. 125.
18. *Film India*, October 1939, p. 21-23.
19. D.G. Tendulkar, *Mahatma*, Publications Division, Government of India, New Delhi, 1951.
20. *Collected Works of Mahatma Gandhi* (Electronic Book), Vol. 49, p. 455.
21. *Navajivan*, 30 September 1928.
22. Nandalal Bose, 1940, *Visva-Bharati Quarterly*, December 1987.
23. *The Collected Works of Mahatma Gandhi* (Electronic Book), Vol. 84, p. 233–234.

8: *Mahatma Gandhi*, starring Mahatma Gandhi

1. A.K. Chettiar, *In the Tracks of the Mahatma: The Making of a Documentary*, edited by A.R. Venkatachalapathy, translated from Tamil by S. Thillainayagam, Orient Longman Private Limited, Chennai, 2007, Kindle edition, p. 162.
2. *Variety*, 13 May 1953.
3. *Educational Screen*, April 1955.
4. *New York Times*, 1953.
5. A.K. Chettiar, *In the Tracks of the Mahatma: The Making of a Documentary*, edited by A.R. Venkatachalapathy, translated from Tamil by S. Thillainayagam, Orient Longman Private Limited, Chennai, 2007, Kindle edition, p. 24.
6. *Film India*, March 1940.
7. C.M. Shankaralingam, *Documentary Invades India*, Talk-A-Tone, September 1940.
8. A.K. Chettiar, *In the Tracks of the Mahatma: The Making of a Documentary*, edited by A.R. Venkatachalapathy, translated from Tamil by S. Thillainayagam, Orient Longman Private Limited, Chennai, 2007, p. 49-50.
9. *Motion Picture Herald*, 20 November 1937, p. 60.
10. *The Hindu*, 'The Making of Mahatma Gandhi', 29 September 2002.
11. *Film India*, March 1940.
12. *The New York Times*, 24 October 1939.
13. *Motion Picture Herald*, 30 March 1940.
14. *The New York Times*, 7 April 1940.
15. *The New York Times*, 7 April 1940.
16. *Business Screen* magazine.
17. A.K. Chettiar, *In the Tracks of the Mahatma: The Making of a Documentary*, edited by A.R. Venkatachalapathy, translated from Tamil by S. Thillainayagam, Orient Longman Private Limited, Chennai, 2007, p. 7.
18. A.K. Chettiar, *In the Tracks of the Mahatma: The Making of a Documentary*, 2007, edited by A.R. Venkatachalapathy, translated

from Tamil by S. Thillainayagam, Orient Blackswan Private Limited, Chennai, 2007, p. 49.

19. *The New York Times*, 7 April 1940.
20. H.Y. Sharada Prasad, *The Book I Won't Be Writing and Other Essays*, Chronicle Books, New Delhi, 2003, p. 210.
21. *Screen*, 28 February 1969, p. 8.
22. *Screen*, 26 September 1969, p. 12.
23. Amit Tyagi, an interview by author, 12 July 2020.

9: God Needs No Sleep

1. Sudhir Kakar, *Mira & the Mahatma*, Penguin India, New Delhi, 2004, p. 107.
2. Jagmohan, *Dr P.V. Pathy*, Monograph, NFAI, Poona, 1972.
3. *The Journal of the Motion Pictures Society of India*, August 1937.
4. *Harijan*, 31 July 1937.
5. Maurice Lancaster, 'Assignment India', *Documentary Newsletter*, Jan–Feb 1944, pp. 9-10.

10: Walking for Peace

1. B.D. Garga, *From Raj to Swaraj: The Non-fiction Film in India*, Penguin Books India, New Delhi, 2007, p. 83.
2. *The Collected Works of Mahatma Gandhi*, 93: 378.

11: Hollywood Loves Gandhi

1. *The New York Times*, 15 October 1931, p. 6.
2. *The Collected Works of Mahatma Gandhi* (Electronic Book), Vol 52, p. 17.
3. *Motion Picture Herald*, 23 May 1931.
   Mordant Hall, *New York Times*, 12 May 1931.
4. William L. Shirer, *Gandhi: A Memoir*, Simon and Schuster, 1963, pp. 148-149.

5. Cesar Saerchinger, *Hello America! Radio Adventures in Europe*, Houghton Mifflin Company, 1938, p. 129.
6. Cesar Saerchinger, *Hello America! Radio Adventures in Europe*, Houghton Mifflin Company, 1938, p. 129.
7. Cesar Saerchinger, *Hello America! Radio Adventures in Europe*, Houghton Mifflin Company, 1938, p. 131.
8. Cesar Saerchinger, *Hello America! Radio Adventures in Europe*, Houghton Mifflin Company, 1938, p. 132.
9. Cesar Saerchinger, *Hello America! Radio Adventures in Europe*, Houghton Mifflin Company, 1938, p. 132.
10. *Radio Digest*, November 1931, p. 26.
11. *Radio Digest*, November 1931, p. 27.
12. A.K. Chettiar, *In the Tracks of Mahatma: The Making of a Documentary*, edited by A.R. Venkatachalapathy, translated by S. Thillainayagam, Orient Longman Private Limited, Chennai, 2007, p. 56.
13. *Movie Makers*, February 1929, p. 97.
14. Prem Chowdhry, *Colonial India and the Making of Empire Cinema: Image, Ideology and Identity*, Manchester University Press, Manchester, 2000, p. 159.
15. *Photoplay Studies*, Vol. V. No. 2, 1939.
16. *Film India*, February 1939, p. 26-27.
17. *Motion Picture*, April 1932, p. 106.
18. *Motion Picture*, April 1932, p. 106.
19. *New Movie Magazine*, September 1931, p. 96.
20. *Picture Play*
21. *Hollywood*, June 1941, p. 21.
22. *Motion Picture Daily*, 4 September 1934.
23. *Film India*, December 1939, p. 4.
24. *Photoplay*, October-December, 1937, p. 17.
25. *World Film News*, April 1937, p. 11.
26. *Motion Picture Herald*, October 1933.
27. *The Indianapolis Times*, 22 October 1931, p. 10.
28. *Box Office*, 10 March 1945, p. 95.
29. *Motion Picture Herald*, 28 October 1933, p. 17.

12: Champagne Glass Dance for Gandhi

1. Padma Subrahmanyam, an interview with author on 29 December 2021.
2. *Screen*, 14 March 1969, p. 1.
3. K.A. Abbas and Pragji Dossa, *Barrister-at-Law: A Play About the Early Life of Mahatma Gandhi*, Orient Paperbacks, New Delhi, 1977, p. 138.
4. *Screen*, 25 July 1969, p. 13.
5. *Screen*, 16 May 1969, p. 2.

13: Three Shots to Eternity

1. *Box Office*, 4 March 1963.
2. *Movieland*, Madras, 5 January 1962, p. 1.
3. *Motion Picture Exhibitor*, 4 April 1962.
4. *Screen*, 10 May 1962.
5. *The Times of India*, 3 January 1963.
6. Lok Sabha Debates, Session No. 42, 27 February 1963, pp. 990–992.
7. Lok Sabha Debates, Session No. 42, 27 February 1963, pp. 990–992.
8. Lok Sabha Debates, Session No. 42, 27 February 1963, pp. 990–992.
9. Lok Sabha Debates, Session No. 42, 27 February 1963, pp. 990–992.
10. Lok Sabha Debates, Session No. 42, 27 February 1963, pp. 990–992.
11. Vijaya Mulay, *From Rajahs and Yogis to Gandhi and Beyond: Images of India in International Films of the Twentieth Century*, Seagull Books, Kolkata, 2010.
12. *Daily Mail*, March 1963.
13. *Motion Picture Exhibitor*, 21 March 1962.
14. *Star & Style*, 25 July 1969, p. 17.
15. *Madhuri*, 8 August 1969, p. 21.
16. *Madhuri*, 8 August 1969, p. 20.
17. *Madhuri*, 8 August 1969, p. 20.
18. *Madhuri*, 8 August 1969, p. 20.
19. *Screen*, 4 July 1969, p. 10.
20. *Madhuri*, 8 August 1969, p. 21.
21. *Madhuri*, 8 August 1969, p. 21.

22. Anmol Vellani, an interview with author on 12 June 2020.
23. Vikas Desai, an interview with author on 13 June 2020.
24. *Gazette of India*, 3 October 1970, Part III, section 4, p. 1115.
25. *The Times of India*, 30 November 1969, p. 19.
26. *Star & Style*, 25 July 1969, p. 18
27. *The Times of India*, 9 February 1970.
28. *The Times of India*, 22 April 1973.
29. *The Times of India*, 23 April 1973, p. 6.

14: These Gandhis Didn't See the Light

1. *The New Movie Magazine*, May 1934, p. 16.
2. *The Film Daily*, 24 September 1947.
3. *The Film Daily*, 1 April 1948.
4. *Film India*, April 1948.
5. *Film India*, April 1948.
6. *Film India*, May 1948. p. 61.
7. *Film India*, May 1948. p. 61.
8. *Film India*, July 1948.
9. *Variety*, 8 August 1951.
10. *Variety*, 1 March 1950.
11. *Variety*, 8 August 1951.
12. *Variety*, 8 August 1951.
13. *Film India*, July 1948.
14. Valerie Pascal, *The Disciple and His Devil: Gabriel Pascal and Bernard Shaw*, McGraw Hill, 1970, p. 231.
15. *Variety*, 26 December 1951.
16. Valerie Pascal, *The Disciple and His Devil: Gabriel Pascal and Bernard Shaw*, McGraw Hill, 1970, p. 232.
17. *Film India*.
18. *Variety*, 22 August 1951.
19. *Motion Picture Daily*, 15 July 1960.
20. *The New York Times*, 18 June 1960.
21. *Motion Picture Daily*, 28 July 1960.
    Motion Picture, December 1961.

22. *Variety*, 24 June 1959.
23. *Broadcasting*, 1961.
24. *Broadcasting*, 1961.
25. *Motion Picture*, December 1931.
26. *Motion Picture Daily*, 23 December 1954.
27. *Independent Film Journal*, January 1955.
28. *Motion Picture Daily*, 9 December 1954.
29. *Variety*, 14 December 1954.
30. Letter from Fred Zinnemann to Christopher Mann, British Library, London, 10 October 1966.
31. Letter from Robert Bolt to Fred Zinnemann, British Library, London, 10 October 1966.
32. Letter from Robert Bolt to Fred Zinnemann, British Library, London, 10 October 1966.
33. Letter from Robert Bolt to Fred Zinnemann, British Library, London, 10 October 1966.
34. Letter from Robert Bolt to Fred Zinnemann, British Library, London, 10 October 1966.
35. Memorandum by Fred Zinnemann, 21 October 1966.
36. Letter from Fred Zinnemann to Christopher Mann, 21 December 1966.
37. Letter from Geoffrey Ashe to Margaret Ramsay, 11 March 1967.
38. Letter from Sidney Kaufman to Robert Bolt, 19 May 1967.
39. Letter from Robert Bolt to Laurence Harbottle, 22 June 1967.
40. J.E. Smyth, *Fred Zinnemann and the Cinema of Resistance*, University Press of Mississippi/Jackson, 2014.
41. Vijaya Mulay, *From Rajahs and Yogis to Gandhi and Beyond: Images of India in International Films of the Twentieth Century*, Seagull Books, Calcutta, 2010.
42. Kevin McDonald, *Emeric Pressburger: The Life and Death of a Screenwriter*, Faber and Faber Limited, 1994.
43. David Lean: Interviews, edited by Steven Organ, University Press of Mississippi, 2009, p. 98.
44. Letter from Robert Bolt to Margaret Ramsay, 1 February 1968.
45. Letter from Margaret Ramsay to B. Griffie Williams, 29 March 1968.

46. Letter from B Griffie Williams to Margaret Ramsay, 2 April 1968.
47. Letter from Margaret Ramsay to Laurence Harbottle, 26 June 1968.
48. Letter from Robert Bolt to Motilal Kothari, 10 December 1969.
49. Letter from Richard Attenborough to Margaret Ramsay, 27 June 1973.
50. David Lean: Interviews, edited by Steven Organ, University Press of Mississippi, 2009, p. 136.
51. Sandra Lean with Barry Chattington, *David Lean: An Intimate Portrait*, Universe Publishing, New York, 2001, p. 200.
52. David Lean: Interviews, edited by Steven Organ, University Press of Mississippi, 2009, p. 86.
53. Sandra Lean with Barry Chattington, *David Lean: An Intimate Portrait,* Universe Publishing, New York, 2001, p. 202.

15: Kothari and Attenborough: The Men Behind *Gandhi*

1. *Filmfare*, 5 March 1965, p. 19.
2. *Filmfare*, 5 March 1965, p. 19.
3. *Filmfare*, 5 March 1965, p. 19.
4. Richard Attenborough, *In Search of Gandhi*, Bodley Head Ltd., London, 1982, p. 19.
5. Letter from Margaret Ramsay to Motilal Kothari, 31 October 1961.
6. Letter from Motilal Kothari to Margaret Ramsay, 8 November 1961.
7. Letter from Margaret Ramsay to Motilal Kothari, 25 January 1962.
8. Letter from Motilal Kothari to Margaret Ramsay, 24 January 1962.
9. https://www.hindustantimes.com/columns/the-aam-aadmi-behind-attenborough-s-gandhi/story-MnQTQj7haxzxtQoCAiEDkN.html
10. Richard Attenborough, *In Search of Gandhi, Bodley Head Ltd.*, London, 1982, pp. 110–111.
11. *Filmfare*, 5 March 1965.
12. *Screen*, 8 January 1965.
13. *Screen*, 8 January 1965.
14. *Filmfare*, 4 February 1966.
15. *Filmfare*, 17 February 1967.
16. Richard Attenborough, *In Search of Gandhi*, Bodley Head Ltd. London, 1982, p. 137.

17. Letter from Fred Zinnemann to Christopher Mann, 10 October 1966.
18. Letter from Robert Bolt to Fred Zinnemann, 16 October 1966.
19. Letter from Robert Bolt to Fred Zinnemann, 16 October 1966.
20. Letter from Robert Bolt to Fred Zinnemann, 16 October 1966.
21. Letter from Margaret Ramsay to Lee Steiner, 25 March 1968.
22. D.G. Tendulkar Papers, NMML, New Delhi.
23. Madhura Pandit Jasraj, *The Man Who Changed Indian Cinema*, Hay House India, New Delhi, 2015.
24. Ram Gabale, *Aatmacharitra*, Padmagandha Prakashan, Pune, 2006, p. 180.
25. Richard Attenborough, *In Search of Gandhi*, Bodley Head Ltd., London, 1982, p. 144.
26. Richard Attenborough, *In Search of Gandhi*, Bodley Head Ltd., London, 1982, p. 120.
27. Barbara Crossette, 'A 20-Year Struggle Puts Gandhi on Screen', *The New York Times*, 28 November 1982.
28. Naseeruddin Shah, *And Then One Day*, Hamish Hamilton, New Delhi, 2014, p. 289.
29. Naseeruddin Shah, an interview by author, 31 August 2020.
30. Naseeruddin Shah, *And Then One Day*, Hamish Hamilton, New Delhi, 2014, p. 291.
31. Naseeruddin Shah, an interview by author, 31 August 2020.
32. Naseeruddin Shah, an interview by author, 31 August 2020.
33. Roger Ebert, https://www.rogerebert.com/reviews/gandhi-1982.
34. Ashish Rajadhyaksha, 'Gandhiana and Gandhiology', *Framework*, 22/23, 1983.

16: Gandhi in Many Avatars

1. YouTube interview, https://www.youtube.com/watch?v=yEiXGQuQDSU
2. YouTube interview, https://www.youtube.com/watch?v=yEiXGQuQDSU
3. Interview in documentary 'Imaging Gandhi/Imagining the Mahatma', by Nandan Kudhyadi, National Museum of Indian Cinema, Mumbai, 2017.

4. Interview in documentary 'Imaging Gandhi/Imagining the Mahatma', by Nandan Kudhyadi, National Museum of Indian Cinema, Mumbai, 2017.
5. D.G. Tendulkar, *Mahatma*, Publications Division, Government of India, New Delhi, 1951, Vol. 7, p. 146.
6. Jahnu Barua, interview by author.
7. Jahnu Barua, interview by author.
8. Jahnu Barua, interview by author.
9. Jahnu Barua, interview by author.
10. *The Collected Works of Mahatma Gandhi* (54: 84).
11. Pyarelal, *Epic Fast*, Navajivan Trust, Ahmedabad, 1932, p. 59.
12. Dr Jabbar Patel, interview by author.
13. Naseeruddin Shah, interview by author, 1 September 2020.
14. Naseeruddin Shah, *And Then One Day*, Hamish Hamilton, New Delhi, 2014, p. 289.
15. Naseeruddin Shah, interview by author, 1 September 2020.
16. Dr Gowri Ramnarayan, 'Matriarch of Music', *Frontline*, 14 August 2009.
17. *The Hindu*, 9 November 2019.

17: Imagining Gandhi in the Present Times

1. Feroz Khan interview in documentary 'Imaging Gandhi/Imagining the Mahatma', by Nandan Kudhyadi, National Museum of Indian Cinema, Mumbai, 2017.
2. Darshan Jariwala interview in documentary 'Imaging Gandhi/ Imagining the Mahatma', by Nandan Kudhyadi, National Museum of Indian Cinema, Mumbai, 2017.
3. Feroz Khan interview in documentary 'Imaging Gandhi/Imagining the Mahatma', by Nandan Kudhyadi, National Museum of Indian Cinema, Mumbai, 2017.
4. *Bhagavad Gita*, II.18 and II.20.
5. C.B. Dalal, *Gandhi 1915–1948 Detailed Chronology*, Gandhi Peace Foundation New Delhi and Bharatiya Vidya Bhawan Bombay, 1971.
6. *New Indian Express*, 18 January 2014, Bengaluru.

7. Press Trust of India, 30 January 2019.
8. https://www.mkgandhi.org/articles/kasturba-gandhi.html
9. Official website of P. Sheshadri.
10. *The Week*, 22 June 2019.
11. Naseeruddin Shah, interview by author, 1 September 2020.
12. Naseeruddin Shah, interview by author, 5 September 2020.
13. Naseeruddin Shah, interview by author, 31 August 2020.
14. https://www.dnaindia.com/entertainment/report-attenborough-responsible-for-lage-raho-munnabhai- rajkumar-hirani-2037250
15. Rajkumar Hirani, *Gandhigiri: Making Gandhi Cool Again*, Gandhi@150, Jaico Publishing House, Mumbai, 2019, p. 44.
16. Abhijat Joshi interview on Youtube.
17. Dilip Prabhavalkar's interview in documentary 'Imaging Gandhi/Imagining the Mahatma', by Nandan Kudhyadi, National Museum of Indian Cinema, Mumbai, 2017.
18. Dilip Prabhavalkar, interview by author.
19. https://www.dnaindia.com/entertainment/report-attenborough-responsible-for-lage-raho-munnabhai- rajkumar-hirani-2037250
20. https://www.hindustantimes.com/entertainment/bollywood/rajkumar-santoshi-faces-protest-due-to-alleged-non-payment-of-dues-to-gandhi-vs-godse-workers-101653633271106.html
21. Twitter @manjrekarmahesh, 2 October 2021.
22. https://indianexpress.com/article/entertainment/bollywood/mahatma-gandhi-birth-anniversary-film-on-his-assassin-godse-announced-7548252/

18: Kurmavatara: The Gandhian Ideas for Salvation

1. Girish Kasaravalli, interview by author.
2. Shikaripura Krishnamurthy's interview in documentary 'Imaging Gandhi/Imagining the Mahatma', by Nandan Kudhyadi, made for National Museum of Indian Cinema, 2017.

Postscript

1. *TOI*, 8 September 2020.

Bibliography

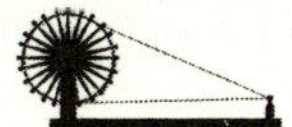

Abbas, K.A., *Barrister-At-Law*, Orient Paperbacks. 1977.

Addison, Paul, 'The Political Beliefs of Winston Churchill', *Transactions of the Royal Historical Society*, 5th Series, Vol. XXX, 1980.

Attenborough, Richard, *In Search of Gandhi,* The Bodley Head Ltd, 1982.

Baskaran, S. Theodor, *The Eye of the Serpent*, East West Books, Madras, 1996.

Behn, Mira, *The Spirit's Pilgrimage*, Longmans Green, London, 1960.

Bhatt, Vijay, www.vijaybhatt.in

British Universities Film and Video Council, *Filming History: The Memoirs of John Turner*, London, 2001.

Chettiar, A.K., *In the Tracks of the Mahatma*, Orient Longman, 2007.

Chowdhry, Prem, *Colonial India and the Making of Empire Cinema: Image, Ideology and Identity*, Manchester University Press, Manchester, 2000.

Dalal, C.B. *Gandhi:1915–1948: A Detailed Chronology*, Gandhi Peace Foundation, New Delhi, 1971.

Damle, V. and S. Fattelal, 'A Monograph, Bapu Watve', NFAI, Pune, 1985.

Fischer, Louis, *The Life of Mahatma Gandhi*, Harper & Brothers, 1950.

Gabale, Ram, *Aatmacharitra*, Padmagandha Prakashan, Pune, 2006.

Gandhi, M.K., *Letters to Sardar Vallabhbhai Patel*, Navajivan Publishing House, Ahmedabad, 1957.

Gandhi, Rajmohan, *Mohandas: A True Story of a Man, His People and an Empire*, Penguin Viking, 2006.

Garga, B.D., *From Raj to Swaraj: The Non-Fiction Film in India*, Penguin Books India, 2007.

Government of India, *Report of the Indian Cinematograph Committee 1927–1928*.

———, *The Collected Works of Mahatma Gandhi* (Electronic Book). Publications Division, New Delhi, 1999.

Grohsgal, Leah Weinryb, 'Newsreel or Not Real', *Humanities Magazine*, Spring, 2019.

Huff, Theodore, *Charlie Chaplin*, Henry Schuman, New York, 1951.

Jasraj, Madhura Pandit, *The Man Who Changed Indian Cinema*. Hay House India, 2015.

Jones, E.S., *Mahatma Gandhi*, Hodder and Stoughton, London, 1948.

Kakar, Sudhir, *Mira and the Mahatma*, Viking, 2004.

Kaul, Gautam, *Cinema and Indian Freedom Struggle*, Sterling Publications, New Delhi, 1998.

Lester, Muriel, *Entertaining Gandhi,* Ivor Nicholson and Watson, Essex, 1932.

McDonald, Kevin, *Emeric Pressburger: The Life and Death of a Screenwriter*, Faber and Faber Limited, 1994.

Mills, James A., 'Filming Mahatma Gandhi', *Bell & Howell Filmo Topics Magazine*, 1932.

Mulay, Vijaya, *From Rajahs and Yogis to Gandhi and Beyond: Images of India in International Films of the Twentieth Century*, Seagull Books, 2010.

Nanda, B.R., *Mahatma Gandhi: A Biography, Complete and Unabridged*, Oxford University Press, 1958.

NFAI Oral History Project, Interview of JBH Wadia of Wadia Movietone, Pune, 1984.

Pascal, Valerie, *The Disciple and His Devil: Gabriel Pascal and Bernard Shaw*; McGraw Hill, 1970.

Pathy, P.V., Monograph by NFAI, 1972, Poona.

Peden, Charles, *Newsreel Man*, Doubleday Doran & Company, New York, 1931.

Prasad, H.Y. Sharada, *The Book I Won't Be Writing and Other Essays*, Chronicle Books, New Delhi, 2003.

Pyarelal, *Epic Fast*, Navajivan Trust, 1932.

Rajkumar Hirani, *Gandhigiri: Making Gandhi Cool Again*, Gandhi@150, Jaico Publishing House, 2019.

Sadanand More, *Lokmanya Te Mahatma*, Rajhans Publication, Pune, 2007.

Shah, Naseeruddin, *And Then One Day*, Hamish Hamilton, 2014.

Shahani, Kumar, 'The Saint-Poets of Prabhat', *Filmworld*, Bombay, 1980.

Shantikumar, *Gandhijina Sansmarano Ane Biji Saambharano*, Balgovind Prakashan, Ahmedabad, 1963.

Shirer, William, *Gandhi: A Memoir*, Simon and Schuster, 1963.

Smyth, J.E., *Fred Zinnemann and the Cinema of Resistance*, University Press of Mississippi/Jackson, 2014.

Tendulkar, D.G., *Mahatma,* Publications Division, Government of India, New Delhi, 1951.

Acknowledgements

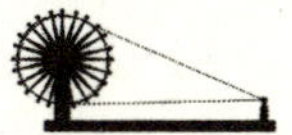

IT IS NOT EASY to write something new about Mahatma Gandhi when there is so much literature available. Even then, I ventured upon this task out of sheer curiosity. When the world started celebrating the 150th anniversary of Gandhi's birth in 2019, various events were planned at all levels, including at the premier film archive of India, NFAI, which I had the privilege to head. While conceiving such programmes, essentially focusing on how cinema has portrayed Gandhi, the irony behind it struck me. Despite Gandhi not liking cinema as a medium, I observed that there are many films celebrating him and his ideas. I decided to dig further into the archives and realized that there exist a vast number of films and footages shot on Gandhi. I was intrigued by it and this book is the result of exploring a rather strange combination of Gandhi and cinema.

The rich archive of films and publicity material at NFAI made my job easier. This journey of looking at Gandhi through cinema was pleasurable due to a passionate team of my colleagues. P.A. Salam, a projectionist of great calibre and a representative of now a disappearing art, was always at hand to show me films and newsreels. The film preservation officer, Kiran Dhiwar, who passed away suddenly last year, helped me in identifying and connecting the dots on this rather unusual subject. For days together, these two gentlemen showcased reels after reels featuring Gandhi on a small flatbed machine at NFAI and I recall their cooperation with gratitude. I spent hours watching Gandhi on those grainy images and these form some of my fondest memories that I carry from my NFAI days. Arti Karkhanis, a walking encyclopedia on the vast film publicity material and head of documentation section, assisted me at every stage providing vital details. She responded to every query of mine and provided the material concerning Gandhi from all regional cinemas. The book library at NFAI is a treasure trove for any cinephile who wants to do research on Indian cinema. Veena Kshirsagar, the librarian, helped me dig the huge database of old film magazines and journals. A rare catalogue of Censor Records beginning with 1920s was of immense help to look at the early era of newsreels. Anuradha Vajire, the librarian at Film and Television Institute of India (FTII) also assisted me while accessing the *Collected Works of Mahatma Gandhi*. My young and passionate colleagues Amit Patil, Aparna Subramanian, Leenali Khairnar and Bhavesh Singh not only encouraged me but also helped in referencing databases of foreign film archives and sourcing old newspaper reports. I am also indebted to all the staff at NFAI that supported my research in many ways.

An archivist and eminent author, Nasreen Munni Kabir, was the one who first suggested me that there could be a book on this idea while I was coordinating Gandhi's 150th birth anniversary celebrations at NFAI. She guided me at every stage of writing, which was very valuable for a debut author like me. Her words of encouragement were a constant source of inspiration and I am truly grateful to her. Veteran film scholar and an authority on Indian silent cinema, Virchand Dharamsey, is like a father figure, and was a guiding force to me during this journey. With a child-like curiosity for anything to do with Indian cinema, he offered me valuable suggestions and gave references. I was fortunate to have benefited from many long conversations with him. Prof. Ravi

Vasudevan, another eminent film historian, encouraged me from time to time while supplying details on short films in pre-Independence era. While working at NFAI, I could build some relationships that went beyond professional limits and I was fortunate that renowned filmmakers such as Shyam Benegal, Jahnu Barua, Rajkumar Hirani, Naseeruddin Shah, Girish Kasaravalli, Arun Khopkar, Vikas Desai, Dr Jabbar Patel, Nandan Kudhyadi and Amit Tyagi opened their minds to give me their perspectives on the subject. I value and cherish their trust and wisdom.

Veteran gramophone records collector Suresh Chandvankar constantly encouraged me by saying how valuable this work could be. A connoisseur of music and a Shankar–Jaikishan fan, Sandeep Apte, was a regular collaborator and kept supplying me news clippings whenever required. Harini Srinivasan, a former civil services colleague turned author, gave the confidence and helped me overcome the initial nervousness a first-time author encounters. I also thank Yaseer Usman, author of many accomplished biographies on film stars, for his encouragement. Film Society activist and founder of Aashay Film Club in Pune, Satish Jakatdar, was a pillar of support throughout the writing of this book. Senior writer Prof. Shyamala Vanarase and author–publisher Ramdas Bhatkal gave valuable suggestions after reading the first draft. Noted political commentator Prof. Suhas Palshikar not only read the entire draft but gave various insights that greatly helped me in fine-tuning the chapters as well as the narrative. I am grateful to Adv. Arpan Banerjee who helped me with certain important references. It was Dr Thea Buckley who came to my rescue while I was searching for some details. Along with Dr Arani Ilankuberan, she facilitated getting many documents from British Library, London in quick time and I thank both of them. I also value the guidance and inputs given by senior editor at Times of India and national award winning author Avijit Ghosh.

I fondly remember Keshav Desiraju, a senior civil servant and author of an excellent biography on M.S. Subbulakshmi. I had called him to ask for some references on other subject and during the course of the conversation, I mentioned about this book. He was kind enough to connect me with HarperCollins just after reading two chapters.

Unfortunately, he passed away this year and I am really sad that he is not there to see this book.

Siddhesh Inamdar, the commissioning editor at HarperCollins liked the idea of this book and I thank him in believing and nurturing it at every stage. Like the *Gandhi* biopic, this book also went through many hands and publishers before finding a home at HarperCollins, particularly when the entire publishing industry was in a bad shape due to the Covid pandemic. Shreya Lall took over and supervised the editing, along with Kripa Raman. Their crisp comments and inputs have benefited me in shaping this book. The vast archive of the newsreel collections of Fox Movietone, Hearst Metrotone News at UCLA Film and Television, Paramount News, Pathe News, Universal News, British Movietone, Moving Image Research Collections at University of South Carolina and the YouTube channel of GandhiServe has been of great help in sourcing many stories for this book. I chanced upon the personal papers of D.G. Tendulkar at the Nehru Memorial Museum and Library at New Delhi and thank their helpful staff in making it accessible.

When I started writing the book, a deadly virus struck the world. To contain the spread of the Covid-19 outbreak, a lockdown was enforced and it became really difficult to travel to conduct research and meet people. In such challenging times, I was immensely benefited by an online portal, Lantern, an open access production of the Wisconsin Centre for Film Theatre Research at the University of Wisconsin Madison that enabled me to go through American film trade magazines.

My obsession with Gandhi in cinema for the last two years couldn't have been possible but for the support of my family! My wife, Veena, my batchmate in civil services who resigned to pursue academics and obtained PhD in Sanskrit, was a constant sounding board in my writing process. My sons, Aditya and Rajvardhan, kept me in good mood, debated points and even saw *Gandhi*, the film, once again with me. I also acknowledge my parents, Sushila and Bhupal Magdum, for their unconditional love and support.

Index

About the Author

Prakash Magdum is a civil servant with interest in films.

30 Years *of*

HarperCollins *Publishers* India

At HarperCollins, we believe in telling the best stories and finding the widest possible readership for our books in every format possible. We started publishing 30 years ago; a great deal has changed since then, but what has remained constant is the passion with which our authors write their books, the love with which readers receive them, and the sheer joy and excitement that we as publishers feel in being a part of the publishing process.

Over the years, we've had the pleasure of publishing some of the finest writing from the subcontinent and around the world, and some of the biggest bestsellers in India's publishing history. Our books and authors have won a phenomenal range of awards, and we ourselves have been named Publisher of the Year the greatest number of times. But nothing has meant more to us than the fact that millions of people have read the books we published, and somewhere, a book of ours might have made a difference.

As we step into our fourth decade, we go back to that one word – a word which has been a driving force for us all these years.

Read.